W9-CKF-558

GREAT PREACHING ON

THE HOLY SPIRIT

GREAT PREACHING ON

THE HOLY SPIRIT

COMPILED BY
CURTIS HUTSON

SWORD of the LORD
PUBLISHERS
P. O. BOX 1099, MURFREESBORO, TN 37133

Copyright 1988 by

SWORD OF THE LORD PUBLISHERS

ISBN 0-87398-329-7

Printed and Bound in the United States of America

Preface

A favorite story of A. J. Gordon was that of an American who wanted his English friend to see Niagara Falls. Taking him to the foot of the Falls, he said, **"There's the greatest unused power in the world."**

"Ah, no," replied the Englishman, **"that's not so. The greatest unused power in the world is the Holy Spirit of the living God."**

When many people hear the minister speak about the Holy Spirit, they have only a very vague idea of what he means. Some Christians have indulged in such extreme fanaticism concerning this subject as to cause others to shy away from it altogether.

But it is precious to know that the Holy Spirit is a Person—not an influence, but a real Person. He is a Person just as Jesus is a Person. He is God just as the Heavenly Father is God. The Holy Spirit is here taking Jesus' place on earth. He lives in the body of believers.

So the best and simplest definition we know for the Holy Spirit is this: The Holy Spirit is God in the believer's body.

What does the Holy Spirit do in this world? Many things. Among them are: He convicts of sin. He regenerates. He gives the new life. He seals us unto the day of redemption. He comforts in time of sorrow. The same Holy Spirit who convicts and regenerates the unsaved, must fill and equip with power those who are saved: we cannot win men with our own words or our own wisdom. If we are in doubt about anything, the Holy Spirit will teach us God's will. And He gives us power to overcome the Devil.

There is no power in us apart from the Holy Spirit.

The command to Christians, "Be filled with the Spirit," is as much a command as repent, believe, be baptized or any other command in the Word of God. And a once-for-all filling is not taught in the Word of God. We are leaky vessels, Moody used to say, and need to be continually replenished.

The authors give a simple explanation of some of these deepest truths of the Bible. They show plainly what the filling of the Holy Spirit is, what it is not, what it will do for you, and how you and every Christian may have this mighty filling of the Holy Spirit. They deal kindly but plainly with "tongues" and other so-called works of the Spirit in our day.

The Spirit-filled ministers of the Gospel represented in this volume are qualified to write on the subject and are outstanding examples of what God can do with a life dedicated to Him. These messages, when preached by the greatest preachers of this and past generations, have resulted in thousands finding a new source of power. We believe this will continue to be so as they are put in book form.

Each message is full of fire. One yearns, as one reads them, for the fullness of the Spirit.

There is not only challenge here; there is comfort and soul blessing for Christians. The reading of this book should make a difference in you! Do you want to be changed? Do you want to be challenged? Do you want to be charged with a new desire to serve? What does the Holy Spirit mean to you? What about your relationship to Him? Do you want Him to be your constant companion? Do you take Him with you wherever you go? These and many other heart-searching questions are raised and answered in *Great Preaching on the Holy Spirit.*

Our all-consuming purpose in this book is to lead our readers into the rich and real experience that is possible to all believers, and we sincerely trust that this useful volume will point the way to victory, successful service and power FOR YOU!

May the yearning and prayer of all Christians be that of Isaac Watts:

Come, Holy Spirit, heavenly Dove,
With all Thy quick'ning powers;
Kindle a flame of sacred love
In these cold hearts of ours.

Sword of the Lord Publishers

Table of Contents

I.

God's Atomic Energy

R. P. "FIGHTING BOB" SHULER

"Not by might, nor by power, but by my spirit, saith the Lord of hosts." —Zech. 4:6.

Failure on the part of the church to magnify the Holy Ghost in His ministry and activity has produced paralysis. A deadness has come upon us, and all our efforts to make the world believe that life is there are vain. The modern undertaker has learned the art of making dead folks look even lovelier than in life and of preparing their faces so they seem about to open their lips and speak. But they are dead. And the church, with all its beautiful ritual and elegant externals, without the presence and power of the Holy Spirit is just as dead. "Thou hast a name that thou livest, and art dead," was not more applicable to the church at Sardis than it is to many churches of these terrible times.

HOW WE NEED POWER!

Power is the most talked of thing in the world, and the most sought after. Dictators seek power as nothing else. They desire engines and instruments of power that they may win victories. The cry of this day is for power. The atomic and nuclear bomb, radar, the rocket, the harnessing of nature's forces—it is man's mad race for power.

If you had stood with me a few years ago on the rim of the great canyon looking down upon the ever-muddy Colorado of the West, the river that buries its dead in the depths of red silt, you would have seen hundreds of men engaged in an attempt to hold back the waters of that turbulent stream and impound the then greatest inland sea within the nation. Mighty machines worked tirelessly in the depths of that canyon. There was the constant hum of wheels and pulleys and cogs and pistons, as man conspired to win his fight over nature's forces.

A great cable stretched from mountain to mountain, and on it moved buckets that held tons of earth and stone. Men were digging a channel back through the mountain to divert the flow of the river while they dropped thousands of tons of concrete where once the river flowed.

If you had turned, you would have seen on a building this blazing electric sign: WE FURNISH THE POWER.

Push the button, and man's genius prevailed. A river that had flowed undisturbed for centuries between those mountains was being conquered. Turn the current off, and the work ceased. There was a silence that screamed of hopeless, helpless inactivity. The buckets hung idly on the great steel cables. The machines in the depths of the canyon were silent. Men stopped in their tracks. Something had happened, something deadly. The river flowed on.

The church of this tragic hour has more wire stretched and less juice on it than in any other day that I have ever known. We have superlative equipment without any vitalizing force to bring it into action. We are continually building sanctuaries that are oftentimes as devoid of spiritual life as tombs. Our altars are no longer places of penitential tears and the birth of new souls. They are places where we burn candles as though the dead were there. When I was a boy in my native mountains, we always burned candles when the light went out.

We have our retreats, our cultural programs, our training, our "credits," our diplomas, our degrees, our worship services, our anthems, our ritual, our "new moons" and "Sabbaths," as in another hour that broke the heart of God. But where is our power? Where is the power that turns the world upside down? Ours is the tragedy of which the prophet spoke when he said, "This day is a day of trouble, and of rebuke, and blasphemy: for the children are come to the birth, and there is not strength to bring forth."

Power is at the center of all life. We hear much talk these days about "living the life." We are told that these times call not for creeds, but for life. Our experts have much to say about "the Jesus way of life." There can be no life without this power I speak of. It is at the very core. We sometimes call it vigor, sometimes vitality, sometimes force. It is that which bulges from below and lifts the whole, which draws like a magnet and exalts in spite of barriers and hindrances. It is that which pushes out, which bursts the shell, which explodes the husk in which the germ lives. It is irresistible. Give it time, and it will conquer all opposition. This is power. This is that without which there can be no life.

The Holy Ghost is power. He is the God of power. He is the dynamic force in spiritual life. He comes into the heart, not alone to possess it, but to invigorate it, to make it vital with God, to make it live in Christ Jesus who indeed is life. Thus the promise of Christ was lifted like a beacon in the darkest moment of seeming defeat: "But ye shall receive power."

The Jewish mob was howling for blood. The Roman government was intent upon putting down this fanatical heresy. No organization existed, no financial backing, no institutions, no heritage of the past, no prospect for the future. What could there be for those who came down from Mount Olivet after the ascension? Jesus had told them, "Ye shall receive power."

There is altogether too much artificiality in the church of our times. We make a marvelous show. I am sometimes saddened and amazed at the emphasis placed upon the administration of the Lord's Supper at our conferences, when I know that there are ministers piously engaging in that solemn performance who do not believe in the blood atonement, the bodily resurrection of Jesus, or His coming again—doctrines which enter vitally into Christ's inauguration of this practice. We pretend. We are indeed arch pretenders.

God abhors artificiality, pretense, pharisaism, the white upon the sepulchers. When I was a boy preacher, I preached to congregations where almost every lady present wore a profuse bouquet of flowers upon her hat. There were all kinds of flowers before me: petunias, roses, violets, and even touch-me-nots. I have seen sunflowers on women's hats in church.

But I never smelled the fragrance of those flowers. It was a dead garden out in front. Those flowers had never bloomed. Some artist who could not paint a sunset or a great desert scene had daubed color on their petals. They were put together with glue and done up on wire.

God despises such! He wants a flower that blooms, that gives its fragrance to the weary pilgrim as the evening takes on the purple of the coming night.

In days immediately preceding those, I used to sit with my mother in the old "meetinghouse" and look about at the birds upon the women's hats—bluebirds, redbirds, robins, wrens, everything but a crow. I listened with the hope that they might join in the singing, but they never did.

They had no song. Their wings had never stretched and soared. They had never built their homes in the treetops. They were not birds at all. They had little bead eyes and celluloid bills. They were feathered hypocrites. God wants a bird that soars and sings and feeds its nestlings in the branches of the trees.

In my city I often see a very beautiful woman standing behind a plate-glass window. She seems to have everything: form, apparel, poise; and on her face every tint—from the faintest hue of the lilac to the red of my father's old barn! But I have never yet seen a man down on his knees on the sidewalks of Los Angeles, or even of New York, pleading with that woman to go home with him that he might love and cherish her and that she might be the mother of his children. I did see a clerk carrying one of those women up a stairway once, and he was the most disgusted man I have ever seen.

What's the matter with her? She is beautiful. She is well dressed. She has poise and bearing. What's wrong? You know what's wrong. Everything is wrong. She is a make-believe. She is a decorated fraud. She is a dressed and painted lie. And whether she is standing behind the plate-glass window or walking down the street with a cigarette in her mouth, beware of her! "But she that liveth in pleasure is dead while she liveth." And whether she be man or woman matters not at all. She is not only dead but deadly. She spreads death.

The dead artificial pretense that has taken the place of living Christianity is the bane and blight of these times. The "form of godliness" is not godliness.

The challenge today is for a living church. The world will not be content with deadness in the name of a living Christ. We need a living altar, a living pulpit, a living pew. Indeed, our God is interested in life. He bestowed it in the beginning. He redeemed it. He saves it. He empowers it. With such a God, why should we live "at a poor dying rate"? It is our privilege to live buoyantly, gloriously, victoriously! "I am come that they might have life, and that they might have it more abundantly."

And now may I bring to you what I conceive to be the five fundamental functions of the Holy Ghost in imparting and maintaining this life?

The Holy Ghost is God—not God standing out on the rim of creation surveying His handiwork, not even God at Bethlehem or Calvary, but God moved in. He is God dwelling in men's hearts. His one interest is to bring life to men—the life that Christ, by His redemption, has made possible. We must forever remember that the Holy Ghost not only came at the promise of Jesus, but came to show Jesus to men. He came, if you please, to enlarge the fact of Jesus, to emphasize Jesus, to magnify Jesus, to introduce Jesus personally, and to make Jesus real.

Jesus Christ is the Way, the Truth, and the Life. There is no other route. There is no truth outside of Him. He is the author of eternal life. The Holy Ghost is forever His ambassador, His announcer, His spokesman, His agent. "He shall testify of me." "For he shall receive of mine, and shall show it unto you."

I. THE HOLY SPIRIT CONVICTS OF SIN

The enemy of life is sin. He who sinneth, dies. Death is the wage. Unless Jesus Christ shall purge, wipe out, wash away sin, then we are dead in trespasses and in sins. Therefore, the Holy Ghost has as His first office work the conviction of men's hearts as to the fact of sin. It is His task to make sin bare, to uncover its ugliness, to expose its pernicious character and its horrible result. He announces that sin is high treason against God. The Holy Ghost takes the truth of God, the gospel message, earnestly and honestly and fearlessly preached, and convicts of sin.

It is by the "foolishness of preaching" that this result is attained. Whatever may be said of a teaching ministry—and there is a large place in the world for such a ministry—it is the preaching ministry that is used of the Holy Ghost in seeking to free men's souls from sin. The history of the Christian movement bears this out abundantly. The cry of our barren day is for great preaching!

And right here the church, interested in life both here and hereafter, needs to face up with a cold, blunt, harsh fact. The truth is that we of this generation have minimized the fact of sin. In our message to the world we have not been courageous enough to proclaim the truth as to the nature of sin—the fact that sin is innate, is a part of us, is wrought into the very fiber of our souls as part of our fabric, and must be dethroned, washed out, removed from our hearts, so that our wills are released from their chains and we become free. Such a Gospel was preached by our fathers. The Holy Ghost blessed their ministry, and the altars of the church were filled with penitential seekers after God.

But a blight has taken hold of the ministry of their sons, and no more are we conscious that

> **. . . Heaven comes down our souls to greet,
> While glory crowns the mercyseat.**

Our ministry has become barren. There are fewer and fewer sons and daughters being actually born into the fellowship of believers, and the reason is plain: we have backed off from the fact of sin.

We no longer preach the penalties of sin. Especially do we "take the siding" when it comes to the eternal penalties of sin. Eternal retribution is a lost note in the gospel message.

We have become "mouthers" of the love of God, lifting the love of God out of its proper relationship to the justice of God, the wrath of God against sin, the eternal vengeance which God declares is His.

We talk of the final restoration of all things, the annihilation of the wicked—as though there were comfort in such a thought—the possibility of a state of penance, a kind of Protestant purgatory out beyond death; and we finally arrive at some kind of conclusion that God in His goodness could not be true to His loving nature and at the same time forever banish lost souls to a place of eternal suffering and despair. The fact that the whole picture we thus draw is contrary to the truths of Scripture and to the teaching of historic Christianity does not seem to bother us. Sin is no longer declared "exceeding sinful." We are content in our day of softness thus to soften our message, and the result is that the Holy Ghost withdraws from us. Our preaching does not convict.

The Holy Ghost has been the ally of the prophet in all times. The prophet has been fearless, bold, uncompromising. The prophet has proclaimed. He was not the violin in the orchestra but the trumpet. The prophet cried out against the sins of kings and lost his own life. He stood against the sin of the court, and his head was served in a charger.

The prophet forgot himself. He forgot his salary. He forgot his bracket. Promotion was not within his thought. He was God's messenger, proclaiming the sins of the people and pointing to the wrath of God against evil. He did not wince or whine. He was not a whimperer. He thundered. And the Holy Ghost backed him to the last syllable.

Thus, down by way of Paul, Martin Luther, John Wesley, Jonathan Edwards, Dwight L. Moody, Sam Jones, Billy Sunday, and tens of thousands who have marched courageously by their sides and after them, the Holy Ghost has blazed a glorious revival trail; and hundreds of thousands have been convicted of their sins, have repented, have looked with faith to Jesus, and have been saved.

In repentance and the exercise of saving faith, the Holy Ghost is ever present; but since these steps are so intimately connected with this Gospel of conviction of sin, I am content to say that in the whole process the Holy Ghost blesses the gospel message to where it becomes so powerful that men, dead in sin, come to live in Christ Jesus the Lord.

II. THE HOLY GHOST REGENERATES

The second office work of the Holy Ghost is in the conversion of men and women, boys and girls, from a life of rebellion against God to one of obedience and the giving of the witness, an unmistakable witness, that such a work of grace has been accomplished. Paul would leave no doubt here. He declared: "The Spirit itself beareth witness with our spirit, that we are the children of God: and if children, then heirs; heirs of God, and joint-heirs with Christ."

Christ is our Saviour. I love to think of the Holy Ghost's bringing Christ into the heart of the penitent sinner, who is face to face with the fact of his sin, and introducing him to that sinner as the only sufficient Saviour. The act of salvation, or what we call conversion, is accomplished when the sinner faces Jesus, introduced by the Holy Ghost, and accepts Him.

The Holy Ghost will not introduce Jesus as Saviour to a man who is not penitent, willing to turn from sin, and anxious to be saved. But when that moment comes, in walks the Holy Ghost with this new Guest, who now is to abide within the heart.

It is merely a matter of changing tenants. The old tenant moves out. The new tenant moves in. That is why we read that, when this transaction is accomplished, things once lovely are now hateful, and things once despised become most lovely indeed.

But the transaction goes even deeper than that, and here is where the fact of life looms large. When Christ moves in and takes charge, He makes new. He does not simply make you feel new; He *makes you new!* He makes you new, it matters not how you feel. He gives you a new nature. It is as mysterious as the blowing of the winds, but it is one of the clearest facts of Christian experience. "Therefore if any man be in Christ, he is a new creature: old things are passed away; behold, all things are become new."

III. THE HOLY SPIRIT WITNESSES, GIVES ASSURANCE OF SALVATION

And since you are now a new man, a son of God in a spiritual life that is divinely bestowed, it becomes the duty and joy of the Holy Ghost to witness that fact to your inner consciousness. "Because ye are sons, God hath sent forth the Spirit of his Son into your hearts." "Ye were sealed with that holy Spirit of promise."

We speak of this as "heartfelt" religion. In other words, it is deeper than the sensibilities, than the physical emotions. It affects them tremendously. They are its channels.

But this witness is a contract between God and the soul of man, signed by the Holy Ghost. It is the new covenant. It is the blood of Jesus applied by the pen of the Holy Ghost. The blood makes the affirmation. The Holy Ghost is the divine agent and instrument.

A man saved by the grace of Jesus Christ has a right to know that so glorious a thing has happened in his soul. The Holy Ghost came upon such a mission. Our "experience of religion" is predicated upon the fact that this new life, this eternal life, is ever publicized in our hearts by the Holy Ghost. "Now he which stablisheth us with you in Christ, and hath anointed us, is God, who hath also sealed us, and given the earnest of the Spirit in our hearts." And as long as we live by faith within the will of God, this witness remains. Experimental religion is therefore a triumphant fact.

IV. THE HOLY SPIRIT GUIDES, TEACHES AND GROWS THE OBEDIENT CHRISTIAN

And now I come to the doctrine of Christian probation, in many quarters fast fading out. By Christian probation we do not mean that men are probably saved or conditionally saved, depending upon future behavior. When a man is saved, he is saved.

However, that salvation is the beginning of a life. And life is a developing process. The moment life stands still, it stagnates, disintegrates, and the processes of death set in. The Holy Ghost is present in the processes of maturing life. All grace is a bestowal, a gift, a divine deposit in the human heart. But from the experience of that new life which comes when grace is given, there grows the mustard plant of a full-statured Christian, and there goes out the leaven which affects the whole lump. Thus the kingdom of God begins in men's hearts and grows.

It is with this growing process that I am now concerned. Whatever the experience, there is always the necessity of this growth and development.

The fathers were right when they preached growth in grace. "But grow in grace, and in the knowledge of our Lord and Saviour Jesus Christ" was the exhortation of Peter, which carries its full content of meaning to this very hour.

Salvation is full, but never complete. Salvation is a total manifestation of divine grace in the heart of man which starts a process of development into which grace constantly feeds and which at last brings the man to full stature in Christ Jesus, described by Paul as "the measure of the stature of the fullness of Christ." All starts with salvation. It ends in Christian perfection, which within itself allows of growth, advance, progress.

Personally I believe that, after the redeemed have been in Heaven for ten thousand years, these processes will still be working. The spiritual life can never become stagnant.

It matters not as to the manifestations of grace along the way, the glorious contributions made by the Holy Ghost as we pilgrimage; the journey still continues. It is a journey upward. There is ever higher ground ahead. We travel from "glory to glory."

And so it is that to those who are born again the Holy Ghost stands as guide along the Christian's way.

Back in the mountains where I was born, some enterprising mountaineer had gone to the sawmill and secured slabs. He sawed out crude hands with fingers pointing and nailed them up at the forks of the road—7 miles to Fox Creek, 9 miles to Comers' Rock, 11 miles to Turkey Cove, 14 miles to Sarvis Flats. Indeed, all you had to do was to look at the signposts, follow the direction the finger pointed, and travel.

The Holy Ghost is the signpost. "He will guide you into all truth." The finger has never yet pointed wrong.

Every now and then some lovely girl comes to me and asks, "Is it wrong to dance?" I have had women ask my opinion about bridge playing for prizes, or jackpots, and petty gambling socially. I have had men ask me as to Sunday golf. That's dangerous business, for we preachers are very fallible. We are never invincible guides. We are sometimes too cowardly to tell you the truth when we know it.

But there is a guide who never fails. I challenge you who hesitate about some worldly practice to fall upon your knees and ask for directions from the Holy Ghost. Never yet has He compromised or softened the truth. He will not guide you into error and sin. The Holy Ghost does not close shop at conversion. He lives in your heart to point the way, to give the strength and power, to supply the cleansing and purification, that the life may be full and complete. Never in this process does He coerce the human will. Never does He force or compel. He simply acts as guide. He keeps the heart sweet with the fragrance of Heaven. He undergirds. He is the never-ceasing dynamo. And thus our Christian lives go forward and upward.

V. THE HOLY SPIRIT ENDUES WITH POWER
AND CLEANSES

As I come to the last function of the Holy Ghost in the life and destiny of the believer, I hesitate. I do not hesitate because of any doubt of my position. I know that if the Book of God is true, I am right in what I am about to say. My hesitancy comes from the fact that a most precious Bible doctrine has been all but wrecked by its own advocates. I sincerely desire not to do hurt to that doctrine in this message. I am speaking now of the work of the Holy Ghost in the sanctification of believers.

What a tragedy that such doctrines as holiness and the second coming of Jesus have been surrounded by so much real fanaticism and near insanity. Yet I am personally determined that all the wildfires that have been built by faddists and zealots shall not rob me of these precious truths.

There is nothing taught more certainly in the Book of God than the doctrine of a holy life. When early Methodism went about the gracious task of spreading scriptural holiness throughout the land, she was certainly on the Lord's business. And God blessed her and prospered her to where men stood astonished at her success and achievement.

I am not interested in the adjectives that are used in speaking of holiness. I am not concerned with men's shibboleths or with the processes that some schools of thought have made more important in their teachings than the fact itself.

I am not now speaking of "blessings." I am speaking of the pentecostal experience. I am speaking of that overwhelming of the believing heart by the dominating power of the Holy Spirit, so that suddenly the Christian life becomes absolutely victorious. Here again it is grace. It is a bestowal of grace. It is the coming of the Holy Ghost as at Pentecost.

But nowhere in the Word of God is it so much as hinted that this work stops with this pentecostal experience. That there was growth and development following Pentecost is certain.

There are those who claim that this experience is effective in the complete eradication of the carnal nature. There are others who claim that it is an act of empowering to the extent that man has enough of God ever present with and in him to enable him to fight the good fight of faith in victorious fashion. One school specializes on taking something out of man. The other school specializes on bringing something into man.

Both schools are undoubtedly feeling after the truth. The Holy Ghost operates negatively and positively. He uproots and He enthrones. He digs out and He plants. Sanctification, as conversion, is the beginning of a glorious process. Pentecost started cowardly men out with the boldness of martyrdom in their hearts. Before Pentecost they were running from Caesar. After Pentecost they were shaking Caesar's throne, so that the Jews mobbed the house of Jason and together with the Roman leaders of the city cried out: "These that have turned the world upside down have come hither also."

They did not simply shout at Pentecost. It was not enough to preach to the assembled multitudes. They went out to live and to die gloriously. And their living and dying shook the world!

Through it all we find that the Holy Ghost is interested in life. He furnishes the vital spark. He lights the heart. Without His presence the church walks its weary, defeated way back into the darkness of pagan despair.

As I have watched the church of my day become self-serving and self-promoting, swallowed up with ritualism and ceremony, content to be a kind of social club of a character a bit more decent than other social clubs about it and give itself to a ministry of culture, often hollow and empty to the core, I feel as though we need a return of Jeremiah with his weeping eyes and sobbing voice:

"Be astonished, O ye heavens, at this, and be horribly afraid, be ye very desolate, saith the Lord. For my people have committed two evils; they have forsaken me the fountain of living waters, and hewed them out cisterns, broken cisterns, that can hold no water."

Where is the blessedness I knew?
. . . .
Where is the soul-refreshing view?

When I was a boy, back many miles from the railroad, a neighbor went over the mountain to Wytheville and came back with a horseshoe magnet. He placed it in his little boy's stocking as a gift from Santa Claus. That magnet was the sensation of the countryside. With wide-open eyes we watched it perform. I turned my pockets wrong side out and offered that boy everything I had for that magnet. But he was adamant. He knew what he had.

I saw it lift iron filings which were brought from the blacksmith shop. I saw it fill nails with a strange power until they lifted other nails. I saw something go out of it without seeming to lessen what remained and make particles of iron like unto it in their ability to draw to themselves.

I did not know what magnetism was. Really, the greatest scientist on earth has not been able to find the innermost secret of that which holds the universe together. You cannot touch magnetism. You cannot see it. You cannot define it. But who doubts it?

Once Jesus said that you do not know the birthplace of the winds, but they fan your cheeks. The Holy Ghost, that blessed Third Person in the adorable Trinity, is too deep, too high, too abounding for me. I cannot grasp the thought. The thought is too eternal, too infinite, too belonging to the very nature of God Himself.

But I have seen the glorious power of the Holy Ghost manifested and have felt the tug at my own heart. My mountain mother was filled with Him and drew her six children up against her knees, and He possessed their hearts. This is the truth I bring.

(From the book, *What New Doctrine Is This?*)

R. A. TORREY
1856-1928

ABOUT THE MAN:

Torrey grew up in a wealthy home, attended Yale University and Divinity School, and studied abroad. During his early student days at Yale, young Torrey became an agnostic and a heavy drinker. But even during the days of his "wild life," he was strangely aware of a conviction that some day he was to preach the Gospel. At the end of his senior year in college, he was saved.

While at Yale Divinity School, he came under the influence of D. L. Moody. Little did Moody know the mighty forces he was setting in motion in stirring young R. A. Torrey to service!

After Moody died, Torrey took on the world-girdling revival campaigns in Australia, New Zealand, England and America.

Like many another giant for God, Torrey shone best, furthest and brightest as a personal soul winner. This one man led 100,000 to Christ in a revival that circled the globe!

Dr. Torrey's education was obtained in the best schools and universities of higher learning. Fearless, quick, imaginative and scholarly, he was a tough opponent to meet in debate. He was recognized as a great scholar, yet his ministry was marked by simplicity.

It was because of his outstanding scholastic ability and evangelistic fervor that Moody handpicked Torrey to become superintendent of his infant Moody Bible Institute. In 1912, Torrey became dean of BIOLA, where he served until 1924, pastoring the Church of the Open Door in Los Angeles from 1915-1924.

Torrey's books have probably reached more people indirectly and helped more people to understand the Bible and to have power to win souls, than the writings of any other man since the Apostle Paul, with the possible exceptions of Spurgeon and Rice. Torrey was a great Bible teacher, but most of all he was filled with the Holy Spirit.

He greatly influenced the life of Dr. John R. Rice.

II.

The Power of the Holy Spirit

R. A. TORREY

"Power belongeth unto God." The Holy Spirit is the Person who imparts to the individual believer the power that belongs to God. This is the Holy Spirit's work in the believer, to take what belongs to God and make it ours. All the manifold power of God belongs to the children of God as their birthright in Christ. "All things are your's" (I Cor. 3:21).

But all that belongs to us as our birthright in Christ becomes ours in actual and experimental possession through the Holy Spirit's work in us as individuals. To the extent that we understand and claim for ourselves the Holy Spirit's work, to that extent do we obtain for ourselves the fullness of power in Christian life and service that God has provided for us in Christ. A very large portion of the church knows and claims for itself a very small part of that which God has made possible for them in Christ because they know so little of what the Holy Spirit can do and longs to do for us.

Let us study the Word, then, to find out what the Holy Spirit has power to do in men.

We shall not go far before we discover that the same work which we see ascribed in one place to the power of the Word of God is in other places ascribed to the Holy Spirit. The explanation of this is simple. The Word of God is the instrument through which the Holy Spirit does His work. The Word of God is "the sword of the Spirit" (Eph. 6:17). The Word of God is also the seed the Spirit sows and quickens (Luke 8:11; I Pet. 1:23). The Word of God is the instrument of all the manifold operations of the Holy Spirit.

If, therefore, we wish the Holy Spirit to do His work in our hearts, we must study the Word. If we wish Him to do His work in the hearts of others, we must give them the Word.

But the bare Word will not do the work alone. The Spirit must Himself use the Word. It is when the Spirit Himself uses His own sword that it manifests its real temper, keenness and power. God's work is accomplished by the Word and the Spirit, or rather by the Spirit through the Word.

The secret of effectual living is knowing the power of the Spirit through the Word. The secret of effectual service is using the Word in the power of the Spirit.

Some seek to magnify the Spirit but neglect the Word. This will not do at all. Fanaticism, baseless enthusiasm, wildfire are the result.

Others seek to magnify the Word but largely ignore the Spirit. Neither will this do. It leads to dead orthodoxy, truth without life and power.

The true course is to recognize the instrumental power of the Word through which the Holy Spirit works, and the living, personal power of the Holy Spirit who acts through the Word.

But let us come directly to the consideration of our subject: What has the Holy Spirit power to do?

1. The Holy Spirit Has Power to Reveal Jesus and His Glory to Man

Turn to I Corinthians 12:3:

"Wherefore I give you to understand, that no man speaking by the Spirit of God calleth Jesus accursed: and that no man can say that Jesus is the Lord, but by the Holy Ghost."

The Holy Spirit has power to reveal Jesus Christ and His glory to man. When Jesus spoke of the Spirit's coming, He said:

"But when the Comforter is come, whom I will send unto you from the Father, even the Spirit of truth, which proceedeth from the Father, he shall testify of me."—John 15:26.

And it is only as He does testify of Christ that men will ever come to a true knowledge of Christ. You send men to the Word to get a knowledge of Christ; but it is only as the Holy Spirit takes the Word and illuminates it, that men ever get a real living knowledge of Christ. "No man can say that Jesus is the Lord, but by the Holy Ghost."

If you wish men to get a true knowledge of Jesus Christ, such a view that they will believe on Him and be saved, you must seek for them the testimony of the Holy Spirit. Neither your testimony nor that of the

Word alone will suffice, though it is your testimony, or that of the Word, which the Spirit uses.

But unless your testimony is taken up by the Holy Spirit and He Himself testifies, they will not believe. It was not merely Peter's words about Christ that convinced the Jews at Pentecost. It was the Spirit Himself bearing witness. If you wish men to see the truth about Jesus, do not depend upon your own powers of exposition and persuasion, but cast yourself upon the Holy Ghost and seek His testimony. If you wish yourself to know Jesus with a true and living knowledge, seek the witness of the Spirit through the Word. Many a man has a correct doctrinal conception of Christ, through a study of the Word, long before he has a true personal knowledge of Christ through the testimony of the living Spirit.

2. The Holy Spirit Has Power to Convict the World of Sin

Now let us turn to John 16:8-11:

"And when he is come, he will reprove the world of sin, and of righteousness, and of judgment: Of sin, because they believe not on me; Of righteousness, because I go to my Father, and ye see me no more; Of judgment, because the prince of this world is judged."

The Holy Spirit has power to convict the world of sin. This is closely connected with the preceding; for it is by showing Jesus and His glory and His righteousness that the Holy Spirit convicts of sin and of righteousness and of judgment.

Note the sin of which the Holy Spirit convicts, "Of sin, because they believe not on me." It was so at Pentecost, as we see in Acts 2:36,37.

You can never convict any man of sin because that is the work of the Holy Spirit. You can reason and reason, and you will fail. The Holy Spirit can do it very quickly.

Did you never have this experience? You have shown a man passage after passage of Scripture and he was unmoved, and you have wondered why the man did not break down. Suddenly it has occurred to you, *Why, I am not looking in my helplessness to the mighty Spirit of God to convict this man of sin, but I am trying to convince the man of sin myself.* Then when you cast yourself upon the Spirit of God for Him to do the work, conviction came. The Spirit can convince the most careless, as experience has proven again and again.

But it is through us that the Spirit produces conviction. In John 16:7,8, we read, "I will send him unto you. And when he is come, he will reprove the world of sin, and of righteousness, and of judgment." It was the Spirit sent to Peter and the rest who convicted the three thousand through Peter and the others on the day of Pentecost.

It is ours to preach the Word and to look to the Holy Spirit to produce conviction (see Acts 2:4-37).

3. The Holy Spirit Has Power to Regenerate

In Titus 3:5, we read,

"Not by works of righteousness which we have done, but according to his mercy he saved us, by the washing of regeneration, and renewing of the Holy Ghost."

The Holy Spirit has power to renew men or make men new, to regenerate. Regeneration is the Holy Spirit's work. He can take a man dead in trespasses and sins and make him alive. He can take the man whose mind is blind to the truth of God, whose will is at enmity with God, and set on sin, whose affections are corrupt and vile, and transform that man, impart to him God's nature so that he thinks God's thoughts, wills what God wills, loves what God loves, and hates what God hates.

I never despair of any man when I think of the power of the Holy Spirit to make new, as I have seen it manifested again and again in the most hardened and hopeless cases. It is through us that the Holy Spirit regenerates others (I Cor. 4:15). In another message I showed that the Word has power to regenerate; but it is not the bare word, but the word made a living thing in the heart by the power of the Holy Spirit. No amount of preaching, no matter how orthodox it is, and no amount of mere study of the Word will regenerate unless the Holy Spirit works. Just as we are utterly dependent on the work of Christ for us in justification, so we are utterly dependent upon the work of the Holy Spirit in us in regeneration.

When one is born of the Spirit, the Spirit takes up His own abode in him (I Cor. 3:16; 6:19). The Holy Spirit dwells in everyone who belongs to Christ (Rom. 8:9). We may not have surrendered our lives very fully to this indwelling Spirit; we may be very far from being "full of the Spirit"; we may be very imperfect Christians; but, if we have been born again, the Spirit dwells in us, just as Paul said to the Corinthians, who were certainly very far from perfect Christians, that He did in them.

What a glorious thought it is that the Holy Spirit dwells in me! But it is a very solemn thought. If my body is the temple of the Holy Spirit, I certainly ought not defile it, as many professed Christians do. Bearing in mind that our bodies are temples of the Holy Spirit would solve many problems that perplex young Christians.

4. The Holy Spirit Has Power to Give Everlasting Satisfaction

We find a further thought about the power of the Holy Spirit in John 4:14:

"But whosoever drinketh of the water that I shall give him shall never thirst; but the water that I shall give him shall be in him a well of water springing up into everlasting life."

You may not see at first that this verse has anything to do with the Holy Spirit, but compare John 7:37,39, and it will be evident that the water here means the Holy Spirit. The Holy Spirit, then, has power to give abiding and everlasting satisfaction.

The world can never satisfy. Of every worldly joy it must be said, "Whosoever drinketh of this water shall thirst again." But the Holy Spirit has power to satisfy every longing of the soul. The Holy Spirit and He alone can satisfy the human heart. If you give yourself up to the Holy Spirit's inflowing, or rather upspringing, in your heart, you will never thirst. You will not long for the theater, or the ballroom, or the card party, or worldly gain, or honor.

Oh, with what joy unutterable and satisfaction indescribable the Holy Spirit has poured forth His living water in many souls! Have you this living fountain within? Is the spring unchoked? Is it springing up into everlasting life?

5. The Holy Spirit Has Power to Set Us Free From the Law of Sin and Death

In Romans 8:2, we read,

"For the law of the Spirit of life in Christ Jesus hath made me free from the law of sin and death."

The Holy Spirit has power to set us free from the law of sin and death. What the law of sin and death is, we see in the preceding chapter (Rom. 7:9-24). Read this description carefully.

We all know this law of sin and death. We have all been in bondage to it. Some of us are still in bondage to it, but we do not need
to be. God has provided a way of escape. That way is by the Holy
Spirit's power.

When we give up the hopeless struggle of trying to overcome the
law of sin and death, of trying to live right in our strength, in the power
of the flesh; and in utter helplessness surrender to the Holy Spirit to
do all for us; when we live after Him and walk in His blessed power;
then He sets us free from the law of sin and death.

Many professed Christians today are living in Romans 7. Some go
so far as to maintain that this is the normal Christian life, that one must
live this life of constant defeat. This would be true, if we were left to
ourselves; for in ourselves we are "carnal, sold under sin." But we are
not left to ourselves. The Holy Spirit undertakes for us what we have
failed to do ourselves (Rom. 8:2-4).

In Romans 8 we have the picture of the true Christian life, the life
that is possible to us and that God expects from each one of us; the
life where not merely the commandment comes, as in chapter 7, but
where the mighty Spirit comes also and works obedience and victory.

The flesh is still in us, but we are not in the flesh (Rom. 8:12,13,
compare vs. 9). We do not live after it. We "live after the Spirit."
We, "through the Spirit do mortify the deeds of the body." We "walk
in the Spirit," and do "not fulfil the lust of the flesh" (Gal. 5:16).

It is our privilege, in the Spirit's power, to get daily, hourly, constant victory over the flesh and over sin. But the victory is not in ourselves, not in any strength of our own. Left to ourselves, deserted
of the Spirit of God, we would be as helpless as ever. It is all in the
Spirit's power. If we try to take one step in our own strength, we
shall fail.

Has the Holy Spirit set you free from the law of sin and death?
Will you let Him do it now? Simply give up all self-effort to be free
from "the law of sin and death," to give up sinning; believe in the
divine power of the Holy Spirit to set you free; and cast yourself
upon Him to do it. He will do it. Then you can triumphantly cry
with Paul, "For the law of the Spirit of life in Christ Jesus made me
free from the law of sin and of death" (Rom. 8:2, American Revised
Version).

6. The Holy Spirit Strengthens the Believer With Power in the Inward Man

We find a closely allied but larger thought about the Holy Spirit's power in Ephesians 3:16 (A.R.V.):

"That he would grant you, according to the riches of his glory, that ye may be strengthened with power through his Spirit in the inward man."

The Holy Spirit strengthens the believer with power in the inward man. The result of this strengthening is seen in verses 17 to 19. Here the power of the Spirit manifests itself not merely in giving us victory over sin, but (a) in Christ's dwelling in our hearts; (b) our being "rooted and grounded in love"; (c) our being made "strong to apprehend with all the saints what is the breadth and length and height and depth, and to know the love of Christ which passeth knowledge . . . " (Eph. 3:18,19). It all ultimates in our being "filled unto all the fulness of God."

7. The Holy Spirit Has Power to Lead Us Into a Godlike Life

We find a still further thought about the Holy Spirit's power in Romans 8:14 (A.R.V.):

"For as many as are led by the Spirit of God, these are sons of God."

The Holy Spirit has power to lead us into a holy life, a life as "sons of God," a Godlike life. Not merely does the Holy Spirit give us power to live a life well-pleasing to God when we have discovered what that life is; He takes us by the hand, as it were, and leads us into that life. Our whole part is simply to surrender ourselves utterly to Him to lead and to mold us. Those who do this are not merely God's offspring, which all men are (Acts 17:28); neither are we merely God's children: "These are sons of God."

8. The Holy Spirit Bears Witness With Our Spirit That We Are Children of God

Further down in the chapter there is a new thought. Romans 8:16 (A.R.V.):

"The Spirit himself beareth witness with our spirit, that we are children of God."

The Holy Spirit bears witness with the spirit of the believer that he is a child of God. Note that Paul does not say that the Spirit bears witness *to* our spirit, but *with* it—"together with our spirit" is the exact force of the words used. That is, there are two who bear witness to our sonship: first, our spirit bears witness that we are children of God; second, the Holy Spirit bears witness together with our spirit that we are children of God.

How does the Holy Spirit bear His testimony to this fact? Galatians 4:6 answers this question, "And because ye are sons, God sent forth the Spirit of his Son into your hearts, crying, Abba, Father" (A.R.V.). The Holy Spirit Himself enters into our hearts and cries, "Abba, Father."

Note the order of the Spirit's work in Romans 8:2,4,13,14,16. It is only when "the law of the Spirit of life in Christ Jesus hath made me free from the law of sin and death" (vs. 2), and so "the righteousness of the law might be fulfilled" in me "who walk not after the flesh, but after the Spirit" (vs. 4), and I "through the Spirit of God do mortify the deeds of the body" (vs. 13), and when I am surrendered to the Spirit's leading (vs. 14), it is then, and only then, that I can expect verse 16 to be realized in my experience, and that I have the clear assurance of sonship that comes from the Spirit of God testifying together with my spirit, that I am a child of God.

There are many seeking this testimony of the Holy Spirit in the wrong place; namely, as a condition of their surrendering wholly to God and confessing the crucified and risen Lord as their Saviour and Lord. The testimony of the Holy Spirit to our sonship comes after all this is done.

9. The Holy Spirit Gives Us Christlike Graces of Character

An exceedingly important thought about the Holy Spirit's power is found in Galatians 5:22,23:

"But the fruit of the Spirit is love, joy, peace, longsuffering, gentleness, goodness, faith, Meekness, temperance: against such there is no law."

The Holy Spirit brings forth in the believer Christlike graces of character (compare Rom. 5:5; 14:17; 15:13). All real beauty of character, all real Christlikeness in us, is the Holy Spirit's work. It is His "fruit." He bears it; not we.

Note that these graces are not said to be the fruits of the Spirit; they are the "fruit." There is a unity of origin running all through the multiplicity of manifestation; and not some of these graces, but all, will appear in everyone in whom the Holy Spirit is given full control.

It is a beautiful life that is set forth in these verses. Every word is worthy of earnest study and profound meditation: "Love," "joy," "peace," "longsuffering," "gentleness," "goodness," "faith," "meekness," "self-control." Is not this the life we all long for, the Christ life?

It is not natural to us, and it is not attainable by any effort of "the flesh," or nature. The life that is natural for us is set forth in the three preceding verses (19-21). But when the indwelling Spirit is given full control in the one He inhabits; when we are brought to realize the utter badness of the flesh and give up in helpless despair of ever attaining to anything really good in its power, when, in other words, we come to the end of self and just give over the whole work of making us what we ought to be to the indwelling HOLY SPIRIT, then, and only then, these holy graces of character are His "fruit."

Do you wish these graces in your character and life? Renounce self utterly, and all its strivings after holiness, and let the Holy Spirit, who dwells in you, take full control and bear His own glorious fruit.

We get the same essential truth from another point of view in Galatians 2:20 (A.R.V., Am. App.):

"I have been crucified with Christ; and it is no longer I that live, but Christ liveth in me: and that life which I now live in the flesh I live in faith, the faith which is in the Son of God, who loved me, and gave himself up for me."

Settle it clearly and forever that the flesh can never bear this fruit, that you can never attain these things by your own effort, that they are "the fruit of the Spirit."

We hear a good deal in these days about "ethical culture," which usually means a cultivation of the flesh until it bears the fruit of the Spirit. It cannot be done, until thorns can be made to bear figs, and a bramblebush, grapes (Matt. 12:33; Luke 6:44).

We hear also a good deal about "character-building." That is all very well, if you let the Holy Spirit do the building, and then it is not so much building as fruit-bearing. (See, however, II Pet. 1:5-7.)

We hear also about "cultivating graces of character," but we must always bear in mind that the way to cultivate true graces of character is by submitting ourselves utterly to the Spirit to do His work. This is "sanctification of the Spirit" (I Pet. 1:2; II Thess. 2:13).

We turn now to the power of the Holy Spirit in a different direction.

10. The Holy Spirit Has Power to Guide Us Into "All the Truth"

John 16:13 (A.R.V.):

"Howbeit when he, the Spirit of truth, is come, he shall guide you into all the truth: for he shall not speak from himself; but what things soever he shall hear, these shall he speak: and he shall declare unto you the things that are to come."

The Holy Spirit has power to guide the believer "into all the truth." This promise was made in the first instance to the apostles, but the apostles themselves applied it to all believers (I John 2:20,27).

It is the privilege of each of us to be "taught of God." Each believer is independent of human teachers. "Ye need not that any man teach you."

This does not mean, of course, that we may not learn much from others who are taught by the Holy Spirit. If John had thought that, he would never have written this epistle to teach others. The man who is most fully taught of God is the very one who will be most ready to listen to what God has taught others. Much less does it mean that when we are taught of God, we are independent of the Word of God. For the Word is the very place to which the Spirit leads His pupils and the instrument through which He teaches them (John 6:63; Eph. 6:17; Eph. 5:18,19; Comp. Col. 3:16). But, while we may learn much from men, we are not dependent upon them. We have a divine teacher, the Holy Spirit.

We shall never truly know the truth until we are thus taught. No amount of mere human teaching, no matter who our teachers may be, will give us a correct apprehension of the truth. Not even a diligent study of the Word, either in the English or original languages, will give us a real understanding of the truth. We must be taught of the Holy Spirit.

And we may be thus taught, each one of us. The one who is thus taught, even if he does not know a word of Greek or Hebrew, will understand the truth of God better than the one who knows the Greek and Hebrew and all "the cognate languages," and is not taught of the Spirit. The Spirit will guide the one He teaches "into all the truth," not in a day, or in a week, or in a year, but step by step.

There are two special lines of the Spirit's teaching mentioned: (a) "He shall declare unto you the things that are to come." Many say we can know nothing of the future, that all our thoughts on that subject are guesswork. Anyone taught of the Spirit knows better than that; (b) "He shall glorify me [i.e., Christ]: for he shall take of mine, and shall declare it unto you." This is the Holy Spirit's special line with the believer as well as the unbeliever, to declare unto them the things of Christ and glorify Him.

Many fear to emphasize the truth about the Holy Spirit lest Christ be disparaged. But no one magnifies Christ as the Holy Spirit does. We will never understand Christ, nor see His glory, until the Holy Spirit interprets Him to us. The mere listening to sermons and lectures, the mere study of the Word even, will never give you understanding to see the things of Christ. The Holy Spirit must show you, and He is willing to do it. He is longing to do it. I suppose the Holy Spirit's inmost desire is to reveal Jesus Christ to men. Let Him do it. Christ is so different when the Holy Spirit glorifies Him by taking of the things of Christ and showing them unto us.

11. The Holy Spirit Has Power to Bring to Remembrance the Words of Christ

Turning to John 14:26 (A.R.V.), we find again the Holy Spirit's power to teach, but with an added thought:

"But the Comforter, even the Holy Spirit, whom the Father will send in my name, he shall teach you all things and bring to your remembrance all that I said unto you."

The Holy Spirit has power to bring to remembrance the words of Christ. This promise was made primarily to the apostles and is the guarantee of the accuracy of their report of what Jesus said. But the Holy Spirit does a similar work with each believer who expects it of Him and looks to Him to do it. He brings to mind the teachings of Christ and the words of Christ just when we need them, for either the necessities of our own life or of our service.

How many of us could tell of occasions when we were in great distress of soul, of great questioning concerning our duty, or great extremity as to what to say to one whom we were trying to lead to Christ or to help; and just the Scripture we needed, some passage we had not thought of for a long time, and, perhaps, never thought of in this connection, was brought to mind. It was the Holy Spirit who did this; and He is ready to do it even more when we expect it of Him.

Is it without significance that in the next verse after making this great promise, Jesus says: "Peace I leave with you; my peace I give unto you"? Look to the Holy Spirit to bring the right words to remembrance at the right time, and you will have peace. This is the way to remember Scripture just when you need it and just the Scripture you need.

12. The Holy Spirit Reveals to Us the Deep Things of God; and Imparts Power of Discernment

Closely akin to what has been said in the two preceding sections is the power of the Holy Spirit as seen in I Corinthians 2:10-14 (A.R.V.):

"But unto us God revealed them through the Spirit: for the Spirit searcheth all things, yea, the deep things of God. For who among men knoweth the things of a man, save the spirit of the man, which is in him? even so the things of God none knoweth, save the Spirit of God. But we received, not the spirit of the world, but the spirit which is from God; that we might know the things that were freely given to us of God. Which things also we speak, not in words which man's wisdom teacheth, but which the Spirit teacheth; combining spiritual things with spiritual words. Now the natural man receiveth not the things of the Spirit of God: for they are foolishness unto him; and he cannot know them, because they are spiritually judged."

In these verses we have a twofold work of the Spirit: (a) The Holy Spirit reveals to us the deep things of God, which are hidden from and foolishness to the natural man. It is preeminently to the apostles that He does this, but we cannot limit this work of the Spirit to them; (b) The Holy Spirit interprets His own revelation, or imparts power to discern, know, and appreciate what He has taught.

Not only is the Holy Spirit the author of Revelation—the written Word of God; He is also the interpreter of what He has revealed.

How much more interesting and helpful any deep book becomes when we have the author of the book right at hand to interpret it to us! This is what we always may have when we study the Bible. The author—the Holy Spirit—is right at hand to interpret. To understand the book we must look to Him. Then the darkest places become clear. We need to pray often with the psalmist, "Open thou mine eyes, that I may behold wondrous things out of thy law" (Ps. 119:18).

It is not enough that we have the objective revelation in the written Word; we must also have the inward illumination of the Holy Spirit to enable us to comprehend it. It is a great mistake to try to comprehend a spiritual revelation with the natural understanding. It is the foolish attempt to do this that has landed so many in the bog of the higher criticism. A man with no aesthetic sense might as well expect to appreciate the Sistine Madonna, because he is not color blind, as an unspiritual man to understand the Bible, simply because he understands the laws of grammar and the vocabulary of the language in which the Bible was written. I would as soon think of setting a man to teach art merely because he understood paints as to set him to teach the Bible merely because he understood Greek or Hebrew.

We all need not only to recognize the utter insufficiency and worthlessness of our own righteousness, which is the lesson of the opening chapters of the epistle to the Romans, but also the utter insufficiency and worthlessness in the things of God, of our own wisdom, which is the lesson of the first Epistle to the Corinthians, especially the first to the third chapters (see, e.g., I Cor. 1:19-21, 26, 27).

The Jews had a revelation by the Spirit, but they failed to depend upon Him to interpret it to them, so they went astray. The whole evangelical church realizes the utter insufficiency of man's righteousness, theoretically at least. Now it needs to be taught, and made to feel, the utter insufficiency of man's wisdom. That is perhaps the lesson this nineteenth century of overweening intellectual conceit needs most of any.

To understand God's Word, we must empty ourselves utterly of our own wisdom and rest in utter dependence upon the Spirit of God to interpret it to us (Matt. 11:25). When we put away our own righteousness, then, and only then, we get the righteousness of God (Phil. 3:4-7, 9; Rom. 10:3). When we put away our own wisdom, then, and only then, we get the wisdom of God (Matt. 11:25; I Cor. 3:18; I Cor. 1:25-28). When we put away our own strength, then, and only then, we get the strength of God (Isa. 40:29; II Cor. 12:9; I Cor. 1:27, 28). Emptying must precede filling—self poured out that Christ may be poured in. We must be daily taught of the Spirit to understand the Word.

I cannot depend on the fact that the Spirit taught me yesterday. Each new contact with the Word must be in the power of the Spirit. That the Holy Spirit once illumined our mind to grasp a certain passage is not enough. He must do so each time we confront that passage.

Andrew Murray has put this truth well:

Each time you come to the Word in study, in hearing a sermon or reading a religious book, there ought to be as distinct as your intercourse with the external means, a definite act of self-abnegation, denying your own wisdom and yielding yourself in faith to the divine Teacher (*The Spirit of Christ*, p. 221).

13. The Holy Spirit Helps Us Communicate Truth to Others

The Holy Spirit has not only power to teach us the truth, but also to impart power to us in communicating that truth to others. We see this brought out again and again.

"And I, brethren, when I came unto you, came not with excellency of speech or of wisdom, proclaiming to you the testimony of God. For I determined not to know anything among you, save Jesus Christ, and him crucified. And I was with you in weakness, and in fear, and in much trembling. And my speech and my preaching were not in persuasive words of wisdom, but in demonstration of the Spirit and of power: that your faith should not stand in the wisdom of men, but in the power of God."—I Cor. 2:1-5 (A.R.V.).

"Our gospel came not unto you in word only, but also in power, and in the Holy Ghost" (I Thess. 1:5). "But ye shall receive power, after that the Holy Ghost is come upon you" (Acts 1:8). The Holy Spirit enables the believer to communicate to others in "power" the truth he himself has been taught.

We not only need the Holy Spirit to reveal the truth in the first place; and the Holy Spirit in the second place to interpret to us as individuals the truth He has revealed; but in the third place we also need the Holy Spirit to enable us to effectually communicate to others the truth He Himself has interpreted to us. We need Him all along the line.

One great cause of real failure in the ministry, even when there is seeming success, and not only in the ministry but in all forms of service by Christian men and women, is from the attempt to teach by "enticing words of man's wisdom," i.e., by the arts of human logic, rhetoric or eloquence, what the Holy Spirit has taught us. What is needed is Holy Ghost power, "demonstration of the Spirit and of power."

There are three causes of failure in Christian work.

First, some other message is taught than the message which the Holy Spirit has revealed in the Word. Men preach science, art, philosophy, sociology, history, experience, etc., etc., and not the simple Word of God as found in the Holy Spirit's Book—the Bible.

Second, the Spirit-taught message, the Bible, is studied and sought to be comprehended by the natural understanding, i.e., without the Spirit's illumination.

Third, the Spirit-given message, the Word, the Bible, studied and comprehended under the Holy Spirit's illumination, is given out to others with "enticing words of man's wisdom" and not "in demonstration of the Spirit and of power."

We need, we are absolutely dependent upon, the Holy Spirit all along the line. He must teach us how to speak as well as what to speak. He must be the power as well as the message.

14. The Holy Spirit Has Power to Teach Us How to Pray

In Jude 20 (A.R.V.) we read,

"But ye, beloved, building up yourselves on your most holy faith, praying in the Holy Spirit."

Again in Ephesians 6:18 (A.R.V.),

"Praying at all seasons in the Spirit."

The Holy Spirit guides the believer in prayer. The disciples did not know how to pray as they ought, so they came to Jesus and said, "Lord, teach us to pray" (Luke 11:1). "We know not how to pray as we ought," but we have another Helper right at hand to help us (John 14:16,17). "The Spirit also helpeth our infirmity" (Rom. 8:26, A.R.V.). He teacheth us to pray. True prayer is prayer "in the Spirit," i.e., the prayer which the Spirit inspires and directs. When we come into God's presence to pray, we should recognize our infirmity, our ignorance of what we should pray for or how we should pray, and in the consciousness of our utter inability to pray aright, look up to the Holy Spirit and cast ourselves utterly upon Him to direct our prayers, to lead out our desires and guide our utterance of them.

Rushing heedlessly into God's presence and asking the first thing that comes into our minds or that some thoughtless one asks us to pray for, is not "praying in the Holy Ghost" and is not true prayer. We must wait for the Holy Spirit and surrender ourselves to the Holy Spirit. The prayer that God the Holy Spirit inspires is the prayer that God the Father answers.

From Romans 8:26,27, we learn that the longings which the Holy Spirit begets in our hearts are often too deep for utterance; too deep, apparently, for clear and definite comprehension on the part of the believer himself, in whom the Holy Spirit is working. God Himself must "search the heart" to know "what is the mind of the Spirit" in these unuttered and unutterable longings.

But God does know "what is the mind of the Spirit." He does know what those Spirit-given longings mean, even if we do not; and when these longings are "according to the will of God," He grants them. So it comes that He is "able to do exceeding abundantly above all that we ask or think, according to the power that worketh in us" (Eph. 3:20). There are other times when the Spirit's leadings in prayer are so plain that we 'pray with the Spirit and with the understanding also' (I Cor. 14:15).

15. The Holy Spirit Has Also Power to Lead Out Our Hearts in Acceptable Thanksgiving to God

Paul says:

"... Be filled with the Spirit; speaking one to another in psalms and hymns and spiritual songs, singing and making melody with your heart to the Lord; giving thanks always for all things in the name of our Lord Jesus Christ to God, even the Father."—Eph. 5:18-20 (A.R.V.)

Not only does the Spirit teach us to pray, He also teaches us to render thanks. One of the most prominent characteristics of the "Spirit-filled life" is thanksgiving. True thanksgiving is "to God, even the Father," "in the name of our Lord Jesus Christ," "in the Holy Spirit."

16. The Holy Spirit Has Power to Inspire in the Heart of the Believer Worship Acceptable to God

"For we are the circumcision, who worship by the Spirit of God, and glory in Christ Jesus, and have no confidence in the flesh."—Phil. 3:3 (A.R.V.).

Prayer is not worship. Thanksgiving is not worship. Worship is a definite act of the creature in relation to God. Worship is bowing before God in adoring acknowledgment and contemplation of Himself.

Someone has said, "In our prayers we are taken up with our needs; in our thanksgivings we are taken up with our blessings; in our worship we are taken up with Himself."

There is no true and acceptable worship except that which the Holy Spirit prompts and directs. "Such doth the Father seek to be his worshippers" (John 4:23, A.R.V.).

The flesh seeks to enter every sphere of life. It has its worship as well as its lust. The worship which the flesh prompts is an abomination to God.

Not all earnest and honest worship is worship in the Spirit. A man may be very honest and very earnest in his worship and still not have submitted himself to the guidance of the Holy Spirit in the matter, and so his worship is in the flesh. Even where there is great loyalty to the letter of the Word, worship may not be "in the Spirit," i.e., inspired and directed by Him.

To worship aright we must "have no confidence in the flesh." We must recognize the utter inability of the flesh, i.e., our natural self as contrasted with the divine Spirit who dwells in and should mold everything in the believer, to worship acceptably. We must realize also the danger there is that the flesh, self, intrude itself into our worship. In utter self-distrust and self-abnegation we must cast ourselves upon the Holy Spirit, to lead us aright in our worship. Just as we must renounce any merit in ourselves and cast ourselves utterly upon Christ and His work for us for justification; just so we must renounce any capacity for good in ourselves and cast ourselves utterly upon the Holy Spirit and His work in us in living, praying, thanking and worshiping and all else that we are to do.

17. The Holy Spirit's Power as a Guide

In Acts 13:2-4, we read:

"As they ministered to the Lord, and fasted, the Holy Ghost said, Separate me Barnabas and Saul for the work whereunto I have called them. And when they had fasted and prayed, and laid their hands on them, they sent them away. So they, being sent forth by the Holy Ghost, departed unto Seleucia; and from thence they sailed to Cyprus."

The Holy Spirit calls men and sends them forth to definite lines of work. The Holy Spirit not only calls men in a general way into Christian work, but He also selects the specific work and points it out. "Shall I go to China, to Africa, to India?" many a one is asking, and many another ought to ask.

You cannot rightly settle that question for yourselves, neither can any other man settle it rightly for you. Not every Christian man is called to China or Africa or any other foreign field. God alone knows whether He wishes you to go to any of these places. He is willing to show you.

How does the Holy Spirit call? The passage before us does not tell. It is presumably purposely silent on this point, lest, perhaps, we think that He must always call in precisely the same way.

There is nothing to indicate that He spoke by an audible voice, much less that He made His will known in any of the fantastic ways in which some profess to discern His leading, as, e.g., by some twitching of the body or by opening the Bible at random and putting the finger on a passage that may be construed into some entirely different meaning than that which the inspired writer intended by it. But the important point is that He made His will clearly known. He is as willing to make His will clearly known to us today.

The great need in Christian work today is men and women whom the Holy Spirit calls and sends forth. We have plenty of men and women whom men have called and sent forth. We have far too many who have called themselves. There are many today who object strenuously to being sent forth by men, by any organization of any kind, who are, what is immeasurably worse than that, sent forth by themselves, not by God.

How shall we receive the Holy Spirit's call? By desiring it, seeking it, waiting upon the Lord for it and expecting it. "As they ministered to the Lord, and fasted," the record reads.

Many a man is saying, in self-justification for staying out of the ministry or for staying home from the foreign field, "I have never had a call." How do you know that? Have you been listening for it? God speaks often in a still small voice. Only the listening ear can catch it. Have you definitely offered yourself to God to send you where He will? While no man ought to go to China or Africa unless he is clearly and definitely called, he ought to definitely offer himself to God for His work and be ready for a call and listening sharply that he may hear it when it comes. No educated Christian man or woman has a right to rest easy out of the foreign field until they have definitely offered themselves to God for that work and it is clear no call from God has come. Indeed, a man needs no more definite call to Africa than to Boston or New York or Chicago.

18. The Holy Spirit Guides in the
Details of Daily Life

We learn something further about the Holy Spirit's power to guide in Acts 8:27-29.

First, we have the story of Philip:

"And he arose and went: and, behold, a man of Ethiopia, an eunuch of great authority under Candace queen of the Ethiopians, who had the charge of all her treasure, and had come to Jerusalem for to worship, Was returning, and sitting in his chariot read Esaias the prophet. Then the Spirit said unto Philip, Go near, and join thyself to this chariot."

The second word is about Paul and his missionary party:

"And they went through the region of Phrygia and Galatia, having been forbidden of the Holy Spirit to speak the word in Asia; and when they were come over against Mysia, they assayed to go into Bithynia; and the Spirit of Jesus suffered them not."—Acts 16:6,7 (A.R.V.).

The Holy Spirit guides in the details of daily life and service as to where to go and where not to go, what to do and what not to do.

It is possible for us to have the unerring guidance of the Holy Spirit at every turn in our lives. For example, in personal work it is manifestly not God's intention that we speak to everyone we meet. There are some to whom we ought not to speak. Time spent on them would be time taken from work which would be more to the glory of God.

Doubtless Philip met many as he journeyed toward Gaza, before he met the one of whom the Spirit said, "Go near, and join thyself to this chariot." In the same way is He ready to guide us in our personal work. He is ready also to guide us in all the affairs of life: business, study, social life—everything.

We can have God's wisdom, if we will, at every turn of life. There is no promise more plain and explicit than James 1:5: "If any of you lack wisdom, let him ask of God, that giveth to all men liberally, and upbraideth not; and it shall be given him." How shall we gain this wisdom? James 1:5-7 answers. Here are really five steps.

First: That we "lack wisdom." We must be conscious of and fully admit our own inability to decide wisely. Not only the sinfulness but the wisdom of the flesh must be renounced.

Second: We must really desire to know God's way and be willing to do God's will. This is implied in the asking, if the asking be sincere.

This is a point of fundamental importance. Here we find the reason why men ofttimes do not know God's will and have not the Spirit's guidance. They are not really willing to do whatever the Spirit leads them to do. It is "the meek" whom He guides in judgment and the meek to whom "he will teach his ways" (Ps. 25:9). It is he who "willeth to do his will" who "shall know" (John 7:17, A.R.V.).

Third: We must ask, definitely ask guidance.

Fourth: We must confidently expect guidance.

"Let him ask in faith, nothing doubting" (vss. 6,7, A.R.V.).

Fifth: We must follow step by step as the guidance comes. Just how it will come no one can tell. But it will come. It may come with only a step made clear at a time. That is all we need to know—the next step. Many are in darkness because they do not know what God will have them to do next week or next month or next year.

Do you know the next step? That is enough. Take it. Then He will show you the next (see Num. 9:17-23). God's guidance is clear guidance (I John 1:5). Many are tortured by leadings which they fear may be from God but which they are not sure about. You have a right as God's child to be sure. Go to God and say, "Here I am, heavenly Father; I am willing to do Thy will, but make it clear. If this is Thy will, I will do it; but make it clear if it is." He will do it if it is His will and you are willing to do it. You need not and ought not to do that thing until He does make it clear.

We have no right to dictate to God how He shall give His guidance, as, e.g., by "shutting up every other way," or by a sign, or by letting us put our finger on a text. It is ours to seek and expect wisdom, but it is not ours to indicate how it shall be given (I Cor. 12:11).

19. The Holy Spirit Has Power to Give Us Boldness in Testimony

In one more direction has the Holy Spirit power. Read Acts 4:31; 13:9, 10:

"And when they had prayed, the place was shaken where they were assembled together; and they were all filled with the Holy Ghost, and they spake the word of God with boldness."

The Holy Spirit has power to give us boldness in testimony for Christ.

Many are naturally timid. They long to do something for Christ, but they are afraid. The Holy Spirit can make you bold if you will look to

Him and trust Him to do it. It was He who turned the craven Peter into the one who fearlessly faced the Sanhedrin and rebuked their sin (see Acts 4:8-12).

Two things are manifest from what has been said about the power of the Holy Spirit in the believer: first, how utterly dependent we are upon the Holy Spirit at every turn of Christian life and service; second, how perfect is the provision for life and service that God has made, and what fullness of privilege that is open to the humblest believer, through the Holy Spirit's work!

It is not so much what we are by nature either intellectually, morally, spiritually or even physically that is important; but what the Holy Spirit can do for us and what we will let Him do. The Holy Spirit often takes the one who gives the least natural promise and uses him far more than those who give the greatest natural promise.

Christian life is not to be lived in the realm of natural temperament, and Christian work is not to be done in the power of natural endowment; but Christian life is to be lived in the realm of the Spirit, and Christian work is to be done in the power of the Holy Ghost.

The Holy Spirit is eagerly desirous to do for each of us His whole work. He will do for each of us all we will let Him do.

(From the book, *How to Obtain Fullness of Power,* Sword of the Lord Publishers, Murfreesboro, TN 37133)

DWIGHT LYMAN MOODY
1837-1899

ABOUT THE MAN:

D. L. Moody may well have been the greatest evangelist of all time. In a 40-year period, he won a million souls, founded three Christian schools, launched a great Christian publishing business, established a world-renowned Christian conference center, and inspired literally thousands of preachers to win souls and conduct revivals.

A shoe clerk at 17, his ambition was to make $100,000. Converted at 18, he uncovered hidden gospel gold in the hearts of millions for the next half century. He preached to 20,000 a day in Brooklyn and admitted only non-church members by ticket!

He met a young songleader in Indianapolis, said bluntly, "You're the man I've been looking for for eight years. Throw up your job and come with me." Ira D. Sankey did just that; thereafter it was "Moody will preach; Sankey will sing."

He traveled across the American continent and through Great Britain in some of the greatest and most successful evangelistic meetings communities have ever known. His tour of the world with Sankey was considered the greatest evangelistic enterprise of the century.

It was Henry Varley who said, "It remains to be seen what God will do with a man who gives himself up wholly to Him." And Moody endeavored to be, under God, that man; and the world did marvel to see how wonderfully God used him.

Two great monuments stand to the indefatigable work and ministry of this gospel warrior—Moody Bible Institute and the famous Moody Church in Chicago.

Moody went to be with the Lord in 1899.

III.

The Dwelling Place for the Holy Ghost

D. L. MOODY

"And he [Moses] reared up the court round about the tabernacle and the altar, and set up the hanging of the court gate. So Moses finished the work. Then a cloud covered the tent of the congregation, and the glory of the Lord filled the tabernacle. And Moses was not able to enter into the tent of the congregation, because the cloud abode thereon, and the glory of the Lord filled the tabernacle."—Exod. 40:33-35.

Our subject today is the Holy Spirit upon us for service, and I want to call your attention to this distinction. The Holy Spirit dwelling *in* us is one thing; the Holy Spirit *upon* us for service is another thing.

Now we find in Scripture only three dwelling places for the Holy Ghost.

It would appear from Scripture that the moment he finished the work, the moment that Tabernacle was ready, the cloud, the Shekinah, the Holy Spirit came and filled it so that Moses was not able to stand before the presence of the Lord.

I firmly believe that the moment our hearts and minds are emptied of pride and self, emptied of ambition and self-seeking and everything else contrary to God's law, the Holy Ghost will come and fill every corner of our hearts; but if we are full of pride and conceit, full of self-seeking, full of pleasure and the world, there is no room for the Spirit of God. Many a man, praying for God to fill him, is full already with something else.

Before we pray for God to fill us, we should pray for God to empty us. There has to be an emptying before there can be a filling. And when the heart is turned bottom side up and everything is turned out that is contrary to God's holy law, then the Spirit will come and fill it again, just as He did in the Tabernacle.

Now we read in II Chronicles 5:13 and 14:

"It came even to pass, as the trumpeters and singers were as one, to make one sound to be heard in praising and thanking the Lord; and when they lifted up their voice with the trumpets and cymbals and instruments of musick, and praised the Lord, saying, For he is good; for his mercy endureth for ever: that then the house was filled with a cloud, even the house of the Lord; So that the priests could not stand to minister by reason of the cloud: for the glory of the Lord had filled the house of God."

As soon as Solomon had the Temple finished, they were praising God with one heart. The choristers, the singers, the minister were all one. There was no discord, but all were praising God. The glory of God came and filled the Temple and the Tabernacle.

In the New Testament, instead of coming to tabernacles and temples, WE are now the temples of the Holy Ghost. On the day of Pentecost, or just before Peter preached that memorable sermon, as they were praying, the Holy Ghost came in mighty power. Now we pray for the Spirit of God to come and we sing,

Come, Holy Spirit, heavenly dove,
With all Thy quickening power;
Kindle a flame of heavenly love
In these cold hearts of ours.

If we understand the meaning, it is perfectly right; but if we are praying for Him to come out of Heaven down to earth again, that is wrong, because He is already here. He has not been away from this earth for nineteen hundred years. He has been in the church and with the believers. The believers are the called-out ones, called out from the earth; and every true believer is a temple for the Holy Ghost to dwell in.

In John 14:17 we read: "Even the Spirit of truth; whom the world cannot receive, because it seeth him not, neither knoweth him: but ye know him; for he dwelleth with you, and shall be in you."

Greater is He that is in you than he that is in the world. And the Spirit dwelling in us gives us power over the flesh, the world and the enemy. That is what it says: He is dwelling in you and shall be in you again.

That is what Paul represented to the Corinthians: "Know ye not that ye are the temple of God, and that the Spirit of God dwelleth in you?" (I Cor. 3:16).

Years ago a saint was being buried. This aged saint was very poor in this world but very rich in the other world. Men were hastening him off to the grave, wanting to get rid of him. But an old minister, officiating at the grave, said, "Tread softly, for ye are carrying the temple of the Holy Ghost."

Whenever you see a believer, you see the temple of the Holy Ghost. He says again:

"What? know ye not that your body is the temple of the Holy Ghost which is in you, which ye have of God, and ye are not your own? For ye are bought with a price: therefore glorify God in your body, and in your spirit, which are God's."—I Cor. 6:19,20.

I call your attention to another truth. It is clearly taught in Scripture that every believer has the Holy Ghost dwelling in him. He may be quenching the Spirit of God where He doesn't have free course; he may not glorify God as he ought; but if he is a believer on the Lord Jesus Christ, the Holy Ghost dwells in him.

The church is today filled with men and women who have the Holy Spirit dwelling in them but they have not the Spirit of God resting on them in power. In other words, God has a great many sons and daughters without power.

At least nine-tenths of our church members never think of speaking for Christ. If they see a man right near them, perhaps a near relative, just rapidly going down to ruin, they never think of talking to him about his sinful course and of trying to win him to Christ. Certainly there must be something wrong. Yet when you talk with them, you find they have faith. And you cannot say they are not children of God. But they do not have the power, nor the liberty, nor the freedom that sons and daughters of God ought to have.

A great many people are thinking that we need new measures, that we need new churches, that we need new organs, that we need new choirs—those new things. But those are not the church's needs today. It is the old power that the apostles had. And if we have that, there will be new life in our churches. Then we will have some "new" ministers—the same old minister but with new power.

When we were in Chicago and were toiling and working and it seemed as though the car of salvation didn't move on, one minister got up and seemed to cry out from the very depths of his heart, "O God, put new ministers in every pulpit in Chicago next Sunday!"

The next Monday I heard two or three men come up and say, "We had a new minister last Sunday—the same old minister, but he had new power."

That is what most of us want all over America—new ministers in the pulpit and new people in the pews; people quickened by the Spirit of God; the Spirit coming down and taking possession and giving us power.

A man filled with the Spirit will know how to use the sword of the Spirit. If a man is not filled with the Spirit, he won't know how to use this Book. We are told that this is the sword of the Spirit. And what is an army good for that doesn't know how to use its weapons?

Suppose there were a battle going on here and I, the general, had 100,000 able-bodied men full of life, but not one of them could handle a sword, not one of them knew how to use his rifle. What would that army be good for? One thousand well-drilled men with good weapons could rout the whole of them.

The church is being routed today by the enemy because we don't know how to use the sword of the Spirit.

People are trying to fight the Devil with their experience, but he will overcome them every time. People are trying to fight the Devil with theories and pet ideas, but he will always get the victory over them. What we want is to draw the sword of the Spirit, that which cuts deeper than anything else.

He says in Ephesians 6:14-17:

"Stand therefore, having your loins girt about with truth, and having on the breastplate of righteousness; and your feet shod with the preparation of the gospel of peace; Above all, taking the shield of faith, wherewith ye shall be able to quench all the fiery darts of the wicked. And take the helmet of salvation, and the sword of the Spirit, which is the word of God."

". . . which is the word of God." Be filled with the Spirit so you will know how to use this Word.

A Christian man was talking to a skeptic. He was bringing him the Word. The skeptic said, "I don't believe, sir, in the Word." But the man went right on giving him more of the Word. The skeptic repeated, "I don't believe the Word." But the Christian kept giving him more. When he said, "I don't accept it," he kept giving him more until at last the man was reached.

Then the Christian said, "If I had a good sword, I would keep right on using the sword."

Yes, the sword—the Word of God—is powerful to convict and to save.

Skeptics, infidels may say they don't believe in it. It is not our work to make them believe in it; that is the work of the Spirit. Our work is to give them the Word of God, not to preach our theories and our pet ideas but to deliver the message as God gives it to us.

It was the sword of the Lord and of Gideon. Had Gideon gone out without the Word, he would have been defeated. But the Lord Jesus used Gideon.

We find all through the Scriptures that God uses human instruments. You cannot find a case in the Bible where a man is converted without God calling in some human agency, using some human instrument, though we doubt not but what He can do it alone.

I heard a man say once that if you put a man on a mountain peak higher than one of the Alpine peaks, he could come at the whole world under one sermon. But that isn't God's way; that isn't His method. It is the sword of the Lord—**and Gideon.** The Lord **and Gideon** will do the work. If we are willing to let the Lord use us, He will.

Then all through the Scriptures men who were filled with the Holy Spirit preached Christ, not themselves. Speaking of Zacharias, father of John the Baptist, Luke 1:67-70 says:

"And his father Zacharias was filled with the Holy Ghost, and prophesied, saying, Blessed be the Lord God of Israel; for he hath visited and redeemed his people, And hath raised up an horn of salvation for us in the house of his servant David; As he spake by the mouth of his holy prophets, which have been since the world began."

See—Zacharias is talking about the Word. If a man is filled with the Spirit, he will magnify the Word; he will preach the Word; he will give this lost world the Word of the living God.

"And thou, child, shalt be called the prophet of the Highest: for thou shalt go before the face of the Lord to prepare his ways; To give knowledge of salvation unto his people by the remission of their sins, Through the tender mercy of our God; whereby the dayspring from on high hath visited us, To give light to them that sit in darkness and in the shadow of death, to guide our feet into the way of peace. And the child grew, and waxed strong in spirit, and was in the deserts till the day of his shewing unto Israel."

We again find that, when Elizabeth and Mary met, they talked of the

Scripture and of the Spirit. When they were both filled with the Holy Ghost, they at once began to talk of the Word of God.

We find that Simeon, as he came into the Temple and found the young child Jesus there, at once began to quote the Scriptures, and the Spirit was on him.

When Peter stood up on the day of Pentecost and preached that wonderful sermon, it is said he was filled with the Holy Ghost and began to preach the Word to them. It was the Word that cut them. It was the sword of the Lord **and Peter,** the same as it was the sword of the Lord **and Gideon.**

As to Stephen, it says, "None could resist his word." Why? Because he gave them the Word of God. The Holy Ghost came on Stephen, he was full of the Holy Ghost, and "none could resist his word."

When Paul was full of the Holy Ghost, he preached Christ and Him crucified, and many people were added to the church.

Barnabas was full of faith and the Holy Ghost. Read on and find out what he preached; it was the Word, and many were added to the church.

So when a man is full of the Spirit, he begins to preach, not of himself but of Christ. He will give them the Word of God.

When the disciples of Jesus were all filled with the Spirit, the Word was published.

When the Spirit of God comes down and we are anointed, the Word will be published in the streets, in the lanes and in the alleys. There will not be a dark cellar nor a dark attic nor a home but what the Gospel will be carried by some loving heart, if the Spirit comes upon God's people as we want Him and as we are looking for Him.

Now a man may barely have life and be satisfied. A great many are now in that condition. In chapter 3 of John, Nicodemus came to Christ, and he just barely got life. You don't hear of him standing up on the day of Pentecost and the Spirit coming upon him in great power. He got life, though.

Chapter 4 of John speaks of the woman coming to the well of Samaria and Christ holding out the cup of salvation to her. She takes it and drinks the water; then Christ becomes in her "a well of water springing up into everlasting life." That is better than in chapter 3 of John. Here, instead of bubbling up, it came down in a flood into her soul. As someone has said, it came down from the throne of God and carried her back to the throne of God. Water always rises to its level, and if we get the soul filled with water from the throne of God, it will carry us to that throne.

But to get the best class of Christians, turn to chapter 7. It says he that receiveth the Spirit, "out of his belly shall flow rivers of living water."

There are two ways to a well. When I was a boy growing up on a farm in New England, we had a well and an old wood pump. I had to pump water from that well on washing day and to water the cattle. I would pump, pump, pump, pump until this arm got tired many a time.

But there is a better way now. We don't now dig down a few feet and brick up the hole and put the pump in; now we go down through the clay and the sand and the rock, and on down until we strike what they call a lower stream. Then it becomes what we call an artesian well of flowing water. Now we don't have to pump at all.

God wants His children to be sort of an artesian well—not to keep pumping, but to flow right out.

Haven't you seen ministers in the pulpit pumping, pumping and pumping? I have many a time. I have had to do so, too. I know how it is. We stand in the pulpit and talk and talk and talk while people go to sleep. What is our trouble? We don't have the living water. We are pumping when there is no water in the well. We can't get water out of a dry well. We have to get something in the well, or we can't get anything out.

I have seen these wooden pumps where you had to pour water into them before you could pump any water out. So it is with a good many people. We have to get something in them before we can get something out of them. People wonder why it is that they haven't got the power. They get up and talk in meetings but don't say anything. They say they haven't anything to say. We find it out soon enough without their stating it. But they talk because they feel it is a duty, yet say nothing.

Now when the Spirit of God is on us for service, resting upon us, and we are anointed, there will be nothing we cannot do. "I will pour water on him that is thirsty," says God. Oh, blessed thought! "He that hungers and thirsts after righteousness shall be filled!"

I would like to see someone here in St. Louis full of living water—so full that you couldn't contain it; so full that you would have to go out and publish it. When a man gets so full that he can't hold any more, then he is ready for God's service.

When we were in Chicago three years ago, Dr. Gibson got up in a meeting similar to this, looked around and said, "Now, how can we find out who is thirsty?" Says he: "If a boy should come down that aisle bringing a good pail full of clear water and a dipper, we would soon find out who was thirsty. Thirsty men and women would reach out for water. But if he should walk down that aisle with an empty bucket, we wouldn't find it out. People would look in, see that there was no water, and say nothing." Says he: "That is the reason we are not more blessed as a ministry. We are carrying around empty buckets, and when people see that we have nothing in them, they don't come forward."

There is a good deal of truth in that. When people see that we are carrying around empty buckets, they will not come to us until they are filled.

People see that we haven't any more than they have. But when the Spirit of God rests upon us, then we have something that gives the victory over the world, the flesh and the Devil—something that gives the victory over our tempers, over our conceits and over everything else. When we can trample these sins under our feet, then people will come to us and ask, "How did you do it? I want some of what you've got. You have something I don't have."

Oh, may God show us this truth today! We have been toiling all night; now let us throw the net on the right side.

He is not going to give this power to an impatient man. He is not going to give it to a selfish man. He will never give it to an ambitious man whose aim is selfish. Man is to be emptied of self, emptied of pride, emptied of all worldly thoughts. Let it be God's glory and not our own that we seek. When we get to that point, how quick the Lord will bless us for good! Then the measure of our blessing will be full.

Do you know what Heaven's measure is? "Good measure, pressed down, shaken together, and running over." If you get your heart filled with the Word of God, how is Satan going to get in and how is the world going to get in when Heaven's measure is "good measure, pressed down, shaken together, and running over"?

Have you got it? If you don't have it, let us seek it. Let us set out by the grace of God to have it, for it is the Father's good pleasure to give us these things. He wants us to shine down in this world. He wants to lift us up for that work. He has left us in this world to testify for His Son. What did He leave us for? Not to buy and sell and to get gain, but to glorify Christ. But how can we do it without this Spirit?

Now John 20:22 says, "And when he had said this, he breathed on them, and saith unto them, Receive ye the Holy Ghost."

Then see what He says in Luke 24:49: "And, behold, I send the promise of my Father upon you: but tarry ye in the city of Jerusalem, until ye be endued with power from on high."

He raised those pierced and wounded hands over them, breathed upon them the Holy Ghost and said, "Receive ye the Holy Ghost." I haven't a doubt but that they received the Holy Ghost then, but not in such mighty power. It was not His fullness that He was to give them then; but had they been like a good many now, they would have said, "I have enough now; I am not going to tarry; I am going to work."

Some people, thinking they are losing time if they wait on God for this power, go to work without unction, without an anointing, without any power.

After He had said, "Receive ye the Holy Ghost," and had breathed on them, He said, "Now you tarry in Jerusalem until I come."

He was certainly in them, or they could not have believed. They could not have taken their stand for God and gone through what they did; they could not have endured the scoffs and frowns of their friends had they not been converted by the power of the Holy Ghost. But now see what He says in Acts 1:8: "But ye shall receive power, after that the Holy Ghost is come upon you: and ye shall be witnesses unto me both in Jerusalem, and in all Judaea, and in Samaria, and unto the uttermost part of the earth."

The Holy Spirit IN us is one thing; the Holy Spirit ON us is another. Had those Christians gone out and gone to preaching right then and there without the power, would that scene have taken place on the day of Pentecost? Peter would have stood up there and beat against the air while these Jews would have gnashed their teeth and mocked him.

But when they arrived in Jerusalem, they waited ten days. What, with the world perishing and men dying! Do what God tells you. There is no use running before you are sent; there is no use attempting to do God's work without God's power. A man working without this unction, without this anointing, without the Holy Ghost upon him, is losing his time after all.

So we are not going to lose anything here in St. Louis if we tarry till we get this power. The object of the meeting next Monday night is to wait on God, to tarry till we get this power for service.

Then we find that on the day of Pentecost—ten days after Jesus Christ was glorified—power came for service. Do you think Peter, James, John and those other apostles dated it from that very hour? They never doubted it. Perhaps some of you are saying now that, when it came then, it was a miracle; it will never come again in such power.

Turn to Acts 4:31 and you will find power came down a second time. The Spirit came, and the place was shaken, and they were filled the second time. The fact is, we are leaky vessels, so we have to keep right under the fountain all the time to keep full of Christ and get a fresh supply.

The grace God gave me to work in Cleveland last month won't do in St. Louis today. I have to get a fresh supply, a fresh anointing, fresh power for St. Louis.

I believe the mistake a great many of us are making is, we are trying to do God's work with the grace God gave us ten years ago. We say, "If it is necessary, we will go on with the same grace." But what we need is a fresh supply, a fresh anointing, fresh power. And if we seek it with all our hearts, we will get it.

The early converts were taught to look for that power. Philip went to Samaria. News reached Jerusalem that there was a great work being done in Samaria, and many converts. John and Peter went down, laid hands on them, and they received the Holy Ghost for service.

We Christians ought to be looking for the Spirit of God for service— that God may condescend to use us in the building up of His kingdom.

Then we find the twelve men down there at Ephesus. The inquiry was made, "Have you received the Holy Ghost since you believed?" That is a queer thing. When they were asked that, they answered, "We don't know what you mean." I venture to say there are very few who, if asked, "Have you received the Holy Ghost since you believed?" wouldn't say, "I don't know what you mean by that." They would be like those twelve men down at Ephesus who had never heard of such a thing as the Holy Ghost for service.

I firmly believe that the church has just laid this gift aside or mislaid it somewhere; so Christians come into the church without any power. Sometimes taking one hundred members into the church doesn't add to its power. Now that is tragic. If these were anointed by the Spirit of God, great power would also be added to the church.

When I went to California the first time, I went down from the Sierra

Nevada Mountains and dropped into the valley of Sacramento. I was surprised to find on one farm everything was green. The trees were green, the flowers were blooming—everything was green and beautiful, while just across the hedge everything was dried up. There was not a green thing there. I couldn't understand it.

When I made inquiries, I found that the man who had everything green and blooming had irrigated, just poured the water on, while the man's farm next to him was as dry as Gideon's fleece, without a drop of dew.

And so it is with a great many in the church today. You are like these farms in California—as dry as Gideon's fleece, with not a drop of power in you, with no life. You can sit next to one who is full of the Spirit of God and in whom God's blessing is like a green bay tree and who is bringing forth fruit, yet you will not be stirred. What is the difference? God has poured water on him that is thirsty. One has been seeking this anointing and has gotten power. When we want this above everything else, God will give it to us.

The question to us is: do we want it today?

When I first went to England and gave a Bible reading, a great many ministers were there. I knew nothing about English theology. I was afraid I might run against their theology, so I was a little hampered, especially on this very subject about the gift for service.

I remember particularly a Presbyterian minister who had his head bowed on his hand. I thought the poor fellow was ashamed of everything I was saying. Of course, that kind of hampered me.

As soon as I got through, he got his hat and away he went. Then I thought, *Well, I shall never see him again.*

The next meeting I looked around for him, and he wasn't there. The next meeting I looked around, and he wasn't there. I thought, *Well, I have driven him off sure.*

But a few days after that, at a large noon prayer meeting, a man got up with his face shining, as if he had been up in the mountain with God. I looked, and to my great joy, saw it was that man. He said at that Bible reading he heard that there was such a thing as having fresh power to preach the Gospel; and he made up his mind that, if that was for him, he would have it. He said he went home, and never had he had such a battle with himself in his life. He asked God to show him the sinfulness in his heart that he knew nothing about. He cried mightily to God that he might be emptied of self and filled with the Spirit. Then he said, "God has answered my prayer!"

I met this man in Edinburgh six months from that time. He told me he had preached the Gospel every single night since and that he hadn't preached one sermon but that someone remained for conversation and that he had engagements in different churches four months ahead to preach the Gospel every night.

From what he told me, you could have fired a cannon ball right through his church and not hit anyone before he got this anointing; but it was not thirty days after then until the aisles were filled and crowded. He had gotten his bucket full of water, and the people found it out and came flocking to get a drink.

You can't get the stream higher than the fountain. What we want today is this power.

Another man had said, "I have heart disease. I can preach just once a week." He had a colleague preach for him and do the visiting. He was an old minister and couldn't do any visiting. He had heard of this anointing, so he said, "I would like to be anointed for my burial. I would like, before I go hence, to have just one more privilege to preach the Gospel with power." He prayed that God would fill him with the Spirit.

I met him not long after that; and he said, "Mr. Moody, I have preached on an average of eight times a week, and," said he, "I have had conversions all along." The Spirit came on him.

That man hadn't broken down with hard work so much as with working the machinery without oil, without power. It is not the hard work but the toil of working without power.

Oh, that God may give it to us today! Not for the ministry only, but for each of you. You need not be shaking your heads and saying, "That is good for the ministers." No! You people in the pews need it as much as we. There is not a mother but needs it in her house to regulate her family, just as much as the minister needs it in the pulpit or the Sunday school teacher needs it in his Sunday school. We all need it together, and let us not rest until we get it. If that is uppermost in our hearts, if we hunger and thirst for it, God will give it to us. If you say, "God, I will not rest until You give it to me," you will sure get it.

I love to dwell on the very sweet story of Elijah and Elisha. The time had come for Elijah to be taken up, so he said to Elisha, "You stay here at Gilgal, and I will go up to Bethel." There was a kind of a theological seminary there, and some young students, so he wanted to see how they were getting along. But Elisha said, "As the Lord liveth and thy soul liveth, I will not leave thee." So Elisha just kept close to Elijah.

They got to Bethel. The sons of the prophets came out and said to Elisha, "Do you know that your master is to be taken away?"

Elisha said, "I know it, but you keep still."

Then Elijah said to Elisha, "You stay at Bethel until I go to Jericho." But Elisha said, "As the Lord liveth and my soul liveth, I will not leave thee. You shall not go without me."

Then I can imagine Elisha putting his arm in that of Elijah, and I can see those two mighty men walking down to Jericho together. When they get there, the sons of the prophets come and say to Elisha, "Do you know that your master is to be taken away?"

"Hush! Keep still," says Elisha; "I know it!"

Then Elijah says to Elisha, "Tarry here awhile; for the Lord hath sent me to Jordan." But Elisha answers, "As the Lord liveth and my soul liveth, I will not leave thee. You shall not go without me."

Then Elisha gets right close to Elijah, and as they go walking down, I imagine Elisha is after something. When they get to the Jordan, Elijah takes off his mantle and strikes the waters. They separate hither and thither, and the two pass through like giants, dry-shod. Fifty sons of the prophets come to look at them and watch them. They don't know Elijah will be taken up right in their sight.

As they get over Jordan, Elijah says to Elisha, "Now, what do you want?" He knew Elisha was after something. "What can I do for you? Just make your request known."

And Elisha answers, "I would like a double portion of your spirit." I can imagine now that Elijah has given him a chance to ask that. So Elisha says to himself, *I will ask for enough.* He already has a good deal of the spirit; but now says he, "I want a double portion of your spirit."

"Well," says Elijah, "if you see me when I am taken up, you shall have it."

Do you think you could have separated Elisha from Elijah at that moment? I can imagine the two, arm in arm, walking along; and as they walk there comes along the chariot of fire, and before Elisha knows it, Elijah is caught up. And as he goes sweeping toward the throne, Elisha cries, "My father! my father! The chariot of Israel and the horsemen thereof!"

Elisha sees him no more. He takes and rends his mantle and picks up Elijah's and starts toward Jerusalem. As he approaches Jordan, he says, *Elijah has gone, and I, Elisha, am alone.* With that old mantle of Elijah's, he comes to the Jordan and cries for Elijah's God, and the waters separate hither and thither, and he passes through dry-shod. The prophets lift up their voices and say, "The spirit of Elijah is upon Elisha." So it was—a double portion of it.

May the Spirit of Elijah come on you and me today. If we seek for it, we shall have it. Oh, may the God of Elijah answer by fire and consume this day the spirit of worldliness in the church, burn up the dross, and make us wholehearted Christians. May the Spirit come upon us. Let that be our prayer at our family altars and in our closets. Let us cry mightily to God for a double portion of the Spirit. May we not be satisfied with this worldly state of living; but let us, like Samson, shake ourselves and come out from the world that we may have the power of God. Amen.

THOMAS L. MALONE
1915-

ABOUT THE MAN:

Tom Malone was converted and called to preach at the same moment! At an old-fashioned bench, the preacher took his tear-stained Bible and showed Tom Malone how to be saved. He accepted Christ then and there. Arising from his knees in the Isbell Methodist Church near Russellville, Alabama, he shook the circuit pastor's hand; and this bashful nineteen-year-old farm boy announced: "I know the Lord wants me to be a preacher."

Backward, bashful and broke, yet Tom borrowed five dollars, took what he could in a cardboard suitcase and left for Cleveland, Tennessee. Immediately upon arrival at Bob Jones College, Malone heard a truth that totally dominated his life and labors for the Lord ever after—soul winning!

That day he won his first soul! The green-as-grass Tom, a new convert himself, knew nothing of soul-winning approaches or techniques. He simply asked the sinner, "Are you a Christian?" "No." In a few minutes that young man became Malone's first convert.

Since that day, countless have been his experiences in personal evangelism.

Mark it down: Malone began soul winning his first week in Bible college. And he has never lost *the thirst* for it, *the thrill* in it, nor *the task* of it since. Pastoring churches, administrating schools, preaching across the nation have not deterred Tom Malone from this mainline ministry.

It is doubtful if young Malone ever dreamed of becoming the man he is today. He is now Doctor Tom Malone, is renowned in fundamental circles for his wise leadership and great preaching, is pastor emeritus of the large Emmanuel Baptist Church of Pontiac, Michigan, Founder and Chancellor of Midwestern Baptist Schools, and is eagerly sought as speaker in large Bible conferences from coast to coast.

Dr. John R. Rice often said that Dr. Tom Malone may be the greatest gospel preacher in all the world today!

IV.

Why I Know the Holy Spirit Is a Person

TOM MALONE

(Preached in the Emmanuel Baptist Church, Sunday, September 6, 1970)

"And I will pray the Father, and he shall give you another Comforter, that he may abide with you for ever; Even the Spirit of truth; whom the world cannot receive, because it seeth him not, neither knoweth him: but ye know him; for he dwelleth with you, and shall be in you. . . . But the Comforter, which is the Holy Ghost, whom the Father will send in my name, he shall teach you all things, and bring all things to your remembrance, whatsoever I have said unto you. Peace I leave with you, my peace I give unto you: not as the world giveth, give I unto you. Let not your heart be troubled, neither let it be afraid. Ye have heard how I said unto you, I go away, and come again unto you. If ye loved me, ye would rejoice, because I said, I go unto the Father: for my Father is greater than I."—John 14:16,17,26-28.

"Nevertheless I tell you the truth; It is expedient for you that I go away: for if I go not away, the Comforter will not come unto you; but if I depart, I will send him unto you. And when he is come, he will reprove the world of sin, and of righteousness, and of judgment: Of sin, because they believe not on me; Of righteousness, because I go to my Father, and ye see me no more; Of judgment, because the prince of this world is judged."—John 16:7-11.

I speak on the subject, "Why I Know the Holy Spirit Is a Person." Please do not immediately say, "That is too far out and too deep for me; I am not interested." If you believe in the Lord Jesus Christ as your personal Saviour, I doubt you will ever hear anything more important than what I want to talk to you about.

The Lord's people need assurance. These verses I have read speak of a Comforter that would come. Jesus spoke these chapters that last night before His crucifixion. They leave the Upper Room where the Lord's Supper was first instituted for the bloody Garden of Gethsemane. Jesus walks in company with His eleven disciples. Judas had already betrayed Him at the table, had sold Him for thirty pieces of silver, and had separated himself from true believers.

As Jesus walks with the eleven toward the Garden, He speaks about important matters. He talks to them about another Comforter that would come, referring to the Holy Spirit.

Many do not know that the Holy Spirit is a Person. Some think of the Holy Spirit as a good influence. Some think of the Holy Spirit as some good spirit that emanates from God. But the Bible teaches that this Comforter of whom Jesus spoke is a real and active Person.

Much emphasis is given in the Bible to this Person of the Trinity. The first New Testament book begins and ends with the work of the Holy Spirit. The book of Matthew begins with the virgin birth. Of the Virgin Mary, we read, ". . . she was found with child of the Holy Ghost" (Matt. 1:18).

Acts gives God's program for the church—to win people to Christ and to evangelize the world. It is impossible to overemphasize how the Holy Spirit is set forth in this book. In fact, many Bible students say Acts of the Apostles should accurately be called Acts of the Holy Spirit.

In chapter 1 the Holy Spirit is set forth four times, doing four different things.

In verse 2 is the instruction of the Holy Spirit, ". . . he through the Holy Ghost had given commandments unto the apostles whom he had chosen." God emphasizes throughout His Word the personality, the reality, the ministry of the Holy Ghost and sets Him forth as a real Person.

We read in verse 5, "For John truly baptized with water; but ye shall be baptized with the Holy Ghost not many days hence," more accurately translated, "ye shall be baptized in the Holy Ghost not many days hence."

We read in verse 8, "But ye shall receive power, after that the Holy Ghost is come upon you: and ye shall be witnesses unto me both in Jerusalem, and in all Judaea, and in Samaria, and unto the uttermost part of the earth."

In Acts 16 Peter said, "Men and brethren, this scripture must needs have been fulfilled, which the Holy Ghost by the mouth of David spake before. . . . "

We see four phases of His work in Acts, chapter 1, alone:
1. Instruction,
2. Inclusion (into the body of Christ),
3. Enduement,
4. Inspiration.

The first chapter of Acts tells us that the Holy Spirit told all the prophets and all the other human writers of the Bible what to write. So I say again that it is absolutely impossible to overemphasize the reality and personality of the Holy Spirit as set forth in the Word of God.

I want you to see the fourfold ministry of the Holy Spirit in the life of every Christian: His incoming, His indwelling, His infilling, His outflowing.

His Incoming

The incoming of the Holy Spirit is important. In John 3 Jesus spoke to a man about being saved. In verses 5 and 6 Jesus taught that the Holy Spirit comes into a person's life the moment he is saved. You need never ask for the Person of the Holy Spirit after you are converted, for His incoming takes place when you are saved.

Remember that Jesus is talking to Nicodemus. "Verily, verily, I say unto thee, Except a man be born of water and of the Spirit, he cannot enter into the kingdom of God." Then He said, "That which is born of the flesh is flesh: and that which is born of the Spirit is spirit." When you were saved, the Holy Spirit of God took up His abode in your heart, in your life, in your body.

His Indwelling

The Holy Spirit never leaves a truly born-again child of God. You say, "What about Saul, the first king of Israel? It plainly says God took His Spirit away from him."

In the Old Testament, before Calvary, before the resurrection, before Pentecost, the Holy Spirit came and went as God so chose. But in the New Testament, after Calvary, after the resurrection, after the day of Pentecost, there was never one instance where God took His Holy Spirit away from one single Christian.

In John 14:6 Jesus said, "And I will pray the Father, and he shall give you another Comforter, that he may abide with you for ever." So if you believe one is saved through all eternity when he accepts Christ, then you believe that once the Holy Spirit enters at the new birth, He never leaves. In fact, Romans 8:9 says, ". . . Now if any man have not the Spirit of Christ [referring to the Holy Spirit], he is none of his." God said, "If the Holy Spirit is not in you, then you are not a Christian." You can't be saved without having Him. And you can't have Him without being eternally saved. So His incoming and indwelling are clearly taught in the Bible.

His Infilling

Then the Bible speaks of what I would like to call His infilling—that is, the filling of the believer. Ephesians 5:18 commands, ". . . be filled with the Spirit." A lot of Baptists get a little nervous when you talk about the fullness of the Spirit, the fullness of the Holy Ghost, the power of the Spirit; nevertheless, the Bible command is, ". . . be filled with the Spirit."

One time a man had this happen. He was a good preacher, filled with the Spirit.

A young convert came to him at the close of a service and said, "May I ask you a question? Do you believe that you are, right now, filled with the Holy Spirit of God?"

This preacher humbly but with confidence answered, "Yes, I believe that I am filled with the Holy Spirit of God."

What would you say if someone posed that question to you: "Are you, at this moment, filled with the Holy Spirit of God?"

His Outflowing

His incoming, His indwelling, His infilling, then His outflowing. Jesus talked of this. One of the strangest things that Jesus said, if it were not fully explained in its context, would be His words of John 7, ". . . If any man thirst, let him come unto me, and drink" (vs. 37). Then Jesus said, "He that believeth on me, as the scripture hath said, out of his belly [or out of His innermost being] shall flow rivers of living water" (vs. 38).

What did Jesus mean? Read one more verse: "(But this spake he of the Spirit, which they that believe on him should receive: for the Holy Ghost was not yet given; because that Jesus was not yet glorified.)"

Jesus was saying, "In the life of a born-again Christian are rivers of living water, the constant outflow of the Spirit." It is like the dear old lady said, when she talked about her cup being full, "Lord, fill my saucer, too, and fill it until they're both running over!"

The New Testament life for the child of God is to be filled with the Spirit until it runs over. There are fruits of the Spirit, the influence on other lives, the winning of souls—the outflowing of the Spirit of God from the life of a Christian.

You say, "Then, Preacher, why is it that there are so many misconceptions about the Holy Spirit, so much misunderstanding, so little known of this member of the Trinity?"

When someone asked me, "How can it be that one God can be in three different personalities—God the Father, God the Son, and God the Holy Spirit?" there came to me this illustration. Go to a faucet in your home, turn it on and get liquid water. Go to the refrigerator and get a cube of ice. Go to the window and wipe off a bit of vapor. All three are the same. One is hardened, one is a vapor, one is a liquid, but all are of the same substance.

God in His sovereignty has so decreed that He be manifest in three personalities—God the Father, God the Son, and God the Holy Spirit.

Why is it that there has been so little emphasis on the Holy Spirit? First, because of a lack of teaching on it. Paul instructed Timothy in II Timothy 2:2, "And the things that thou hast heard of me among many witnesses, the same commit thou to faithful men, who shall be able to teach others also." Preachers, teachers and believers need to teach on the personality of the Holy Spirit.

Why are there so many misconceptions about Him? Because many who say they are Spirit-filled are not. You say, "Preacher, are you a judge?" No, but I know that Spirit-filled Christians are victorious Christians, soul-winning Christians, working Christians, separated Christians.

There is misconception about what the Bible teaches about the fullness of the Spirit. Every now and then we find someone with a long face and a sad countenance; that one will feign some sort of deeper life and call that the fullness of the Holy Spirit. The power that Christians in Bible times had was evidenced in their lives.

Unfortunate translations cause some misconceptions about the personality of the Holy Spirit. For instance, Romans 8:16 says, "The Spirit *itself* beareth witness with our spirit. . . ." Verse 26, ". . . the Spirit *itself* maketh intercession for us with groanings which cannot be uttered." The Holy Spirit is not an *"it."* The Holy Spirit is a Person. So it should read: "the Spirit *himself.*"

Suppose a lady asks another, "Where is your husband?" and she answers, "*It* is standing over there." Or one would ask some man, "Where is your wife?" and he would answer, "Well, *it* just went out the door." Suppose one would ask about your sweetheart, "Where is he?" or "Where is she?" and you would say, "*It* went away for this weekend." Wouldn't that be stupid! Yet that is all the Holy Spirit is to many people. He is not the glorious, wonderful, divine personality set forth in the pages of the Word of God but merely an influence or an emanation from God.

Why do some misunderstand about the Holy Spirit? Because of tradition or denominational slant or a substitution of other things for the real power of the Spirit.

It is said that Torrey was once speaking in a service on "Why I Know the Holy Spirit Is a Real Person." At that time a relative of his was staying with him. Following the service she came and said, "Reuben, I never thought of it as a Person before."

Dr. Torrey said, "And you didn't get the message. Not, 'I never thought of *it* as a Person before,' but, 'I never thought of *Him* as a Person before.' " The Holy Spirit is a real Person indwelling every believer.

Once a lady said to a preacher, "I got the Holy Spirit last night." (That was wrong terminology unless she had just been saved.)

The preacher said, "I know something better than that."

She said, "What could be better than my getting the Holy Spirit?"

He said, "It would be far better if the Holy Spirit could get all of you."

This is the secret. You have the Holy Spirit, but does the Holy Spirit have you, possess you? Do you believe the Holy Spirit has hold of your life?

WHY DO I BELIEVE THE HOLY SPIRIT IS A PERSON?

1. Because of His Pre-existence as a Personal God

Genesis 1:1,2 says, "In the beginning God created the heaven and the earth. And the earth was without form, and void: and darkness was upon the face of the deep. And the Spirit of God moved upon the face of the waters."

That leads to my opening statement as to why I believe the Holy Spirit is a living Person rather than just a good influence or some impersonal force. It leads me to this thought because of His pre-existence with and as a personal God.

Isn't it exciting, mysterious and wonderful that we find the Holy Spirit in the opening expression of the Bible! "In the beginning God created the heaven and the earth. And the earth was without form, and void; and darkness was upon the face of the deep. And the Spirit of God moved upon the face of the waters." The Jewish Talmud is a more accurate translation even than the King James: "And the Spirit of God **brooded** upon the face of the waters."

Finding the Spirit of God in the very opening of the Bible leads us to know that the Holy Spirit is as pre-existent as God. Before God ever made a star, before He ever made sun and moon, before the creation of this earth, before God ever made man, we find in the very beginning of time the work of the Holy Spirit. He was "brooding." An impersonal force or mere influence could not do that.

Also, in Genesis 1:26, when God was ready to make man, He said, "Let US make man. . . ." To whom could God be speaking? No man, no woman, no intelligent being had been created; yet God is speaking to someone, for He uses the personal pronoun US: "Let US make man. . . ." It is believed by Bible students that God the Father is speaking to God the Son and God the Holy Spirit and saying, "Let us make man in our image. . . ."

God is a Trinity. Man is a trinity also. The Holy Spirit is the Designer and the Creator in the beginning with God. Man has a body, man has a soul, man has a spirit. Man is a trinity made in the image of God.

So I believe the Holy Spirit to be a living Person because He is pre-existent with God the Father and God the Son.

2. He Has All the Components of a Personality

The Holy Spirit has all the components of a personality.

From a psychology book—or any book that deals with what constitutes a personality—you would learn that four things constitute a personality. First, understanding; second, a will; third, affection; fourth, some idea of morality. To have a personality, there must be these four things.

God made many things that could not be called a personality. He made many things without understanding. He made many things without a will. He made many things without affection. He made many things with no relation to morals. But to have a personality, there must be these: understanding, will, affection and morality.

Now apply those four components of a personality to the blessed Holy

Spirit of God. The Bible teaches that the Holy Spirit has complete knowledge and understanding. In I Corinthians 2:1 we read, "For what man knoweth the things of a man, save the spirit of man which is in him? even so the things of God knoweth no man, but the Spirit of God." The Spirit of God has understanding. In fact, God goes so far as to say that no one understands the things of God but that the Holy Spirit of God has complete understanding.

Second, does the Holy Spirit have a will? The Bible says He does: "But all these worketh that one and the selfsame Spirit, dividing to every man severally as he will" (I Cor. 12:11).

"But all these...."; that is, the gifts of the Spirit. There are nine of them. In spite of the fact that it was not the best church, the church at Corinth is the only church mentioned in the Bible that had all nine gifts of the Spirit—not the fruits of the Spirit but the gifts of the Spirit. So God is talking about them. "But all these worketh that one and the selfsame Spirit, dividing to every man severally as he will." The Holy Spirit has a will.

He not only has a will, but He has affection. I do not believe that I have heard more than a half-dozen Christians talk about the love and affection of the Holy Spirit.

Romans 15:30 says, "Now I beseech you, brethren, for the Lord Jesus Christ's sake, and for the love of the Spirit, that ye strive together with me in your prayers to God for me." The Bible speaks of a love of the Spirit. Christian, not only does God love you, not only does Christ love you, but a living Holy Ghost loves you. He has affection. That third component of His personality is love.

It may be a low standard, it may be a mediocre standard, it may be a high standard; but in order to have a personality, there must be some knowledge of morals. Animals have no sense of morals; only a personality does.

Does the Holy Spirit? His very name indicates it—Holy Spirit. Not unholy, not imperfect. Holy Spirit is His name, and we read that He will convict of sin because Jesus said, "they believe not on me." So the Holy Spirit has the highest sense of morality. Thus, in Him, this glorious Person, we have all the components of a personality.

Here is something that I think we don't understand. Does the Holy Spirit have a body with hands, feet, eyes and a tongue to speak as Jesus did? No. Then how can one be a personality without having a body?

In Romans 12:1 Paul says, "I beseech you therefore, brethren, by the mercies of God, that ye present your bodies a living sacrifice, holy, acceptable unto God, which is your reasonable service." God is asking for your body. What for? The Bible teaches that the Holy Spirit indwells the bodies of people. The hour will come when everyone shall have the separation of the spirit from his body. Then, do you cease to be a person when your spirit goes to meet God and you are absent from the body and present with the Lord? You will be no less a personality than that you are right now, for you will still have understanding, you will have a will, you will still have affection, you will still have a sense of longing.

So in order to be a personality, it is not necessary to have what might be called a corporeity, that is, a body. The Holy Ghost has the body of every believer and "dwelleth not in temples made with hands" (Acts 17:24).

Paul said, "What? know ye not that your body is the temple of the Holy Ghost which is in you, which ye have of God, and ye are not your own? For ye are bought with a price: therefore glorify God in your body, and in your spirit, which are God's" (I Cor. 6:19,20).

So the Holy Spirit of God has all the components of a personality. Think of the Holy Spirit not as just an influence, not as an "it," not as just some impersonal force, but as a real Person.

3. Jesus Was a Person, and the Holy Spirit Is Like Jesus

Jesus said in John 14:16, "And I will pray the Father, and he shall give you another Comforter, that he may abide with you for ever." Jesus is going away. So He says, "It is expedient for you that I go away, but I will pray the Father and He will give you another Comforter."

The Greek New Testament has two words for another. I have a song book in my hand, and I say, "I will give you another book." It might be on astronomy or on astrology or on sociology or on history or on something else. "I will give you another book" means I will give you another book but not this song book.

But when Jesus said, "I will pray the Father, and he shall give you another Comforter" [heteros in the Greek], He meant, "I will give you another Comforter just like Me." Hallelujah! We have another Comforter just like Jesus!

How is He like Jesus? Both came to earth. Jesus came by the lowly manger and was born in Bethlehem. The Holy Ghost came on that glorious day of Pentecost.

Not only did both come to earth, but both have become incarnate— Jesus, in a body of His own, conceived by that Holy Ghost in the womb of the Virgin Mary; the Holy Spirit, incarnate in every born-again man and woman.

And both came to do a work. The work of Jesus was finished at Calvary when He cried, "It is finished" (John 19:30). The work of the Holy Spirit continues on. Both are divine, both are God, equal as members of the Trinity.

Strange as it may sound, both will have a second coming. Jesus will come to receive the church. Ezekiel 37 teaches that the Holy Spirit some-day will come back again to this earth and Israel shall be reborn in a day.

So the Holy Spirit is a Person because He is another Comforter just like Jesus.

4. He Has All the Attributes of Deity
or of a Personal God

I know the Holy Ghost to be a real personality because He has all the attributes of Deity. We think of God as being omnipotent—that is, unlimited in power—but so is the Holy Spirit. We see that in creation: "By the word of the Lord were the heavens made; and all the hosts of them by the breath of his mouth" (Ps. 33:6).

Breath and spirit in the Bible are almost synonymous. When we read that God made man out of the dust of the ground, breathed into his nostrils the breath of life and he became a living soul, it is speaking of the spirit that God put into man. He made Him a body out of the ground and breathed into him a spirit, and man became a living soul. So by the breath of His mouth the heavens have been made, meaning that the Spirit of God has done it all.

Job further clarifies this in Job 33:4, "The Spirit of God hath made me, and the breath of the Almighty hath given me life." So the Bible even represents the Holy Spirit as the architect, designer and decorator of all that has ever been made. What a shame that this member of the Trinity has been relegated to some obscure place!

Not only is He omnipotent; the Holy Spirit is omniscient, absolutely unlimited in knowledge. In Isaiah 40:13 we read, "Who hath directed the Spirit of the Lord, or being his counsellor hath taught him?" Further verses in the context in Isaiah 40 show the Holy Spirit to be omniscient. He knows all about you. He knows your every thought. He knows every fiber in your being. The Holy Spirit is absolutely omniscient.

Not only is the Holy Spirit omnipotent and omniscient; He is omnipresent. Just like God can be everywhere at once, so the Holy Spirit can be everywhere at once. He can be across the sea blessing where believers are, and He can be in this church—and He is. He is in my body and in yours, if you are saved. He is omnipresent. David spoke of that in Psalm 139:7-10: "Whither shall I go from thy spirit? or whither shall I flee from thy presence? If I ascend up into heaven, thou art there: if I make my bed in hell, behold, thou art there. If I take the wings of the morning, and dwell in the uttermost parts of the sea; Even there shall thy hand lead me, and thy right hand shall hold me." David said, "To the depths of the sea, or to the heights of the heavens, or to the darkness of the night, I could not escape from the presence of the Holy Spirit." Everywhere you go, He goes. The Holy Spirit is omnipresent.

The Holy Spirit is eternal, just as God is eternal. "How much more shall the blood of Christ, who through the eternal Spirit offered himself without spot to God, purge your conscience from dead works to serve the living God?" says Hebrews 9:14.

Then, just like God, He is absolutely holy.

Five emblems or symbols in the Bible represent the Holy Spirit. One is a DOVE. To show the holiness, the absolute, divine perfection of the Holy Ghost, go back to the ark, which is a type of Christ. Noah is in the ark and has been for months. The water has begun to abate. Noah has two birds, one unclean and one clean. He has a dove and a raven.

Yes, a dove is a symbol of the Holy Spirit. When Jesus was baptized in the River Jordan, the Holy Spirit came in the form of a heavenly dove.

From the ark, Noah releases that dove, and Genesis 8:9 says, "But the dove found no rest for the sole of her foot, and she returned unto him into the ark, for the waters were on the face of the whole earth: then he put forth his hand, and took her, and pulled her in unto him into the ark." The dove returned.

Then Noah sends out the raven. He likes it out there in that filth, so he stays. Not the dove. The Holy Ghost never rests upon anything unclean. He is absolutely holy.

A second symbol of the Holy Spirit in the Bible is *FIRE*. He was manifest as fire on the day of Pentecost. "And there appeared unto them cloven tongues like as of fire, and it sat upon each of them" (Acts 2:3). He was often manifested as fire in the Old Testament, as in the case of the Tabernacle in the wilderness. "So it was alway: the cloud covered it by day, and the appearance of fire by night" (Num. 9:16).

Fire warms, cleanses, illuminates, energizes, attracts; so does the blessed Holy Spirit of God.

OIL in the Bible is a symbol of the Holy Spirit.

For anointing—Leviticus 8:12: "And he poured the anointing oil upon Aaron's head, and anointed him, to sanctify him."

For light—Exodus 25:6: "Oil for the light, spices for anointing oil, and for sweet incense. . . ." Matthew 25:3: "They that were foolish took their lamps, and took no oil with them. . . ."

For invigoration—Psalm 23:5: "Thou preparest a table before me in the presence of mine enemies: thou anointest my head with oil; my cup runneth over."

For healing—James 5:14: "Is any sick among you? let him call for the elders of the church; and let them pray over him, anointing him with oil in the name of the Lord."

For joy—At least twenty-nine times in the Old Testament, oil and wine (joy) are used in the same verse.

For energy—Zechariah 4:6: "Not by might, nor by power, but by my spirit, saith the Lord of hosts." Zechariah 4:11,12: "Then answered I, and said unto him, What are these two olive trees upon the right side of the candlestick and upon the left side thereof? And I answered again, and said unto him, What be these two olive branches which through the two golden pipes empty the golden oil out of themselves?"

WATER is also a symbol of the Holy Spirit in the Bible:

"For I will pour water upon him that is thirsty, and floods upon the dry ground: I will pour my spirit upon thy seed, and my blessing upon thine offspring. . . ."—Isa. 44:3.

"In the last day, that great day of the feast, Jesus stood and cried, saying, If any man thirst, let him come unto me, and drink. He that believeth on me, as the scripture hath said, out of his belly shall flow rivers of living water. But this spake he of the Spirit, which they that believe on him should receive: for the Holy Ghost was not yet given; because that Jesus was not yet glorified."—John 7:37-39.

WIND is a type or symbol of the Holy Spirit.

"And suddenly there came a sound from heaven as of a rushing mighty wind, and it filled all the house where they were sitting."—Acts 2:2.

"Then said he unto me, Prophesy unto the wind, prophesy, son of man, and say to the wind, Thus saith the Lord God; Come from the four winds, O breath, and breathe upon these slain, that they may live. So I prophesied as he commanded me, and the breath came into them, and they lived, and stood up upon their feet, an exceeding great army."—Ezek. 37:9,10.

5. He Can Be Mistreated as a Person

The Holy Spirit of God is a Person because He can be mistreated.

The Bible plainly teaches that He can be lied to. We have in chapter 5 of Acts the record of a man, Ananias, and his wife, Sapphira. They sold a certain piece of property for so much money. No one said, "You have to give it to God." But they came with a portion of it and said, "This is all we have; we are giving it all to God." Peter said to Ananias, "Ananias, why hath Satan filled thine heart to lie to the Holy Ghost, and to keep back part of the price of the land?" (Acts 5:3).

So, one can lie to the Holy Ghost. I wonder how many believers have lied to the Holy Ghost. I wonder how many promises have been made to Him and not kept. I wonder how many believers have promised the Holy Spirit to read their Bibles, promised they would serve the Lord, promised they would tithe their income, promise they would win souls, yet, they have not done it. Oh, yes, He can be mistreated as a Person. He can be lied to.

He can be resisted. Stephen said in Acts 7:51, "Ye stiffnecked and uncircumcised in heart and ears, ye do always resist the Holy Ghost: as your fathers did, so do ye." I have seen people resist. If God is speaking to your heart and you are not a child of God and do not yield to God, you are resisting the Holy Ghost.

Some people say, "Well, I am not going to do what the preacher says. I am not going to walk down that aisle." It isn't tremendously important that you do what this preacher says, but the Bible says that you can resist the Holy Spirit of God.

The Holy Spirit can be mistreated as a Person. He can be lied to, He can be resisted, and the Bible says that He can be grieved. Read

Ephesians 4:30: "And grieve not the Holy Spirit of God, whereby ye are sealed unto the day of redemption." You can't grieve an influence. You cannot grieve an impersonal force. You cannot grieve a mere emanation from God. You can only grieve a person, someone who loves you.

If a total stranger goes down the street and doesn't speak to me, so what? Since I don't know him, there is no special affinity between the two of us. But if someone I know well were to pass me on the street and ignore me, that would grieve me.

You can grieve the Holy Spirit because He loves you and He is as sensitive as that mournful little bird, the dove.

So He can be resisted and grieved, and He can even be despised, according to Hebrews 10:29. "Of how much sorer punishment, suppose ye, shall he be thought worthy, who hath trodden under foot the Son of God, and hath counted the blood of the covenant, wherewith he was sanctified, an unholy thing, and hath done despite unto the Spirit of grace?"

The Holy Spirit can be quenched, for we read in I Thessalonians 5:19, "Quench not the Spirit."

The Holy Ghost can be mistreated as a Person because He can be blasphemed. In Matthew 12:31,32 Jesus spoke of a particular sin for which there is no forgiveness. Jesus was careful to say no forgiveness in the world to come. What is that sin? Jesus said, "Wherefore I say unto you, All manner of sin and blasphemy shall be forgiven unto men. And whosoever speaketh a word against the Son of man, it shall be forgiven him: but whosoever speaketh against the Holy Ghost, it shall not be forgiven him, neither in this world, neither in the world to come."

What is the blasphemy against the Holy Ghost? What is the sin called the "unpardonable sin"? What is the sin that Jesus Christ, the Son of God, said, "For this sin there is no forgiveness"? What is blasphemy against the Holy Ghost? It is attributing the work and power of the Holy Spirit to the Devil. If you ever say, "The work of the Lord is of the Devil," that is blasphemy against the Holy Spirit. If you ever hear some blasphemer say about some born-again Christian, "That is the work of Satan," Jesus said, "That sin will never be forgiven him."

You thought we could be saved from anything. Well, take Jesus at His Word: "And whosoever speaketh a word against the Son of man, it shall be forgiven him: but whosoever speaketh against the Holy Ghost, it shall not be forgiven him, neither in this world, neither in the world to come."

He can be mistreated as a Person.

6. He Acts Like a Person

I know that the Holy Spirit is a Person because He acts like one. He speaks. I read in II Peter 1:21, "For the prophecy came not in old time by the will of man: but holy men of God spake as they were moved by the Holy Ghost." This Bible is speaking of a personal Holy Spirit. ". . .But holy men of God spake as they were moved by the Holy Ghost." The word *moved* can be translated "borne"—borne along, carried along. ". . .but holy men of God spake as they were carried along by the Holy Ghost."

Only a person speaks. Influences do not speak.

In Acts 8:29 Deacon Philip led the Ethiopian eunuch to Christ. "Then the Spirit said unto Philip, Go near, and join thyself to this chariot." So the Holy Spirit is a Person because He speaks and because He loves. Romans 15:30 says, "Now I beseech you, brethren, for the Lord Jesus Christ's sake, and for the love of the Spirit, that ye strive together with me in your prayers to God for me."

The Holy Spirit guides. "Howbeit when he, the Spirit of truth, is come, he will guide you into all truth: for he shall not speak of himself; but whatsoever he shall hear, that shall he speak: and he will shew you things to come" (John 16:13). Here in this verse you find four times the personal pronoun *he*.

The Holy Spirit will guide you.

The Holy Spirit restrains. Acts 16:6,7, talking about Paul's second journey, says, "Now when they had gone throughout Phrygia and the region of Galatia, and were forbidden of the Holy Ghost to preach the word in Asia, After they were come to Mysia, they assayed to go into Bithynia: but the Spirit suffered them not."

The Holy Spirit fellowships—II Corinthians 13:14: "The grace of the Lord Jesus Christ, and the love of God, and the communion of the Holy Ghost, be with you all. Amen." The Bible mentions that we can have fellowship with the Holy Spirit.

7. He Should Be Treated as a Person

Last, the Holy Ghost should be treated as a Person. He should be given complete access to your body. He should possess every fiber in your being. If it be true, and it is, that our body is the only body that the Holy Spirit will ever have, He should have complete access to all of it.

I have had the privilege of going to Athens, Greece and seeing the beautiful buildings erected hundreds of years before Christ. Paul stood on a little mountain called Mars' Hill, looked at all that antiquity and declared, "God that made the world and all things therein, seeing that he is Lord of heaven and earth, dwelleth not in temples made with hands" (Acts 17:24). God doesn't dwell in all these religious buildings; He dwells in the bodies of believers in the Person of the Holy Spirit.

A fine Christian writer was once being entertained in a home. After being shown her bedroom, her hostess said, "We are happy to have one of the servants of the Lord here. This is your bedroom, but no visitor has access to the kitchen." Her hostess, about to leave for a short time, turned again and said, "Also, we ask you not to use the living room. That is where the family meets."

This fine Christian lady sat down on the bed in her room and thought, *I am not welcome in the kitchen, not welcome in the living room; I am only welcome back in this little corner called a bedroom.*

I wonder if the Holy Spirit of God, that living Person who indwells every believer, hasn't often thought, *I am a restricted Guest in this house, in this person. I occupy only a little corner of his mind, heart and body.*

The Holy Spirit, a living Person, wants to fill us with His fullness. The blessed Holy Spirit is a Person.

V.

Back to the Holy Spirit for Power

HYMAN J. APPELMAN

(This sermon first preached in 1946)

"But ye shall receive power, after that the Holy Ghost is come upon you: and ye shall be witnesses unto me both in Jerusalem, and in all Judaea, and in Samaria, and unto the uttermost part of the earth."— Acts 1:8.

Many of you know by heart my text above. I want to impress upon your hearts the first part of the verse, "But ye shall receive power, after that the Holy Ghost is come upon you. . . ."

To tell you that Christianity is the only religion of power is merely to repeat a platitude. To go on to say that the church is an organization (an organism would be better) that is supposed to have in it the power, the driving, the conquering, the overcoming, the sin-destroying, the Devil-defeating power of God's presence, is to repeat a truth that is known to every one of you. To go on to remind you that the church is not only the body of the saved but also of the Saviour (that is, that the Lord God, the Lord Jesus Christ, the Lord Holy Spirit, the Triune God, has delegated to us the responsibility of going afield, to batter down the gates of Hell and to open the gates of Heaven to those who know not Christ now in the pardon of their bitter sins, by our testimony) is just to retell an old, old story familiar to every one of you.

There is one further word, however, before I hasten on with the message.

Denominational differences there have almost always been. Ecclesiastical differences there are now between great Christians of every kind, of every description, of every persuasion. Questions, doubts, arguments in theology, in ecclesiology, there have seemingly ever occurred.

There are what are known as high churches. There are also low churches. Protestantism is divided into hundreds of different sects. No one deplores these tragedies more than I. Yet, the universal fact still remains. Through the ages, the outstanding Christians have had one thing in common. They all agreed and do agree with hardly the shadow of a difference that, next to salvation, the most important essential in the Christian life is the indwelling presence of the Holy Spirit. That is the thought that I seek to write across your souls this night.

Please take an outline.

First—the search for power; second—the source of power; third—the scope of power; fourth—the secret of God that leads to that power. This is an open secret to be sure, yet, because of the frailties of our minds and lives, it seems to be a closed mystery to many.

You will remember that, when I speak of power, I am not referring to the mundane, workaday world. We know that in the world, knowledge is supposed to be power. We know that the great combinations sometimes make for power. We know that in the streets, money is power. We know that out there, political preferment, political advancement, is power. We know that in the haunts and activities of men, great armies, great navies, atomic bombs, great inventive skill, great military equipment, go in to make up what the world calls power. What I am concerned about is religious power, spiritual power, Christian power, the power of God in the affairs of men.

I. THE SEARCH FOR POWER

I refer you again to my first point—the search for power. We have all tried to obtain that power. We have searched for it. We have compassed, seemingly, Heaven and earth in order to obtain it. Some of us have gone the limit of all that we are and have, striving to obtain that power. We have sought for it in holiness, in separation from the world. We thought that, if we refused to comply with the practices, the programs, the procedures of a generation taken over by Satan, we should 'ipso facto,' by the very nature of our life, be flooded with that power. We believed that, if we should never touch liquor, never attend a show, eschew the dance hall, turn our backs on filthy literature, refuse to use rouge and lipstick, not go the route of the world, that would be the avenue to power.

But, alas and alack, too many of us have learned that these things are not enough, that negative holiness does not lead to power with God and, consequently, does not suffice for power with men.

We went on to try organization. Please, I beg of you, do not misunderstand me. I am not criticizing organization. Whoever says our churches are too organized definitely does not know the full facts. Our churches are not overorganized; they are underorganized. Take one illustration.

There is not a church that I know anything about (and God has privileged me to be with a great many churches) that does not have men, women, even young people, who do not have three, four, sometimes a half dozen jobs each. Here is my own church in Fort Worth, with a tremendous membership of almost six thousand. I know a man in that church who is a deacon, a B.Y.P.U. sponsor, the treasurer of the church and one of the church clerks. Now what kind of over-organization is that when one man has four jobs?

I do not know what you think about it, but it seems this way: if a man is really going to do the work of a deacon, he has a full-time job. If a man is really going to be a steward, he has a full-time job. If a woman is really going to teach a Sunday school class, she has a full-time job.

We have tried organization. Oh, how much of every kind of it we do have! There are Youth for Christ, Christian Businessmen's Committees, Gideons, John Brown Schools, Bob Jones Schools, The Bible Institute of Los Angeles, Moody Bible Institute, great denominational schools, and so on, and on. We have missions, evangelistic campaigns, programs such as the one that brings us together here to Los Angeles. We have THE SWORD OF THE LORD, *Moody Monthly, The King's Business,* and my own paper, *The International Evangelist;* organizations, magazines, ad infinitum, almost ad nauseam. We have found, however, that it takes more than organization to obtain the power of God.

Do not misunderstand me nor misquote me. We must have organization. Why, the very electricity which lights this building would not do us a tiny particle of good unless it were piped to us by an organization. We need, however, the power that produces this electricity before the wires, the chandeliers, the lights, the globes, the bulbs, will do us one particle of good.

Not only have we tried separation; not only have we tried organization; but we have tried busyness. We have tried hard work. I do not know of a pastor of any good-sized church who is not worked to death.

Anybody who accuses preachers of being lazy does not know the preachers across the nation. I do not know of a single preacher—and I know thousands across this continent—who really loves the Lord and is in a pastorate anywhere, who is not on the dead run from morning until late at night. Work! Why, we are doing more work in this generation than any three generations of Christians have ever done before. The lesson comes back to us that it takes more than work to obtain the power that cometh down from above.

Who among us does not remember the indicting testimony of the great D. L. Moody? He was a busy man, an organizing man, an extraordinarily hard-working man. Before he was filled with the Holy Spirit, there was no keeping up with him. They say that there were times when he would make as many as two hundred visits in one day, tiring out the men and animals who served him. He would wear his companions down. After he was filled with the Holy Spirit, he worked perhaps just as hard, but there was not that hustling, bustling, busy activity. Much of his life was spent in standing still to see the salvation of God. Moody himself testifies that for every soul he won to Christ before he was filled with the Spirit, with all of his extraordinary busyness, he won perhaps a hundred after his experience with the Third Person of the Trinity.

Permit a very crude illustration. I had a Pontiac automobile which gave me a great deal of trouble. I paid $1,046.00 for it. It was a good car, a beautiful car, one of the first silver streaks. It seemed that all you had to do was to turn on the ignition, step on the starter, gauge it in gear, say, "Skat!" close your eyes, open them again, and you would be at your destination! I have many times driven that car ninety miles an hour on those flat, straight Texas roads.

One morning before sunup, driving from Del Rio, Texas to Fort Worth, the car stopped. I tried everything to get it started again. At first I didn't know what was wrong. The Lord had given us a great victory in Del Rio. I had been thinking of that and just driving along. That very night I was to start another revival near Fort Worth. My time, on that drive, was spent between thanking God for the past victory and praying for the future victory.

After awhile I got out of the car and began to look around. The wheels were still on the ground. The horn worked. The radio worked. So did the lights. I lifted the hood. The engine was still there. I thought perhaps I had dropped it out somewhere along the road. After checking everything, I realized that I was out of gas. It seemed to me then, as it seems to me now, that $1,046.00 worth of automobile ought to travel a few miles without gas! But it just doesn't work that way.

There it stood. There I stood, right in the middle of that dark Texas highway. I started pushing the car along. I know the highway since I have been over it many times. I knew that a little distance away there was a gas station run by some people who knew me. If I could get there, they would give me all the gas I needed. I kept on pushing until I came to the station. I'll guarantee it was a great deal harder shoving that car than it was shoving the throttle to feed it gas!

I wish I had time to go into more detail. But I want to show you that, in a great measure, Christianity, the church of the living God, ought to be carrying us instead of our pushing them. We are working terribly hard, but the results are so meager. I wonder if we have enough of the gas and oil of the Holy Spirit.

We saw that separation by itself will not work. We saw that organization was not enough. We saw that busyness would not turn the trick. We then decided to try something else. We have not quit trying it yet. We were and are going to compete with the world, to put on shows. We would have moving pictures, slides, gymnasiums, swimming pools. We would attract the world by singspirations, by all sorts of musical instruments—singing saws, marimbas, trombones, trumpets, orchestras. However, in this also the Holy Spirit taught us soon enough that that was not the way.

No church in the land can compete with Hollywood. We cannot act like Greta Garbo and Clark Gable. We dare not go in for the stuff which engages those people. We found out that shows would not work. I would not give you very much for all the people that you can get to church by some sort of a show. It is a definite reproach on the drawing power of the Gospel. It is a definite reproach on the name, the fame, the attractiveness of the Lord Jesus Christ. It is a definite slap in the face to the presence and power of the Holy Spirit. Anybody who thinks that the church needs shows to attract people to the proclamation of the Truth which is in Christ Jesus is definitely lacking the Holy Ghost.

II. THE SOURCE OF POWER

Let us, however, hasten on to the second word. Here is the source of power. You know only too well what I am going to say. The all-pervading, all-controlling, all-achieving Holy Spirit is the only source of power. It is not in our schools, not in our churches, not in our organizations. It is not in our separation. It is not in our busyness. It is not in our attractions. It is not in our programs. It is solely the Holy Spirit who gives this power to do exploits for God, to promote the interests of God's kingdom, to overcome Satan, to win the lost round about us. There is no separating of spiritual power from the Holy Spirit. It is not power; it is the Holy Spirit. You cannot have power without the Holy Spirit. You cannot have the Holy Spirit without being flooded by Heaven's power.

The next item in this source of power is a matter of considerable disputation. There it is, though. Argue all you want to about it. Debate over it all you please. Call it by any sort of name that may suggest itself to you. Say fanaticism, "holy rollerism," Four-Square Gospelism—just title it anything you please, as long as you go after it. The Bible teaches and Christian biography proves that there is such a thing as an experience with the Holy Spirit apart from and subsequent to salvation. If this be treason, make the most of it. The mere fact that so many have not experienced this influx of grace doesn't make any difference. If you don't believe me, argue with Paul. If you disagree with me, argue with Wesley. If you refuse to admit it, debate it over with George Whitefield, with Charles G. Finney, with Paul Rader. If you don't believe me, give the lie to Pentecost and to every pentecostal experience that has come to pass in the activities and affairs of God's people through the past ages of Christendom.

If I read my Bible correctly, and I am sure that on this point I do, the power and the presence of the Holy Spirit was the definite, indubitable gift of God to every child of God back yonder in the story of the Bible. The promise still is, however, "Repent, and be baptized every one of you in the name of the Lord Jesus Christ, and ye shall receive the gift of the Holy Ghost. For the promise is unto you and to your children, and to all that are afar off, even as many as the Lord our God shall call." The promise was and is, "Christ hath redeemed us from the curse of the law, being made a curse for us: that the blessing of Abraham might come on the Gentiles through Jesus Christ; that we might receive the promise of the Spirit through faith."

In the apostolic days, by apostolic testimony, by the clearly understandable declaration of God's Word, by the unavoidable revelation of the Bible, the Holy Spirit was not only given to the apostles but to everyone who loved and claimed the Lord Jesus Christ in the pardon of sin.

Beloved, will you agree with me that the source of the Spirit, the promise of power, the promise of the Spirit, the gift of God, the blessing of God, this pentecostal experience, is for us just as definitely as it was for Paul, for Peter, for James, for John, for the hundred and twenty in Jerusalem, for the twelve in Ephesus, for those in the fourth chapter of Acts. May I repeat pressingly that the source of this power is not education, not superlative talent, not personality. It is entirely and altogether of, in, through, by the Holy Spirit. He is the same for you and for me, the same Holy Spirit who has been working in the hearts and lives of God's people through the ages.

III. THE SCOPE OF POWER

The next thing in this story is the scope of that power, how that power works in our lives. Why should we go back to the Holy Spirit anyway? Why should not we go out and multiply organization? Why not advertise more? Why not put on more drives? Why not have more pastors, more evangelists, more books, more tracts? Because, my dear friends, the generations of the servants of the cross have proved beyond cavil that it is only the Holy Spirit who can give us what we need for what needs to be done in the upbuilding of God's kingdom's program.

What will the Holy Spirit do? He will do three basic, three absolutely essential things.

First, He will give us THE PROGRAM FOR CHRISTIAN SERVICE. We have a heresy going around. I accuse the whole church body of this heresy. Here is what I am talking about. We have summer camps, retreats, conferences. We get a great group of our young people together for a week or for ten days. We sing with them. We rouse them early in the morning for prayer meetings. We plead with them all day long for God, for Christ. We have vesper services. We stay up through the night in protracted prayer meetings. We have them stirred up, melted down, literally on fire. Some great orator stands and pleads with them something on this wise: "Those of you who have been called to special service, come, take my hand, dedicate your lives fully to the Lord."

Beloved, I may be as dead wrong as the vilest sinner who ever trod God's green footstool, but I thank God that my call to the ministry came in the quietness of my soul when the Holy Spirit dealt with me. It was not some great, overwhelming, sweeping emotional power, not some extraordinary enthusiastic drive.

Whatever your opinion may be on all of this, you will agree with me that the Holy Spirit is the only One who can give us the real program for Christian service.

First, the program must be worthy of God. God is not magnified by our small buildings. God is not magnified by our critical preaching, putting up the straw men of modernism, of liberalism and knocking them down, when there is not a modernist or a liberal within a hundred miles of our pulpits. God is not magnified by our little picayunish programs. God is not magnified by our half-empty churches. God is not magnified by our niggardly giving. God is not magnified by what we call revivals that so seldom result in the salvation of even half a hundred sinners. No, the program must be as great as God Himself. We must strengthen our stakes and lengthen our cords. We must attempt and, in God's strength, do the impossible.

Second, the Holy Spirit will give us a program that will be of benefit to ourselves. Beloved, you who are engaged in Christian services, whether it be evangelism, pastoral work, Sunday school teaching, distribution of tracts, or anything else, if the work you are doing does not draw you closer to God and make you a better Christian, it is not of God. The very activities that you are engaged in, in the name of the Lord, must be the means of growth in your soul or they cannot be blessed of the Holy Spirit. You are not led into them by the Holy Spirit.

The Holy Spirit will give us a program not only worthy of God, not only of benefit to ourselves, but of superlative blessing to everybody we touch. If we go out to witness in the Holy Spirit, we shall not antagonize very many. If we preach in the demonstration of the Spirit, we are not going to split churches. If we conduct revivals in the Holy Spirit, we are not going to bring the blessed name of evangelism to shame. Everything that we engage in will result in drawing souls round about us—especially the souls of our fellow Christians—closer to God and to the Lord Jesus Christ. If what you do pushes people away from the Lord and away from the church, you may take it for granted that the blessing of God is not upon it.

I beseech you, search your hearts, your motives, your plans, search everything that you are doing, to find the fault, the flaw. Then correct it. God will do the rest.

The second item in the scope of this power is PREPARATION FOR CHRISTIAN SERVICE. The only One who can cleanse us is the Holy Spirit by the application of the shed blood of the blessed Son of God. The only One who can separate us unto the service of the Lord, making us and keeping us pure and holy, is the Holy Ghost.

I sincerely wish I had hours instead of these fleeting minutes to press these points upon you. You do not have the faintest idea of the hell that I went through AFTER I became a Christian. I was not much concerned about these things before. After I accepted the Lord Jesus Christ as my personal Saviour and believed that I was a Christian, with my Jewish background, with the strivings of my flesh, with my early training pulling at me and trying awfully hard to drive me away from God, I had a terrible time. Foolishly, I strove to fight sin and Satan in my own strength. Oh, God be praised for that day when I read in my Bible the assurance of the Apostle Paul, "Work out your own salvation with fear and trembling; For it is God which worketh in you both to will and to do of his own good pleasure." God be eternally praised for that day in my Christian life when I learned that, even though I was a child of God, in my own strength I was no match for Satan; but even Satan was no match for the Holy Ghost. I learned then and there that the Holy Spirit would fight my battles if I gave Him a chance. If I depend upon Him, if I do His will, if I abide in His presence, He will do the rest.

First of all, in this preparation for Christian service, there will come clearness of vision, an extraordinary perception of God, of the plan of salvation, of God's relationship to men and of men's relationship to God. It will do more for us than all the seminaries, than all the commentaries, than all the lexicons, than all the studying put together. God will open our eyes to the beauties of His law. God will unveil our souls to our responsibilities, first to Him, then to a world round about us.

Second, the preparation for Christian service, as the Holy Spirit works upon us, will create within us a spiritual discipline. It will not be rigorous, nor a hardship. It will not seem only a duty, a sad responsibility. It will be a Christian discipline that, in the name of the Lord Jesus Christ, will enjoy denying itself.

How desperately we need this development of Christian character ourselves and in our churches! But one dreadful element is particularly lacking. Our people do not have any more sense of personal discipline than as though they were literal, physical, mental, moral, spiritual babies.

Oh, how necessary this discipline is before we can become spiritual athletes!

Hear me! I would rather have people say about me what my wife said about Gipsy Smith, than to have everything God can give me. I mean every word of it. She said, "Every time that man steps into the pulpit, it is like the Lord Jesus Christ. He shines for Jesus."

Surely I want to be a great preacher. Certainly I want to be a great orator. Certainly I want to be able to sway congregations. Certainly I want to be able to quote pages of God's Word. Certainly I want to be the master of assemblies. But far greater than all these things put together, I want to be a man shining for Jesus, clean, holy, pure, upright, so that the testimony of my life will be infinitely purer and greater than the testimony of my lips.

The third thing in the scope of this power will be POWER IN CHRISTIAN SERVICE. We all desperately need that. All of our efforts are as sounding brass and tinkling cymbal without that. Oh, how our hearts cry out to God for this power! Oh, what revolutionary changes there would be in our ministries if we were immersed in that power, if that power were flowing through us!

First, there would be power in the understanding of the needs of the world. What does this world need? Does it need more prophecy? Preaching about the second coming of our Lord and Saviour? Warning against definite sins? We stand before our classes. We are in our homes, on the streets. We preach, many of us. Some of us head up schools. What shall we tell them? What shall we give these people? What do they need? What is it that they want from God that we can pass on to them?

I do not know. These dear men, whose shoes I am not worthy to lick, let alone to latch, do not know.

But there is One who does know—the Holy Spirit. He will reveal to us the very innermost secrets of the hearts of people. Even in my own poor ministry, time and again I have had folks say to me, "You preached to me tonight." I did not know them from Adam's off ox. I didn't know their names, knew nothing about them. But the Holy Spirit knew, and He had put the words on my lips.

Not only will there be power for Christian service in understanding the need of the world, but also power in understanding the supply of God for that world, in comprehending the message of salvation for lost souls, in being able rightly to divide the Word of Truth.

Hear me! I am not boasting, even though it may sound like it. Jews are almost all like this, especially those reared under the same circumstances in which I was brought up. I know English, Russian, Jewish, German, Latin, Hebrew, Greek and a bit of Spanish. But that is not enough. I spent three years in a seminary in Fort Worth, Texas. I thank God for those wonderful years. But that is not enough. Send your children to good Christian schools where they can get the best of everything.

But if you want to really understand the Word of God, the message of salvation, you must have the Teacher who never graduated from any seminary. You must have the Teacher who does not pass out a diploma. You must have the Teacher who does not mark term papers. That Teacher is the Holy Spirit. The Holy Spirit causes us to realize the needs of the world. He leads us to recognize the message of salvation.

But here is one thing, which I know, yet which I cannot understand. The Holy Spirit places Himself alongside us. He adds His power to our programs, to our preaching, to our teaching, to our witness-bearing. By His presence and power, He makes our stuttering, stammering tongues and lackadaisical efforts mighty unto the pulling down of the strongholds of sin. Do not ask me how He does it—I do not know. All I have to do is to let Him have His way with me, and He will do the rest. I do not have to ask the why's and wherefore's of all of the Spirit's workings. I should hate to have a God whom I could completely understand. I should hate to have a God whom some professor could put on a blackboard and prove by the A equals B equals C process of algebra or geometry. He would be a mighty small God if that were true. This I know: the power of the Holy Spirit, added to our efforts, will do the mighty works of God in and through our lives.

IV. THE SECRET OF POWER

We come to the last word—the secret of power. What must we do to obtain this mighty power? "Ye shall receive power, after that the Holy Ghost is come upon you: and ye shall be witnesses unto me." What must any of us do to be filled with the Holy Spirit? There are three simple things we must do ere we can hope to be flooded with the power from on High. The apostles had to step out on them. And every child of God has to comply with them.

First, there must be a searching of heart constantly. No unconfessed, unforgiven sin must be permitted to abide in our souls. Yes, we may stumble. Yes, we may fall by the wayside. Yes, we may backslide. Yes, we may drift away from God. Yes, we may grieve God. But there is provision made for every one of us so that by the confessing of our sins we are constantly cleansed and kept cleansed from all unrighteousness. There must be a sincere searching of the heart constantly.

Then, there must be a daily surrender of self, of life, consistently. We must say to God, and mean it, "As much as in me is, here are the ways of my life; here are the keys to every room of my existence. Take them over, Lord Jesus. Work out Your will in my life." That must be a consistent practice for every one of us. We are so constituted that we are like Indian givers—giving ourselves to God but having all sorts of strings attached to our gifts. These strings must be cut. The surrender must be consistently complete.

The third thing leads us one step further: **there must be a serving of God consecratedly.** Using opportunities, in the study of God's Word, in rebuking sin, in prayer, in giving of our means, in witness-bearing, in teaching and preaching, in the offices that we hold, in supplying of the wherewithal to the soldiers of the cross on the far-flung missionary fields, our ultimate object must be the coronation of the blessed Son of God. We must serve God without cessation.

When we do these three things: constantly search our hearts, consistently surrender our lives, consecratedly serve our Lord, then, the guarantee of God's Word is, backed up by every drop of Christ's precious blood, sealed by the agony of Calvary's cross, that we too will know the fullness of God's Holy Spirit.

My earnest prayer is: God grant each of us the grace, the wisdom, the power, to make that complete, definite, devoted surrender to God, letting the Holy Spirit have all of His way with us. For Christ's sake. Amen.

VI.

Paul's Secret of Power

HYMAN J. APPELMAN

(Preached at Sword Conference on Evangelism, Church of the Open Door, Los Angeles, California, 1946)

"For though I be free from all men, yet have I made myself servant unto all, that I might gain the more. And unto the Jews I became as a Jew, that I might gain the Jews; to them that are under the law, as under the law, that I might gain them that are under the law; To them that are without law, as without law, (being not without law to God, but under the law to Christ,) that I might gain them that are without law. To the weak became I as weak, that I might gain the weak: I am made all things to all men, that I might by all means save some. And this I do for the gospel's sake, that I might be partaker thereof with you. Know ye not that they which run in a race run all, but one receiveth the prize? So run, that ye may obtain. And every man that striveth for the mastery is temperate in all things. Now they do it to obtain a corruptible crown; but we an incorruptible. I therefore so run, not as uncertainly; so fight I, not as one that beateth the air: But I keep under my body, and bring it into subjection: lest that by any means, when I have preached to others, I myself should be a castaway."—I Cor. 9:19-27.

In addition to the reading I have just finished, I want to add that familiar 13th verse in chapter 4 of Philippians:

"I can do all things through Christ which strengtheneth me."

Combine these two passages of Scripture and you unquestionably have the secret of Paul's power, or Paul's secret of power. May we bow our heads for a word of prayer.

PRAYER: We earnestly beseech Thee, our heavenly Father, that Thy Holy Spirit, who first caused these words to be indicted, will make them clear to us. We know that they are not in the Bible by happenstance, by accident. We know that there is a message for our hearts in this tremendous assertion that comes from the experience of the Apostle Paul.

O our Father, we also want to know by personal assurance what he meant when he cried for the ages, "I can do all things through Christ which strengtheneth me."

We thank Thee that he was a sinner like unto ourselves. We thank Thee that he was saved by the blood of Jesus Christ even as we have been. We thank Thee that the promises, that the provisions that Thou didst make for Paul the apostle, Thou didst make for us also. We thank Thee that we have the same right to claim Thy mercies as he had. We thank Thee for the assurance that there is nothing to keep us from knowing this same vigorous power that seemed to be his constant heritage.

So we pray that Thou wouldst open our eyes, that Thou wouldst search our hearts, that Thou wouldst try our souls, that Thou wouldst lay bare our lives. Make us to see what we have that we should not have, what we do not have that we should have, what we are doing that we should not be doing, what we are not doing that we should be doing.

Give us the grace to obey Thy behest. Give us the grace to respond to Thy invitations. Give us the faith to close with the offer of Thy mercies. Give us the wisdom to understand and the power to do Thy will in our lives, that we too may be able to say, "I can do all things through Christ which strengtheneth me."

Help us, our Father, in this hour, that Thy Word may be written indelibly upon every one of our souls. We ask it trustingly, believingly, gratefully, humbly, yet boldly, by faith in Thy promises, in Jesus' name and for His dear sake. Amen.

*   *   *

May I be permitted to call your attention to some of the things I said in my message last night. I said that with all of our organizations, that with all of our busyness, that with all of our evangelistic conferences, that with all of our great churches of our orthodox fundamentalism, unless we have the power of God motivating us, inspiring, impelling us, we are not going to get very far. Oh, we will accomplish some things; oh, we will do some works—but the greatness of God's grace will not be ours to know. We are not going to do miraculous works, perform the impossible. Yet the promise of God is to us, as it has been to the children of God through the ages, 'Greater things than these shall ye do because I go unto my Father.'

The question comes up: Why is it that most preachers, when they talk about power, after they have spoken of the Holy Spirit, generally call the attention of the people to the Apostle Paul?

There are many reasons for it. The first one perhaps you have never considered. There is a definite difference of opinion among orthodox fundamental scholars on this matter of the baptism with the Holy Spirit, on this matter of the infilling of the Holy Spirit, on this matter of the experience that results when the Holy Spirit comes to possess our souls. I say fundamental orthodox scholars advisedly. Some say that the only kind of an experience that could be had by Christians is the one that happened on the day of Pentecost, and that was the end of it.

When you choose Peter as a criterion for your argument that you must be filled with the Spirit, you fall into the hands of these men who say that the Pentecostal experience was once for all and once for all time.

When, however, you take the life of the Apostle Paul who was not there on the day of Pentecost, who had absolutely no association with the apostolic band on the day of Pentecost, who was not even a Christian on the day of Pentecost, you see that their argument of Pentecost being an experience that happened back yonder once for all, and once for all time, falls to the ground. Paul was not there to have that experience. Paul came after Pentecost. What happened to him, we have a right to expect may happen to us.

But what was the secret of Paul's power? Let us see. Was it because he was a Jew? Of course not. There have been many Jews before Paul and many Jews since Paul. They never have achieved, they never have accomplished the mighty things that seemed to have been the rule rather than the exception in the life of this same Paul.

Was it because he was so brilliant? You will understand me when I say that Paul was not the only brilliant Jew of his day and time, not the only brilliant Jew of the ages, let alone the only brilliant man. There have been people endowed with extraordinary mentality of every nationality throughout the ages. No, I am sure his brilliancy was not the key to his power.

What then was there about him that gave him such tremendous power?

Some time ago, I sat in a hotel room in San Angelo, Texas, with one of our great religious leaders. This man was great in his orthodoxy, great in his power, great in his leadership of the forces of a mighty state. At that time he was my superior in the work in which I was engaged. He had complimented me on some of the things concerning my ministry. Then he had said: "Hyman, you cannot expect to have the great revivals that Moody had back yonder because the times are different. Besides, in every generation God picks out somebody and uses him in an extraordinary way."

I do not believe that at all. I believe that the reason Moody was used more of God than we are being used is, Moody made more of a surrender to God; God had more of that man than He has of us.

You remember the story that is told about General William Booth's interview with Queen Victoria.

Queen Victoria said, "General Booth, you are not the most educated preacher in my realm nor the most talented. You do not have the largest church. Why is it, then, that you are being used so mightily of God?"

Bowing before her, the great, good man humbly said, "Your Majesty, I guess it is because God has all there is of me."

That undoubtedly was the secret of Paul's power. That was the program he pursued. Those were the conditions he met. Those were the steps he followed. That was the gist of his art of operation in life and in his ministry. This was what made him such an outstanding, shining example of what the Holy Spirit can do in the individual soul.

I believe, my dear friends, I have the mind of God, the mind of Christ, the mind of the Spirit, when I call your attention to four or five things in the life of the matchless apostle that explained the secret of his wondrous power.

I. PAUL'S SATURATION WITH THE SCRIPTURES

First and foremost, there was his knowledge of Scriptures, his knowledge of the Bible.

Beloved, the ignorance of the Bible, of Scripture, in the United States of America is appalling. The great majority of our church members, let alone the multitudes of the unsaved, do not know the first thing about Holy Writ. The fact that there are more Bibles being printed and distributed makes not much difference.

You have all read in the papers the laughable, the ridiculous, the almost blasphemous answers that some of our college students give when they are given an examination on the Book of books.

The world is never going to learn the truths of the Bible; the United States of America is never going to know the holy Book; the people of our community are never going to delve into the depths of God's revelation until we teach them. And you and I are not going to teach them the Bible until we know it ourselves. Do not forget that! Hear me now! We are never going to know the Bible ourselves until we obey it, until we live it. That is the thing that counts. That is the thing that stands in the way of any revival meeting—not the lack of organization or anything of that kind, but disobedience to the Word of God.

Listen to me! It is not enough to know John 3:16 or Isaiah 53:6 or the Lord's Prayer or the Beatitudes. It is not enough to be able to parse a sentence in Greek in the Greek New Testament or in Hebrew in the Hebrew Old Testament. There is only one way to know the Bible: read it, study it, obey it. To really live the Word of God, we must make every bit of it our own, even as did Paul the apostle. It must be a roaring flame, a constant constraint in our souls.

We had a man, a Titan, in the south land, Dr. George Truett. I had rather hear him preach than any and every other preacher in all the world. His language was biblical. It was shot through and through with Bible terms. He talked like the Bible. He lived like the Bible.

What is it that we like about John Bunyan, about his *Pilgrim's Progress*, about his *Abounding Grace*, about the rest of his works, his sermons? They are soaked in Scripture. They sound like the very voice of God.

Unquestionably, indubitably, the knowledge of Scripture was the first secret of Paul's power.

II. PAUL'S CONCEPTION OF JESUS CHRIST
AS SAVIOUR AND LORD

The second secret of the apostle was his conception, his great conception, his high conception, his lofty conception of the Lord Jesus Christ both as Saviour and as Lord. There never has been anyone who wrote in such superlative terminology about Jesus Christ as did this man Paul.

He beheld Him as the crucified Christ: "Christ hath redeemed us from the curse of the law, being made a curse for us" (Gal. 3:13). He saw Him as the glorified Christ, the Christ whom God had lifted up from the dead, "declared to be the Son of God with power, according to the spirit of holiness, by the resurrection from the dead" (Rom. 1:4).

On these two pillars Paul stood, preaching dogmatically, positively, proclaiming without an apology the truth of the unsearchable riches of the Son of God. There was no vacillating with him. There was no shaking him. There was no questioning in his mind. Paul knew that Jesus Christ had died for the sins of a lost world, that God had raised Him from the dead. Standing flatfootedly on these two propositions, he threw the lifeline to a world of lost sinners. He saw the Son of God not only as the crucified Christ, not only as the glorified Christ, but also as the indwelling Christ.

What I said about the Bible, my friends, I must say about the Lord Jesus Christ. You do not know the first thing about Jesus until He lives in you. You are not saved until Jesus Christ is reproduced in you.

Not only did Paul see this Christ as the crucified Christ, as the glorified Christ, as the indwelling Christ, but he saw Him as the cosmic Christ, the Christ for the world, the Christ for the Jew, the Christ for the Gentile, the Christ for the rich and the poor, the Christ for the Pharisee and the publican, the Christ into whose hands God had put the reins of authority over all time and eternity. That is what the apostle meant when he said:

"Wherefore God also hath highly exalted him, and given him a name which is above every name: That at the name of Jesus every knee should bow, of things in heaven, and things in earth, and things under the earth; And that every tongue should confess that Jesus Christ is Lord, to the glory of God the Father."—Phil. 2:9-11.

These are the first two steps, the first two conditions that Paul met on his road to Pentecostal power. He had a wonderful knowledge of Scripture, and he lived it out to the full. He had a lofty estimation of the Son of God, the crucified, the glorified, the indwelling, the cosmic Christ. Jesus Christ was real to him in every sense of the word.

III. PAUL'S PRAYER LIFE

The next part of the secret of Paul's power was his prayer life. You knew what I was going to say. That is an open secret. He prayed for everybody. He prayed for everything. He prayed for his friends all around the world. Even as the Lord Jesus Christ cried out on the cross,

"Father, forgive them; for they know not what they do" (Luke 23:34), so the apostle prayed for his worst, for his bitterest enemies, not just once, but all of the time.

Hear me, by your souls! Prayer with him was not a matter of daily gymnastics, not a sort of spiritual "daily dozen." Here is what I am talking about. It almost ruined my Christian life. This is definitely worth listening to, because I am sorely afraid it parallels the experience of many of us.

I had been a Christian for just a part of a year. I was a member of a church in Washington, D.C. The young people decided they wanted to put on a prayer campaign. One young woman had a brainstorm. She got a number of little red cards, slightly smaller than a visiting card, and on that card she put three "D's" in black: **"D-D-D."** She gave them out to us, telling us she would advise us the next time we came together what they were. Next week, all aglow, all a flutter, she told us that these were supposed to be the Devotional Daily Dozen.

That sounds good, does it not? That sounds sweet, does it not? That sounds worthwhile, does it not? But if you are merely praying to do your Devotional Daily Dozen, you are not really praying. If you are merely praying because you have been trained to do it, because it is an exercise that has become a habit, you are not really praying. That is not heart prayer. That is not soul prayer. That is not power-bringing prayer. Oh, I will confess it is better than nothing. Any kind of praying, out of an honest heart, is better than nothing. But that is not the prayer that opens the gates of Heaven. That is not the prayer that brings the showers of power. That is not a good picture of the praying of Paul. His heart was in it. His soul was in it. His mind was in it. He would have infinitely rather missed a day's meals than missed a day's praying.

I learned a long time ago that the quietness of my soul, the assurance of my heart, the little power there may be in my life, is in direct proportion to the time I spend in prayer. It is that way with all of us, if we face it out. You know that old saying: PRAYER IS POWER. MUCH PRAYER IS MUCH POWER. LITTLE PRAYER IS LITTLE POWER. NO PRAYER IS NO POWER.

Further, Paul the apostle prayed in the Spirit. He did not just sound off so many words. He did not do as so many we know do this day.

You and I have been in places and called on men to pray. Some dear, good deacon brother had memorized the prayer of the Odd Fellows or the Masons or the Knights of Pythias. Every time you call on him to pray, he will give you their invocation and finish with their peroration. That is about the extent of it. You call on him to pray Sunday morning, Wednesday night, Sunday night. It is all the same. Whatever the occasion, he will start with Dan, finish with Beersheba, going all around the Sea of Galilee, up and down the Jordan valley, give you a free course in biblical theology, and call it praying.

My friends, it is for us—as it was for Paul—to pray in the Spirit. The Spirit groans within us. The Spirit gives us utterance. The Spirit will make us to know for what to pray.

Hear me! I am passing this on to you for what it is worth, out of personal experience. If you have thirty minutes to pray, it is better for you to spend twenty-five minutes getting ready to pray and five minutes in prayer than the other way around.

We are not ready to pray when we drop down to our knees. We have rushed in from a workaday world, full of faults, full of worldly ideas, with the hold of the flesh upon us. It takes the Holy Spirit time to prepare our hearts, to shut us in with God. It is definitely, in this matter of prayer, not the words but the heart behind the words, that counts.

Paul the apostle prayed with thanksgiving. He was always thanking and praising God. I am sorely afraid that is the missing note with too many of us, most of all with myself. The burdens oppress, depress, repress, suppress. The flesh is weak. The days fly past like a weaver's shuttle. We have so much to do. We have so little with which to do it. We become fretful. We are always bemoaning our lot.

It was not that way with our brother Paul. His lips were framed for shouting the glory of God.

What can you do with a fellow like the Apostle Paul? What can you do with a man who refuses to get angry? What can you do with a person who will turn the other cheek? What will you do with a soul who never, never has any hatred, except for the Devil, in his heart? What can you do with an individual who thanks God for being in jail, for being poor, for being in difficulties? I tell you, not even Satan can do anything with a child of God such as the one I am describing.

Oh, make me like that, Lord Jesus! May He make you like that also. What can you do with a doormat when it is made to kick around? It has a good time when you step on it. Every child of God ought to be a doormat, thanking God for being cuffed about. We should consider ourselves the doormats for the world to walk over as it finds its way to Calvary's cross.

IV. PAUL'S SELF-CRUCIFIXION

The next secret in the life of the Apostle Paul, on the road to his power, was not only his understanding of Scripture, not only his exaltation of the Lord Jesus Christ, not only his prayer life, but the crucifixion of his flesh.

It was not easy for Paul to become all things to all men. It was not easy for Paul to commune, to associate with the offscourings of the earth. It was not easy for that aristocratic, that fine, that wealthy, that talented, that educated, that intellectual giant, to come down to the level of the lowest of the low, the weakest of the weak, to boast in the fact that his friends were the offal as it were of creation. He knew that in the flesh there was no good thing. He knew that power could only be obtained by the crucifying of the flesh.

The first part of Paul's crucifixion of the flesh was entire abandonment. He felt that everything that he was, that everything that he had, belonged to God in the Lord Jesus Christ. His motto was, ". . . Ye are not your own; For ye are bought with a price: therefore glorify God in your body, and in your spirit, which are God's" (I Cor. 6:19,20). In this abandonment of the flesh there was a passionate, an earnest, a crystal clear sincerity.

When people come to say to us, "That was a good sermon," the old Devil makes us feel mighty good. After awhile, we stand in the pulpit trying to preach good sermons, anxious to hear, "You sure did hit the ball that time, brother." All of our desire, all of our longing, all of our ambition must be pleasing to Jesus and present Him clearly to the people.

We come to Sunday school. Here is Sister So-and-So; here is Brother So-and-So; there is that woman, that man. We just love them to death. We cannot wait until Sunday comes around to come to Sunday school. Why? Is it to serve God? Is it to enjoy the fellowship of kindred hearts? You all understand what I am talking about. We subserve the glory, the interest of God, the leadership of the Holy Spirit, the desires of God for our life, to our own sentiment, to our own fleshly inclinations.

There must be a passionate sincerity to do the will of God, a crystal-clear desire to magnify the Lord Jesus Christ. We cannot be mockly pious. We cannot put on a long face, to say we are so good, so clean, so fine, when on the inside of us there is the ravening beast of jealousy, of selfishness, of personal aggrandizing desires. The Lord knows about these things. The Holy Spirit is grieved with them. Abandonment must be utter dedication of self, so that it does not come into any part of our service.

Paul the apostle, because he crucified the flesh constantly, received constant influxes of power—physical power, mental power, moral power, most of all spiritual power—from heavenly sources.

There are a great many things God can do, but there are some things He cannot do. If we are as full of ourselves as an egg is of white and yolk; if we are so full of ourselves that we cannot think of anything or anybody else but me, my, mine; if somebody looking at us sideways makes us mad, causes us to want to quit; if the fact that we are not made captain causes us to take our balls and bats and gloves, to go home—not even God can do a thing with us. But when we are empty of self, when we are sincere in our purposes, when we are looking out for God and for His kingdom and for His glory, then God will flood our souls with the same power that He gave to this chief of apostles.

V. PAUL'S INTENSE CONCENTRATION

One more thing I must say to you. Not only was Paul empowered because of his knowledge of the Scriptures, because of his exaltation of the Lord Jesus Christ, because of his prayer life, because of the crucifixion of the flesh; but it came about also because of the intensity of his concentration.

You heard me right. I did not say consecration. I said concentration.

O beloved, the temptation that comes to us preachers to become known as great, popular, crowd-drawing, soul-winning, money-raising, church-building preachers!

Have you ever heard the story of Charles Haddon Spurgeon? You know he never was ordained. He would not permit any group to ordain him at all. He wanted to go to college, wanted to get an education. Making a date with the president of a certain school yonder in England, he walked into the president's home one day, to be greeted by a maid who, asking him to be seated, told him that the president was not in, but would be back in a little while.

In her household cares, she promptly forgot about the waiting young man. Spurgeon sat there three or four hours waiting for the maid or the president.

After awhile, the maid came in to work in that room. Startled at seeing the young preacher, she abjectly apologized, telling him that she had forgotten all about him. By that time the president was gone for the day and could not be approached.

Spurgeon walked out of that place with his head hanging down, his feet dragging along, thinking he had been mistreated. He did not know what to do, which way to turn, or when he could see the president again.

As he was walking along, there came to his mind, as if spoken from the sky, "Seekest thou great things for thyself? seek them not" (Jer. 45:5). Then and there he turned his back on the chance of a formal education.

Do not misunderstand me nor misquote me. I am for education. I am glad the Lord gave me a chance to go to university, to law school, to seminary. Everybody who has the chance to get an education ought to get it. The moral of this story, the thing I am trying to impress upon your hearts is that there must be concentration of motive. It must all be for the glory of God! "Whatsoever ye do, do all to the glory of God" (I Cor. 10:31).

We must not seek great things, not even small things for ourselves. Why are you here this afternoon? Is it because you know that you are going to hear an orthodox message in the Church of the Open Door? Why are you here this afternoon? Is it because you had nowhere else to go? Why are you here this afternoon? Is it because, having walked up and down town in this glorious Los Angeles sunshine, you are getting a little tired out and want to take a bit of a rest? Why are you here this afternoon? If you are here for any other purpose except to glorify God, I beseech you, confess it as a sin to God, and ask Him to forgive you. Ask God to give you a renewal of your devotion to the Son of God!

Not only must there be concentration of motive, but there must be concentration of aim. What is your desire? What do you want to accomplish? What do you want to do with your life? Why are you investing your service in the Lord?

Do you want a big church? That is not good enough. Do you want a large Sunday school? That is not good enough. Do you want the approval of your fellow men? That is definitely not good enough.

Paul the apostle said, "I am made all things to all men, that I might by all means save some" (I Cor. 9:22). That is the motive that God can honor, that God does honor, that God ever will honor. That is the motive that sends the missionaries to the ends of the earth. That is the motive that was in the heart and mind of R. A. Torrey when he established this institute, when he founded this church. That is the motive in the heart and soul of Dr. John Rice and Dr. Bob Wells and, please God, the rest of us on this program, as we come here to stand before you.

There must be not only concentration of motive, not only concentration of aim, but there must be concentration of talent, of personality, of ability, of weapons, of money, of organization, of efforts.

Every organization in our churches, every institution in our programs must be aimed at one thing: to be an instrument in the hands of the Holy Spirit to do the will of God in advancing the interests of His kingdom, in carrying out the program of the Great Commission.

If there is anything we do, if there is any group to which we belong, if there is anything we permit in our churches that is not aimed toward being a grappling hook in the hands of the Holy Spirit to rescue souls as brands from the burning, I beseech you, dismiss it, close it up, throw it away, cast it from you, have nothing to do with it. Concentrate every effort, every energy, every endeavor toward the one thing of lifting aloft the crucified, resurrected Son of God.

VI. PAUL'S GREAT HOPE

We hasten on. Not only did Paul know the Scriptures; not only did he exalt the Lord Jesus Christ; not only did he pray unceasingly; not only did he crucify the flesh; not only was he intense in his concentration, but he was also buoyed up by the optimistic energy of a great hope. Power flowed to him from that great hope. We also may have the same power through the same great hope.

They tell us nowadays that it is not fashionable to preach the second coming of the Lord Jesus Christ. Beloved, Paul preached it again and again. You and I would rather be old-fashioned with Paul than new-fashioned with anyone else. He knew all about the second coming of Christ. He preached it without hesitation, without fear, without favor. There was the assurance, the confidence, the drive, the intensity, the encouragement, the inspiration of that conquering hope.

First, he thought of the second coming of the Lord Jesus Christ in the consummation of the program of God. Hear me! Things look tough.

Things look hard. I am not minimizing the difficulties, the obstacles. I know them, alas and alack, only too well. I am not a blind optimist. True, I am a Christian optimist. As a Christian, I cannot be anything else but an optimist.

Listen! Show me a Christian who is an incurable pessimist, and I will show you a Christian who is not entirely right with God. That is all there is to it. There is some sin in his or her life that the person is striving to hide by throwing sand into the air, by crying, "Stop, thief!" and pointing out the other fellow's sins.

We might as well face it. Optimism, in the good Christian sense of the word, ought to be the rule rather than the exception of our lives. Sin will drain it out of us. Sin will darken our outlook. Sin will catch up with us. It will show in our walk, in our talk, in our preaching, in our teaching, in the prayers that we utter.

It was not that way with Paul. The times were hard, just as hard, harder even than they are today. Preaching the Gospel was difficult, just as difficult as it is today. I will guarantee you those jail cells were not nearly as comfortable as the seats in the Church of the Open Door! Paul the apostle saw beyond the difficulties the "Son of righteousness with healing in His wings" coming to straighten out this old world. That gave him the blazing challenge of an immortal hope.

There was further, the hope of personal immortality, of a personal resurrection.

What can you do, I say again, with a man who knows that if you kill him, you are doing him a favor?

What can you do with a Christian who knows that, when you bury him, you have blessed him?

What can you do with a person who will stick out his head to say, "Do you want to chop off my head? Go ahead! Do it quickly! For me to die is gain"?

You just cannot do anything with an individual such as this. You cannot hurt him. You might as well go out there to the cemetery, dig up a corpse, kick it in the teeth, for all the impression you can make on a person who turns his back on the world, the flesh, the Devil, and lives for nothing but the glory of Jesus in the hope of His imminent second coming.

Paul knew that his immortality was secure. He knew it by the resurrection of the Lord Jesus Christ from the dead. He knew it by the love of Jesus Christ for His disciples, for all the saints through the ages. He knew it by the constant upsurge of a renewed and renewing experience in his own heart and soul. He knew it by the promises of God. He knew it by the witnessing testimony of the Holy Spirit. He just knew it, knew it all the time. It was in all of his preaching, in all of his praying uppermost; and uttermost in his thoughts.

In that power of a great hope there was also the mighty hope of a reward waiting for him, a crown of righteousness, a crown of rejoicing, a crown of reward. He knew that his tears were recorded in Heaven. He knew that his prayers were bottled up in Glory. He knew that his difficulties had been marked down on the book of God's remembrance. He knew that God would pay it all off with a great usury. He knew that the investment of his life in the Lord Jesus Christ would bring mighty dividends here, and the mightiest of all sorts of dividends in the life to come.

Put all of these things together now. Add a knowledge of the Scriptures to an exaltation of the Lord Jesus Christ, to an incessant Holy Spirit-led, Holy Spirit-inspired prayer life, to a crucifixion of self, to an intensity of concentration, frost it over with a blazing firmness of conviction in the hope of the soon coming of the Lord Jesus Christ. Brother, sister, you will, too, and so will I, count everything but refuse for the excellency of the knowledge of Christ Jesus. When we get to know Him as Paul knew Him, we too will spend and be spent in the one tremendous attack against sin and Satan, particularly in this matter of evangelism, every kind of evangelism, individual personal work, church evangelism, mass evangelism, whatever other program the Holy Spirit may lead us to engage in, in our day, in our time, in our circumstances.

There is not one of us in this congregation but almost envies the power that Paul the apostle had with God. Beloved, we need not envy it. We can have it at the same price and on the same condition that Paul faced, that Paul paid, with which Paul complied.

I have given them to you as God has written them across my own soul. God give us, each of us, all of us, every one of us, and through us, multitudes of others, the grace to step out in this essential program, so that in our souls too, in our lives also, there may be the upsurging, outflowing tide of pentecostal power and victory.

O for that flame of living fire,
Which shone so bright in saints of old!
Which bade their souls to Heaven aspire,
Calm in distress, in danger bold.

Where is that Spirit, Lord, which dwelt
In Abrah'm's breast, and sealed him thine?
Which made Paul's heart with sorrow melt,
And glow with energy divine?

That Spirit which from age to age
Proclaimed Thy love, and taught Thy ways?
Brightened Isaiah's vivid page,
And breathed in David's hallowed lays?

JOHN R. RICE
1895 - 1980

ABOUT THE MAN:

Preacher...evangelist...revivalist...editor...counselor to thousands...friend to millions—that was Dr. John R. Rice, whose accomplishments were nothing short of miraculous. Known as "America's Dean of Evangelists," Dr. Rice made a mighty impact upon the nation's religious life for some sixty years, in great citywide campaigns and in Sword of the Lord Conferences.

At age nine, after hearing a sermon on "The Prodigal Son," John went forward to claim Christ as Saviour. In 1916, with only $9.35 in his pocket, he rode off on his cowpony toward Decatur Baptist College. He was now on the road to becoming a world-renowned evangelist, although he was then totally unaware of God's will for his life.

There was many a twist and turn before Rice rode through the open door into full-time preaching—the army, marriage, graduate work, more seminary, assistant pastor, pastor—then FINALLY, where God planned to use him most—in full-time evangelism.

Dr. Rice and his ministry were always colorful (born in Cooke County, in Texas, December 11, 1895, and often called "Will Rogers of the Pulpit" because of their likeness and mannerisms)—and controversial. CONTROVERSIAL—and correctly so—because of his intense stand against modernism and infidelity and his fight for the Fundamentals.

Dr. Rice lived and died a man of convictions—intense convictions. But, like many other strong fighters for the Faith, Rice was also marked with a sincere spirit of compassion. Those who knew him best knew a man who loved them. In preaching, in prayer, and in personal life, Rice wept over sinners and with saints. But there is more....

Less than seventy-one hours before the dawning of 1981, one of the most prolific pens in all Christendom was stilled. Dr. John R. Rice left behind a legacy in writing of more than 200 titles, with a combined circulation of over 61 million copies. And through October of 1981, a total of 24,058 precious souls reported trusting Christ through his ministries, not counting those saved in his crusades nor in foreign countries where his literature has been translated.

And who but God knows the influence of THE SWORD OF THE LORD magazine which he started and edited for forty-six years!

And while "Twentieth Century's Mightiest Pen"—and man—has been stilled, thank God, the fruit remains! Though dead, he continues to speak.

VII.

The Holy Spirit — Our Best Friend

How He Loves Us; What He Will Do for Us; How We Should Treat Him

JOHN R. RICE

Your best Friend is the one who loves you the most and does the most for you and stays the closest by you. And that Friend is the Holy Spirit of God.

In Romans 15:30 Paul says,

"Now I beseech you, brethren, for the Lord Jesus Christ's sake, and for the love of the Spirit, that ye strive together with me in your prayers to God for me."

Paul was led by the Holy Spirit to ask Christians at Rome to pray for him. They were to pray for him for Jesus' sake—that is, because the work Paul was doing honored the Lord Jesus, and it would please our Lord for them to be partakers in his ministry by prayer. They were to pray also because of the love of the Spirit.

The Holy Spirit loved Paul and the Christians at Rome. With unspeakable concern He longed to bless Paul in the ministry and to bless these Christians who would have a part in Paul's ministry by prayer.

So Paul is led to ask them to pray for him because of the love of the Holy Spirit for him and them. It is as if Paul said, "The Holy Spirit loves me so much that He wants you to and will lead you to pray for me."

"The love of the Spirit"! The Holy Spirit loves us! This unseen Person who loves us so is our best Friend.

The Holy Spirit is the personal representative of God and of Christ on earth. He is called many times "the Spirit of God" (Matt. 3:16; Gen. 1:2), and God many times speaks of "my Spirit" (Gen. 6:3;

Isa. 44:3; Joel 2:28; Acts 2:17,18). He is also called "the Spirit of Christ" (Rom. 8:9).

In John 14:16-26 the Saviour told His sorrowing disciples that through the Holy Spirit both He and the Father would manifest themselves to the disciples and would come and make their abode with Christians.

The Holy Spirit is God's executive officer in dealing with mankind.

The Holy Spirit dictated the Bible. "Holy men of God spake as they were moved by the Holy Ghost" (II Pet. 1:21). We are told that the things God has prepared for us are not known by eye, nor ear, nor heart of man; "but God hath revealed them unto us by his Spirit" (I Cor. 2:10).

Even the very words of divine revelation are given by the Holy Spirit: "Which things also we speak, not in the words which man's wisdom teacheth, but which the Holy Ghost teacheth; comparing spiritual things with spiritual" (I Cor. 2:13). The Holy Spirit is the author of the Bible. So the Word of God is fittingly called "the sword of the Spirit" (Eph. 6:17).

But as wonderful as is the fact that the Holy Spirit is the author of the Bible, here is a fact even more wonderful: the entire ministry of Jesus Christ on earth was wrought in the power and wisdom of the Holy Spirit!

It was by the Holy Spirit that Christ was conceived in the womb of a virgin girl (Matt. 1:20; Luke 1:35). Joseph was told, "That which is conceived in her is of the Holy Ghost"; and the Angel Gabriel explained to Mary, "The Holy Ghost shall come upon thee, and the power of the highest shall overshadow thee: therefore also that holy thing which shall be born of thee shall be called the Son of God."

And all the ministry of the Lord Jesus, including creating the world, was NOT in His power as the Son of God, but in the power of the Holy Spirit. He never worked a miracle nor healed the sick nor cleansed a leper nor preached a sermon nor won a soul until His baptism when, praying, the Holy Spirit came upon Him. After that, He did His first miracle at Cana of Galilee and then went to Nazareth and in the synagogue read and explained Isaiah 61:1:

"The Spirit of the Lord is upon me, because he hath anointed me to preach the gospel to the poor; he hath sent me to heal the brokenhearted, to preach deliverance to the captives, and recovering of sight to the blind, to set at liberty them that are bruised, to preach

the acceptable year of the Lord."—Luke 4:18, 19.

Then Jesus said, "This day is this scripture fulfilled in your ears" (Luke 4:16-21).

Thereafter Jesus did His work under the Holy Spirit's complete anointing. (See Acts 10:38.)

Even after His resurrection, He gave His apostles instructions through the power and wisdom of the Holy Spirit (Acts 1:1,2). When Jesus returns to the earth to reign, His reign will be as the Spirit-filled Son of man. "And the spirit of the Lord shall rest upon him, the spirit of wisdom and understanding, the spirit of counsel and might, the spirit of knowledge and of the fear of the Lord" (Isa. 11:2). That is why we may do the same work that Jesus did. We may have the same power and wisdom that was given to Him through the same Holy Spirit.

It is the Holy Spirit who convicts sinners: "When he is come, he will reprove the world of sin, and of righteousness, and of judgment" (John 16:8).

Every soul that is regenerated is literally "born of the Spirit." Just as God breathed His Spirit or breath into the nostrils of Adam, the first man whom He had made out of dust and he became a living soul; so the Holy Spirit of God comes into the body and life of a poor lost child and makes him into a child of God. He is "born of the Spirit."

It is perfectly proper to say, "Let Jesus come into your heart." But in truth the Lord Jesus has a human body. He has scars in His hands and His feet. He ate and drank before the disciples. Their hands handled Him. When Jesus comes again, it will be the same Jesus; and every eye shall see Him, this Christ with a human body, with hands and feet and flesh and bones.

So, in a sense, Christ could not come into your heart. What we mean is that when we get converted we let the Spirit of Christ come into our hearts. Christ's own representative, doing His work, took us over, regenerated us, and made us children of God.

Now this blessed Holy Spirit dwells literally in our bodies.

"What? know ye not that your body is the temple of the Holy Ghost which is in you, which ye have of God, and ye are not your own? For ye are bought with a price: therefore glorify God in your body, and in your spirit, which are God's."—I Cor. 6:19,20.

Since the day Jesus rose from the dead and breathed on the disciples and said, "Receive ye the Holy Ghost," the Holy Spirit of God has lived literally in the body of every Christian (John 7:37-39; John 20:22). When you were converted, the Holy Spirit, who made you a member of the body of Christ, buried you into this body as a stone is buried in the mortar and other stones of a wall so as to become a part of the building (I Cor. 12:13; I Pet. 2:5; Eph. 2:19-22). All this work is done by the Holy Spirit as the representative of God and Christ on the earth.

I. WHAT THE LOVING HOLY SPIRIT DOES FOR A CHRISTIAN

One can thus see how intimate is the relationship of the Holy Spirit to the Christian. If God loved the whole world enough to give His Son, and if Christ loved poor sinners with such infinite compassion that He gladly went to the cross, then how the Spirit of God must love His own!

How much He must love those He has sought and convicted of sin, those whose hearts He has changed, those into whose bodies He has come to dwell forever, those He has made a part of that mystical body of Christ which will be called together at the rapture and assembled in Heaven, the church of the firstborn.

Romans 15:30 urges us to pray one for another "for the love of the Spirit." The Holy Spirit loves us with a tender compassion. The Holy Spirit is our best Friend.

And now, keeping always in mind how the Holy Spirit loves us and yearns over us, let us see some of the things that the Holy Spirit does for a Christian.

1. The Holy Spirit Comforts

He is called by our Saviour "the Comforter," that is, one called alongside to help. Acts 9:31 tells us how the churches "were edified; and walking in the fear of the Lord, and IN THE COMFORT OF THE HOLY GHOST, were multiplied."

New Testament Christians and many thousands of others have been comforted by this Holy Spirit who loves us, who lives within us, and who does the work of God within us. Romans 14:17 tells us, "For the kingdom of God is not meat and drink, but righteousness, and peace, and joy in the Holy Ghost."

It is the Holy Spirit who sets the songs singing in our heart, as you see from Ephesians 5:18,19: ". . . be filled with the Spirit; speaking to yourselves in psalms and hymns and spiritual songs, singing and making melody in your heart to the Lord."

So the Holy Spirit is the Author of spiritual songs; the Holy Spirit makes melody in the heart of a Christian. He is the Comforter, the joy of the redeemed!

God promises to despised and hated Israel that one day He will comfort them. "As one whom his mother comforteth, so will I comfort you" (Isa. 66:13). When Jews cease to reject the Saviour and are born again and the Spirit of God comes and abides in their bodies, then they, too, will know the Comforter that the saints of God know when they let the Holy Spirit have His way.

God comforts His people through the Holy Spirit.

This verse indicates that the mother-work of God is done by the Holy Spirit. God is a masculine God. The pronouns *He* and *Him* are used of God the Father. But there is something so intimate, so personal, so affectionate, so detailed about the way the Holy Spirit of God, the indwelling Comforter, warms and consoles the heart that God says, "As one whom his mother comforteth, so will I comfort you."

For seventy-eight years I have missed my mother. How strangely my mind goes back to certain little details of a mother's love and affection.

Mother cooked the loveliest birthday cakes and wrote my name on them with little cinnamon drops! Mother made the straight little trousers out of a pair of my father's worn ones and made the little red waist with the big collar. She brushed my hair so nicely and said how fine I looked when she took me to church. She had me sing out of her book (though I could not read), and called me her preacher boy! Many long, orphaned years went by after my mother died before I got another birthday cake, made just for me!

Mother knew just what to do when I exploringly pushed a pea up my nose. After she took me out and had me look at the sun and I had sneezed violently and the pea shot out, how we laughed together! And when I tried a circular washer on my hand and it fit so tight I couldn't get it off, it was Mother who assured me I would not have to wear it all my life, as I had feared. She knew the marvel that soapy water would work in just such a case!

Even now, there are many times when I long for my mother. What a comfort it would be if I could only kneel down at her knees or lay my head in her lap or have her hands on my face or hear her praise me or strengthen me or comfort me!

But, bless God, I have One who can comfort me "as one whom his mother comforteth." The blessed Holy Spirit does this blessed mother's work in my heart! Does not this picture how sweetly the Spirit loves us?

2. The Holy Spirit Is "the Spirit of Wisdom" (Eph. 1:17; Isa. 11:2)

Do not be misled by the fact that sometimes the Bible does not spell *Spirit* with a capital *S*. The translators could not always decide; and in the original languages capitalization of words did not mean always the same as it does in English.

The Lord Jesus called Him "the Spirit of truth" (John 14:17). And again He promised, "When he, the Spirit of truth, is come, he will guide you into all truth: for he shall not speak of himself; but whatsoever he shall hear, that shall he speak: and he will shew you things to come. He shall glorify me: for he shall receive of mine, and shall shew it unto you" (John 16:13,14).

Thus spiritual wisdom is given by the blessed Holy Spirit who is indwelling the Christian's body. He reveals the things of Christ to us. He will guide us into all truth. Not only that, but He will help us remember spiritual truths; for Jesus said, "But the Comforter, which is the Holy Ghost, whom the Father will send in my name, he shall teach you all things, and bring all things to your remembrance, whatsoever I have said unto you" (John 14:26).

Always teaching, always reminding, always guiding—that is the work of the Spirit, who loves us and is anxious to tenderly guide us into all truth.

When we come to read or study the Bible, we should be conscious of the Spirit's presence. We should always ask Him to teach us the Word of God. Many times when I write an article or preach a sermon, I earnestly pray for the Spirit to bring to my remembrance the Scriptures on the subject and to help me understand them. And often when I am in the pulpit, Scriptures come to mind that I did not think about when I prepared the sermon. And oftentimes after I have read the Scriptures in the pulpit, there will come such light on the Word of God as I did not have in the study and preparation. That happens only as I am led by the Spirit of God and when I am surrendered to Him and have a receptive heart. He is our Comforter, our Guide, our Teacher.

In this dark world every Christian needs a guide. How can I know which way to turn, what to do? A thousand details must be settled day after day. The preacher must know what text to preach on, what illustrations to use, whether to accept this invitation and reject another, or vice versa. What is the will of God about this matter, or that, or that? The only way that we can day by day *know* that we are following the will of God for us is by the clear leading of the Holy Spirit.

And every Christian may have that leading. Isaiah 30:21 says, "And thine ears shall hear a word behind thee, saying, This is the way, walk ye in it, when ye turn to the right hand, and when ye turn to the left." Every Christian can hear that word of direction from the Holy Spirit.

The way may be dark, but I can say, "Though I walk through the valley of the shadow of death, I will fear no evil: for thou art with me."

How clearly the Holy Spirit led Christians in the Bible! Note how "the angel [messenger or agent] of the Lord spake unto Philip, saying, Arise, and go toward the south unto the way that goeth down from Jerusalem unto Gaza, which is desert" (Acts 8:26). It seems likely that this is simply another way of saying that the Spirit of God told Philip what to do. He may or may not have spoken with an audible voice, but Philip knew exactly what to do.

We read on in verse 29: "Then the Spirit said unto Philip, Go near, and join thyself to this chariot." The Spirit taught Philip how to win the eunuch to Christ, then "the Spirit of the Lord caught away Philip, that the eunuch saw him no more."

Now read in chapter 10 of Acts how the Holy Spirit dealt with Peter, preparing him to go to speak to Cornelius and win him and his family to Christ. How definite was the leading of the Holy Spirit! And how wonderful the results when Peter obeyed!

Read how the Holy Spirit directed the praying group of workers at Antioch to "separate me Barnabas and Saul for the work whereunto I have called them."

How clearly and definitely the Holy Spirit led Paul in his work is indicated by Acts 16:6-10:

"Now when they had gone throughout Phrygia and the region of Galatia, and were forbidden of the Holy Ghost to preach the word in Asia, After they were come to Mysia, they assayed to go into Bithynia: but the Spirit suffered them not. And they passing by Mysia came down to Troas. And a vision appeared to Paul in the night; There stood a man of Macedonia, and prayed him, saying, Come over into Macedonia, and help us. And after he had seen the vision, immediately we

endeavoured to go into Macedonia, assuredly gathering that the Lord had called us for to preach the gospel unto them."

O Christian, the dear Holy Spirit wants to lead you in the will of God. You can walk day by day with sweet assurance that you are where God wants you, that you are busy about the things that please Him, that you are acting in His wisdom.

3. The Holy Spirit Is Our Help in Prayer

When God promises to pour upon the house of David and the inhabitants of Jerusalem "the spirit of grace and of supplication" so that they will see the Saviour and know He is their Messiah and will seek Him with mourning and confession, He means that the Holy Spirit will be poured upon them. In fact, again and again God does promise to pour out the Holy Spirit upon Israel, as in Joel 2:28, quoted in Acts 2:17. So "the spirit of supplication" is simply the Holy Spirit doing His blessed work in helping people pray!

And if the Holy Spirit would create a hunger in the heart of a lost man and lead him to be convicted and seek God, how much more will the Spirit help a Christian to pray! We are told in Romans 8:26,27:

"Likewise the Spirit also helpeth our infirmities: for we know not what we should pray for as we ought: but the Spirit itself maketh intercession for us with groanings which cannot be uttered. And he that searcheth the hearts knoweth what is the mind of the Spirit, because he maketh intercession for the saints according to the will of God."

You know how our mothers pray for us. My mother prayed for me to be a preacher, giving me to God when I was born.

The Syrophenician woman came to Jesus and said, "Have mercy on me, O Lord, thou son of David; my daughter is grievously vexed with a devil" (Matt. 15:22).

Many a mother has written to a judge asking leniency for her wayward boy who was charged with a crime.

The mother of James and John came to Jesus interceding for them that they should sit on His right hand and on His left in the coming kingdom.

How many times has my good wife come to me when there was a question of punishing one of our daughters and said, "But, Daddy, she is such a little girl."

The Holy Spirit pleads to God for us. He is "the spirit of supplication," and the Spirit "maketh intercession for us with groanings which cannot be uttered."

So the Holy Spirit helps us to pray. He puts in our minds what we should pray for, gives us a heart to pray if we wait on Him and listen to His tender wooing and follow His loving leading. When a Christian really prays aright, then be sure that the Holy Spirit is helping him pray.

The blessed Spirit always prays in the will of God. "He that searcheth the hearts knoweth what is the mind of the Spirit, because he maketh intercession for the saints *according to the will of God.*"

People are often timid about praying. They tell me that they dare not be very bold since they may be asking something contrary to God's will. But usually a Christian can pray in the will of God. One can know ahead of time whether the prayer he wants to bring is according to the will of God—first, by the Scriptures; and second, by the sweet whispering of the Holy Spirit in his heart.

When the Holy Spirit helps, every prayer is born in Heaven, a request that is patterned after the answer God wants to give; and such a prayer is always heard!

Oh, we are not orphans! We need not be untaught, unguided in our ignorance and frailty when we come to pray. The Spirit of God prays with and for us!

I was a guest for two weeks in a pastor's home during a revival campaign. Each morning we joined hands around the breakfast table as each one prayed. The father, holding his five-year-old son's hand, put the words in his mouth as he prayed. As we kneeled in the home, the father took the little one down on the floor beside him and with his arms about him, whispered into his ear, the words a line at a time, that he should pray. And that baby boy prayed sensible, wise prayers, such prayers as if he knew well the Bible and as if he had a mature, well-disciplined heart; all because he was taught and helped to pray by such a Christian father.

Just so the Holy Spirit kneels with every Christian who prays and, as if loving arms were about us, as if a loving voice whispered in our ears, we may know what we should pray for and how to pray. And we may hear Another praying with us—the Holy Spirit joining us in prayer for the things that please God and that He has revealed as His sweet will for us.

Thank God for the love of the Spirit as shown in His help in prayer!

So a Christian can know how to pray, can pray for the right things and can have a sweet assurance that God hears him when he prays! A Christian need only submit himself to the Spirit and to the will of God. Then he can pray in the will of God, pray with faith, joy and victory and get the answer to a prayer that has already been made in Heaven!

4. The Only Power a Christian Can Have Is Power of the Holy Spirit

In Acts 1:8 Jesus promised the disciples, "But ye shall receive power, after that the Holy Ghost is come upon you: and ye shall be witnesses unto me both in Jerusalem, and in all Judaea, and in Samaria, and unto the uttermost part of the earth."

And Jesus commanded the disciples, "And, behold, I send the promise of my Father upon you; but tarry ye in the city of Jerusalem until ye be endued with power from on high" (Luke 24:49).

Pentecost was an example of Christians under the mighty power of the Holy Spirit carrying out the Great Commission. As D. L. Moody said, "Pentecost is simply a specimen case of what God can do when people are filled with His Spirit." When the Holy Spirit controls and fills and masters Christians, He brings revivals and gives wonder-working power to the people of God.

That is what the prophet means when he says, "Not by might, nor by power, but by my spirit, saith the Lord of hosts" (Zech. 4:6). Again I quote D. L. Moody: "It is foolish to try to do the work of God without the power of God."

None of us knows the secrets of unsaved hearts. None of us by nature or training has the keys to unlock the sealed vaults of the will. Only the Spirit of God knows how to convict the sinner and bring him to repentance and faith in Christ.

Our fruitfulness in soul winning must depend altogether on having the power of the Holy Spirit, being filled with Him, controlled, mastered and used by Him. His loving heart yearns to use our hands, our feet, our voices, our heart's love in winning souls. Because of His love for us, He longs for us to have that highest honor, that sweetest joy, that greatest reward that can ever come to a child of God—the honor, joy and reward of soul winning.

5. The Holy Spirit and the Christian's Body

The body is not the soul. A Christian's body is not as important as his spirit. The Scripture says, "Keep thy *heart* with all diligence; for out of it are the issues of life" (Prov. 4:23). Yet the bodies of those we love are dear to us.

To a baby, a mother is not just a spirit, but a loving spirit and a maternal body all in one. Mother's lap, Mother's soft breast, Mother's tender hands, Mother's gentle smile and Mother's goodnight kiss—these go to make up Mother. Our personalities are woven up, in part, of the fleshly body; and we want the bodies of our loved ones.

Every marriage should be a marriage of heart, but it is obviously and properly a marriage of human bodies. God prepared husband for wife and wife for husband. Every mother and father watch little bodies grow with delight. They match little hands and feet by Father's and Mother's, kiss every dimple, love the bare, clear, baby skin, the soft hair, the wet little smile, the fat little creases, the first little teeth.

And since the Holy Spirit loves us, He also has much to do with our bodies. In fact, He lives in the body of every Christian. Again notice I Corinthians 6:19,20:

"What? know ye not that your BODY is the temple of the Holy Ghost which is in you, which ye have of God, and ye are not your own? For ye are bought with a price: therefore glorify God in your BODY, and in your spirit, which are God's."

It is only partly true to say that we have Christ in our hearts or the Holy Spirit in our hearts. Actually, the Holy Spirit is in our bodies. When we go to serve and glorify God, we are to glorify Him first in our bodies and then in our spirits.

So when a Christian is baptized and his body is buried in the watery grave, picturing the burial and resurrection of the Saviour, it also means that the Christian counts his old body and the fleshly nature dead; and he is commanded to reckon himself alive from the dead. His body is no longer his own but is counted as belonging to God alone.

In Romans 12:1 we are commanded, "I beseech you therefore, brethren, by the mercies of God, that ye present your BODIES a living sacrifice, holy, acceptable unto God, which is your reasonable service." We deceive ourselves when we talk about giving our hearts to God and making Him first in our hearts, if we do not really give Him our *bodies*.

Every Christian should offer his body freely to God. It belongs to Him. Of course that means he is to put his body under the control of the Holy Spirit who lives within.

Your body is dear to the Holy Spirit. He wants it to be a holy body, a living sacrifice, acceptable unto God, so that every member of it will be used to God's glory and for your own good.

When the body is defiled, it grieves the Spirit. We are told, "If any man defile the temple of God, him shall God destroy; for the temple of God is holy, which temple ye are" (I Cor. 3:17). This indicates that Christians who defile their bodies will die prematurely; and we know that some died in the church at Corinth because of their sins (I Cor. 11:29-32).

It is the Holy Spirit who heals the body. James 5:14,15 tells us that when the elders of the churches are called upon to do so, they shall anoint the sick with oil, and the prayer of faith shall save the sick. The oil here is a symbol of the Holy Spirit of God, the loving, brooding, indwelling Presence in every Christian's body. The meaning of the anointing with oil must be that it is the Holy Spirit which heals the body when God gives the faith for healing.

Thus our sins grieve the Holy Spirit. When we defile the body and misuse it, whether it be the mouth, the stomach, hands or eyes or feet, we sadden the Holy Spirit who loves us so. Ill health and sickness are often the result of such sins. The Holy Spirit longs to cleanse us of our sins and to heal our bodies of the diseases that sin brings.

The Holy Spirit never leaves a Christian. As the angels of God, sent forth to be ministers to those who shall be the heirs of salvation constantly watch over us, go with us and surround us, as the angels in chariots of fire surrounded Elisha at Dothan, so the Holy Spirit always goes with the Christian wherever he goes. Jesus said in Matthew 28:20, "Lo, I am with you alway, even unto the end of the world."

The always abiding Presence of the Holy Spirit is consciously felt with obvious power and joy when He is in control; He is unobtrusive and rather passive when the Christian is worldly-minded and not walking in the Spirit nor filled with the Spirit. But always the abiding Holy Spirit goes with the Christian, staying where he stays and abiding within his body.

Sometimes He manifests Himself happily, revealing the truth of God, giving us light on the way and power for our tasks, comforting our hearts. Other times He seems to speak only reluctantly and sadly because He is so grieved by our sins.

But whether happily or sadly, the Spirit stays within the body of a child of God. That is His home, His temple, and He never leaves.

I have heard Christians say, "If you go to the tavern, the Holy Spirit will not go with you." Or, "If you go to the theater or the dance hall, the Holy Spirit will not go with you there." But wherever a child of God goes, the Holy Spirit goes. That body belongs to Him. It is in His charge; it is His temple, His home.

How ashamed and heartsick many a child of God will be when Jesus comes unexpectedly and the Christian is found in sin. Some may be in theaters, some in taverns, some engaged in business that will terribly embarrass them before Christ.

Don't say no Christian ever goes where he should not. Many a Lot, vexing his righteous soul, will be in the midst of some wicked Sodom when Jesus comes. Many a David, after God's own heart in other matters, may be with some Bathsheba when Jesus comes. Many a Peter will be warming by the Devil's fire and denying his Lord. It will still be of grace, not of works, and we who deserve to be left behind but have trusted in the blood shed for sinners will be taken with our Saviour when He comes for those He has purchased. Christ will not seize an arm and a leg of His bride and leave the body here. It will be a rapture, not a rupture.

But how shamed, how sad, will be those who are not pleasing the Lord Jesus when He comes, "ashamed before him at his coming," as the Holy Spirit puts it. So many Christians will have tears of sorrow and shame over themselves when they meet the Saviour.

Since He always goes with us everywhere, sleeping or waking, working or playing, laughing or crying, living holily or carnally, then how earnestly we must seek to please Him and always be conscious of His presence.

When the Christian dies, he is still not done with the blessed Holy Spirit. The Holy Spirit will raise up our mortal bodies and make them glorified bodies. "But if the Spirit of him that raised up Christ from the dead shall also quicken your mortal bodies by his Spirit that dwelleth in you" (Rom. 8:11).

It was the Holy Spirit who raised Christ from the dead. The same Holy Spirit who overshadowed Mary, conceived the Holy Son of God and formed the child in her womb, was the Holy Spirit that came upon Jesus with wisdom and power for all His ministry. Then the same Holy Spirit raised His body from the grave! Now the same Holy Spirit dwells in us who are saved, and He that raised Christ from the dead shall also quicken our mortal bodies by the same Holy Spirit!

Dr. J. Wilbur Chapman, preaching at Dayton, Ohio at a Bible conference of ministers and workers, said:

> I was sitting in my home in the country reading the account of an address delivered by Dr. Moorehead at a Bible conference. He said he believed it was true that, when one became a son of God, the Spirit of God came into him to dwell and He continued to dwell always.
>
> "I don't know but that in some way unknown to me He will continue to abide, even though in the tomb, until the resurrection morning. But," said he, "if any of my brethren deny me the privilege of this belief, I will say, when I became a son of God, the Spirit of God came into my life, and He continues to abide through life, and then if I am placed in the tomb He will still hover over me. He hovers over that tomb keeping watch until the day breaks in glorious resurrection."
>
> I could not read the closing sentences, for the tears had filled my eyes. I told my man to hitch the horse to the carriage.
>
> My wife and I rode out to the little grave where we had buried our firstborn boy, and as we stood there that morning we said, "Thank God, He is keeping watch!" Peace filled our souls.
>
> And I shall never forget going across the country to stand beside the grave of my mother, and I said, "Thank God! Thank God! For thirty years He has been keeping watch, and when the morning breaks He will lift them up to be united by the Spirit again—the body in the grave and the spirit in His presence."

That is the work of the Holy Ghost.

The loving Holy Spirit of God will then complete the sanctification which He has been working in our natures and then will completely perfect these bodies which He has inhabited and loved and cared for so long.

Blessed, loving Holy Spirit!

6. How Christians Should Treat This Best Friend

There are four plain commands for Christians about the Holy Spirit.

The first of these is in Ephesians 4:30: "And grieve not the Holy Spirit of God, whereby ye are sealed unto the day of redemption."

1. If we have an important and greatly respected guest in the home, how careful we are to see that nothing offends. There are clean towels in the room. The housewife is so careful to see that just such food is served as will please the guest.

The guest is given the best bed, a place of honor at the table; the best silverware is brought out, the loveliest cut glass and china. Dad tries to be more than usually entertaining; Mother makes her choice desserts, and the children try to be on their best behavior.

But how a sensitive and cultured guest might be grieved if there were filth in the home, if there were wrangling, quarreling, profane language and drunkenness!

And how do you suppose the Holy Spirit feels, He who dwells always lovingly within the body of the Christian, when the life is given over to things unclean and worldly?

Many people are made physically ill by tobacco smoke. When I ride on a plane where people smoke, I have a headache. When I visit in a home where tobacco is used, I can usually smell it afterward on my clothes. When I sit at restaurant tables and the ash try has been used, I ask that it be removed. I have not developed a tolerance for tobacco.

But how do you suppose the Holy Spirit feels about the same foul-smelling stuff? How do you think He feels about tobacco stains on fingers that ought to be holy and tobacco smell on a breath that ought to speak only of the praise of God!

How does He feel about the use of beer in a Christian's body? about Christian eyes that look on the foul scenes of the movies? and Christians who enjoy the lust of the dance? and of promiscuous petting?

But in this passage where we are urged, "And grieve not the Holy Spirit," several sins of the tongue are mentioned: corrupt communications, bitterness and wrath and anger and clamour and evil speaking. God also mentions here malice and fornication and all uncleanness, covetousness and filthiness as sins that grieve the Holy Spirit.

2. Again the Scripture says, "Quench not the Spirit" (I Thess. 5:19). As water quenches fire and as discouragement quenches enthusiasm, so rebellion of heart by a Christian quenches the Holy Spirit's leadership.

Perhaps someone reads this who no longer feels the leading of the Spirit, does not hear His voice, is not conscious of His presence. Do not feel that the Holy Spirit has left you. He has not, nor will He ever leave His temple. But rebellion may have so broken His heart that He cannot make His way clear to you nor give in your heart the witness of your salvation nor help you pray until you have renounced your rebellion and confessed and forsaken this grievous sin.

We should well remember that the tender Holy Spirit is the most sensitive of all beings. The purest and most fastidious woman would not be offended by anything ugly or unclean as soon as would the dear Holy Spirit. The gentlest and most trusting and loving child would not be hurt as soon by neglect and harshness as He.

I remind you that it is only against the Holy Spirit that a lost man can commit the unpardonable sin. So sin can grieve the Spirit, and so rebellion can quench His leadership in the life.

If you have been quenching the Spirit, offering alibis, excuses, rebellion, instead of listening to every command, instead of following where He leads, then I beg you to today confess to Him your sin, surrender your will and resolve to follow anywhere He leads.

3. Another command of the Holy Spirit is, "Walk in the Spirit" (Gal. 5:16,25). A Christian may walk in the *conscious* fellowship of the Spirit, may know day by day that he is in the sweet will of God. The presence of the Spirit is one thing; but consciously walking together, led by Him, listening to the slightest call, would be walking in the Spirit.

4. The next command I will mention is, "And be not drunk with wine, wherein is excess; but be filled with the Spirit" (Eph. 5:18). Oh, to be filled with the loving Holy Spirit! To have His power, His wisdom, to bear His fruits!

That will mean a surrender of the will; that will mean a conscious and deliberate confessing and forsaking of sin. It will mean waiting on God until He prepares your heart and life for the perfect fullness of the Spirit. He who lives in your body wants to take charge of you, soul and body.

How foolish to live in our barrenness when we may have His fullness and fruitfulness!

Then, Christians, let us seek, long, pray, wait and surrender to be filled with Him. Thus in our lives we may have shown all the fullness of God, and the marvelous results that followed New Testament Christians will follow us, too.

Your best Friend is the Holy Spirit. I hope you will rejoice in "the love of the Spirit," and for His sake, as well as for Christ's sake, do God's will.

VIII.

The Power of Pentecost
JOHN R. RICE

(Preached at the National Conference on Soul Winning and Revival at the Dallas Convention Center, Dallas, Texas, 1975)

"But Peter, standing up with the eleven, lifted up his voice, and said unto them, Ye men of Judaea, and all ye that dwell at Jerusalem, be this known unto you, and hearken to my words: For these are not drunken, as ye suppose, seeing it is but the third hour of the day. But this is that which was spoken by the prophet Joel; [So He reads it.] *And it shall come to pass in the last days, saith God, I will pour out of my Spirit upon all flesh: and your sons and your daughters shall prophesy, and your young men shall see visions, and your old men shall dream dreams: And on my servants and on my handmaidens I will pour out in those days of my Spirit; and they shall prophesy: And I will shew wonders in heaven above, and signs in the earth beneath; blood, and fire, and vapour of smoke: The sun shall be turned into darkness, and the moon into blood, before that great and notable day of the Lord come: And it shall come to pass, that whosoever shall call on the name of the Lord shall be saved."*—Acts 2:14-21.

Tonight I will discuss Pentecost. I will not retreat because some ride a hobby and get off on loose ends, seeing the incidentals instead of the fundamentals.

I am not going to quit preaching on baptism because some think you have to get baptized to be saved.

I am not going to quit preaching that we ought to pray for the sick because some go to extremes. God does heal in answer to prayer, if it is His will.

So I won't quit preaching on the power of the Holy Spirit just because some may misunderstand the Scripture.

Now, as an introduction and out of lovingkindness I explain some errors about Pentecost. Then I will launch right into the exegesis and the explanation of this passage of Scripture.

I. MISUNDERSTOOD PENTECOST

There are some misunderstandings about Pentecost.

1. Talk About Pentecost and Some Think Talking in Tongues

Now you ask, "Do you believe the gift of tongues is for this age? Do you believe the gift of tongues has passed away? In the Bible there is a gift of tongues. Can it be had today?"

Yes, if there is occasion for it. If there were a place where some needed what they got at Pentecost, surely God could meet that need. But it is not for everybody. The Holy Spirit divides these gifts severally as He will. But we are to "covet earnestly the *best* gifts," not the least, the Scripture says.

What happened at Pentecost? A great multitude of Jews came out of every nation under Heaven—sixteen different languages are named. The Lord has just given to them the Great Commission, saying, "Tarry in Jerusalem until you be endued with power from on high," then, "Repentance and remission of sins should be preached in his name among all nations, beginning at Jerusalem," and "Behold, I send the promise of my Father upon you: but tarry ye in the city of Jerusalem, until ye be endued with power from on high" (Luke 24:47-49).

Now they are supposed to win souls and have power; so they prayed ten days. Then what? Many visitors did not understand the Aramaic language that was common in all Palestine; so these Christians prayed, and God gave them power to speak to other people *in their own tongue in which they were born.*

Tongues means "languages." *Glossa* is the Greek word for language.

They prayed. Here are people from many countries saying, "Are not all these which speak Galileans? How do we hear every man in our own tongue, wherein we were born? . . . . We do hear them speak in our own tongues the wonderful works of God."

Now if anyone here has a need to talk to a Chinese who can't understand English and you don't know the Mandarin or Cantonese language—the two most prominent Chinese languages—what will you do? Pray. And if God gives you power to tell him how to be saved in his own tongue in which he was born, you do so. That is what it means.

I say this sadly. I was in Toronto at the Avenue Road Church preaching to a crowd estimated at 1700, which filled the balcony and the chairs put in the aisles. Another crowd waited in the vestibule to come in for a second service, when I would preach again.

God was there, and about fifteen people were saved after I had preached. Workers took them in another room for further instruction and to get their names and addresses.

As I stepped out of the pulpit, a man stepped up and asked, "Brother Rice, have you been baptized with the Holy Ghost?"

I said, "That depends on what you mean. Some sweet power of God has helped me see tens of thousands of sinners saved. Drunkards, harlots, infidels, Catholics and Jews, old men and young men have come down the aisles and have taken Christ as Saviour. If you mean that, in some sweet measure, the hand of God is on me—yes! Is that what you mean?"

"No, I mean, do you talk in tongues?"

"If you didn't mean that, then why did you ask me? I talked in the English tongue tonight. Could you understand me?"

"Yes."

"And as far as I know, everyone present understood me. Why should I talk in any other tongue?"

"But I don't mean that, Brother Rice. Oh, you don't know! You just turn loose, and something comes on you, and you don't know what you are saying. You feel light as a feather. Oh, you feel so good!"

I said, "If I see sinners coming down the aisle, I am going to feel mighty good. Now let me ask you: have you ever won a soul?"

"Well, I pray for them."

"I know, but have you ever won a soul?"

"Oh, I witness to them."

I said, "Quit dodging! Did you ever take your Bible and show a man he was a sinner, show him that Christ died for him, show him how to trust the Lord and get him to pray for mercy and trust the Lord and claim Him and set out to live for Him? Did you ever win a soul?"

"I don't think I ever did," was his reply.

I said, rather sternly I am afraid, "Then don't you ever again go to some man who has been used of God to win thousands and pretend to have something better than he has. God may kill you for that kind of blasphemy!"

I am not so much against those who want to talk in tongues; I am just against their missing the main part—the power of God to win souls.

If you don't win souls, you don't have it, brother! You don't have the power of God. I mean that in kindness. Pentecost is misunderstood.

2. Pentecost Did Not Involve Sanctification

We hear them say, "At Pentecost people got the second blessing. They got the old carnal nature burned out. They got sanctified."

There is a simple Bible doctrine of sanctification. You know that all saved people are called saints. Read Hebrews, chapter 10 and verse 14: "For by one offering he hath perfected for ever them that are sanctified." The word *sanctified* means "set apart for God." So each one who is saved is set apart for Heaven and God, sanctified, a saint. Not a perfect sinner—no.

When the Bible talks about the "holy" mountains, it doesn't mean the mountains do not sin. It is talking about being "set apart for God." When we say the "holy" city of Jerusalem, do we mean nobody sins there? No. It is set apart for God.

So when one is saved, he is set apart for Heaven and God, "sanctified."

Another element in sanctification is that we grow in grace day by day and are more and more set apart for God. Jesus prayed in the high priestly prayer, "Father, sanctify them through thy truth: thy word is truth" (John 17:17). The more one trusts and loves the Bible and lives by it, the more he is set apart from this old world and for Jesus Christ. That is a growth in sanctification.

In Acts, chapter 20, Paul called the elders of Ephesus together and said, "I commend you to God, and to the word of his grace, which is able to build you up, and to give you an inheritance among all them which are sanctified" (vs. 32).

A preacher can get sanctified by reading and loving the Word of God so that it changes him and he becomes a little queer to the world.

A Christian can be set apart for God as he waits on God and grows in grace and in the knowledge of the truth. The Word of God sets him apart.

Then one of these days our sanctification will be finished, when we hear the voice of the archangel and the trump of God and when all Christians rise up to meet the Lord. I will then never anymore have to say, "Lord, I am sorry." I will never anymore have to say, "I wish I had done what I promised, Lord." That will all be done away when I awake in His likeness. My sanctification will then be complete.

That never happened at Pentecost. Not a word is said in the Bible about sanctification at Pentecost. Something else happened there. They were endued with power from on High to carry out the Great Commission and to win souls.

II. THE LAST DAYS—THE WHOLE NEW TESTAMENT AGE

"These are not drunken, as ye suppose, seeing it is but the third hour of the day." You couldn't get drunk with their light wine at nine o'clock in the morning. What is it then? This is that which was spoken by Joel.

"And it shall come to pass in the last days, saith God, I will pour out of my Spirit upon all flesh: and your sons and your daughters shall prophesy, and your young men shall see visions, and your old men shall dream dreams: And on my servants and on my handmaidens I will pour out in those days of my Spirit; and they shall prophesy."

When will it come to pass? In the last days. What are the last days?

The modernists do not use the Bible honestly. When they say "the Gospel," they mean the United Nations, the CARE packages, teaching people to read, raising money for the uncultured hordes of the earth, etc. They talk about a "social gospel," but the Bible defines the Gospel as "how that Christ died for our sins according to the scriptures, and that he rose again the third day according to the scriptures."

It is wrong to use Bible terms to mean something else. The World Council of Churches expressly says in its Constitution that W.C.C. is based upon Jesus Christ as Saviour and Lord. But the principal men who run it do not believe He died to save people, do not believe He is God in the flesh, do not believe in the atoning blood. Most of them have not even been converted. So it is hypocrisy and wicked for them who are called preachers to claim their tax exemption when they don't believe the Bible nor truly preach it. It is wrong for modernists to use Bible names in a crooked way.

But it is all right for a fundamentalist to do wrong, isn't it! It is all right for a fundamentalist to use Bible terms, then interpret Scripture his way, isn't it!—to say, "We are in those last days. We are about to the end. I can see it coming. We are right there." A fundamentalist ought also to use Bible terms to mean what God means.

1. Last Days Include Pentecost and on
to "Day of the Lord"

Joel said, "It shall come to pass in the last days. . . I will pour out of my Spirit upon all flesh." "This is it," he said.

In the Bible the last days means all the New Testament Age. This goes right on down through the ages. ". . . and your sons and your daughters shall prophesy, and your young men shall see visions, and your old men shall dream dreams: And on my servants and on my hand-maidens I will pour out in those days of my Spirit; and they shall prophesy. . . . The sun shall be turned into darkness, and the moon into blood." (There will come a great tribulation time. Then what?) ". . . before that the great and notable day of the Lord"—when Christ returns to reign on the earth.

So here are the last days, including Pentecost and right on through the whole age, down through the Rapture and the Tribulation, until Christ returns to set up His kingdom on the earth. All are included in the last days.

2. Before Christ Came, Called "Time Past";
After Christ Came, "The Last Days"

Turn to Hebrews 1:1,2: "God, who at sundry times and in divers manners spake in time past unto the fathers by the prophets, Hath in these last days spoken unto us by his Son."

Here are two periods of time: the time past, the Old Testament time when God spoke to our fathers by the prophets—Isaiah, Jeremiah, Elijah, Elisha and all those; and these last days, when God hath spoken to us by His Son.

When are the last days? The life and ministry of Jesus was in the time called the last days. So the whole New Testament Age and right on down to the coming of Christ and when His reign starts on earth is called "the last days."

Two divisions: in Old Testament time (past) God spoke unto the fathers by the prophets; and these last days He has spoken to us by His Son.

3. In Apostle John's Day, It Was Already
"The Last Time"

Turn to I John 2:18:

"Little children, it is the last time: and as ye have heard that the

antichrist shall come, even now are there many antichrists; whereby we know that it is the last time."

It was already the last days or last times in John's ministry.

4. Perilous Times Promised in II Timothy 3:1-6 Were the Whole Ages, Including Timothy's Day

Turn to II Timothy, chapter 3:

"This know also, that in the last days perilous times shall come. For men shall be lovers of their own selves, covetous, boasters, proud, blasphemers, disobedient to parents, unthankful, unholy, Without natural affection, trucebreakers, false accusers, incontinent, fierce, despisers of those that are good, Traitors, heady, highminded, lovers of pleasures more than lovers of God."

You say, "That is the way our young people are getting to be." Yes, but that is the way the prodigal son was, too, when Jesus was here! Read on:

"Having a form of godliness, but denying the power thereof. . . ."

"Oh, that is just the way the modernists are," you declare. "They have the form without any power." Yes, but the Pharisees and Sadducees had the same in Jesus' time!

But wait:

". . .from such turn away."

To whom is he writing? Timothy. Whom is he telling to turn away from these bad people? "Timothy, stay away from that crowd."
Read on:

"For of this sort are they. . . ."

Tell me, is the "are they" here present or future? Does that mean right now? or does it mean after two thousand years? That crowd was there. "Timothy, they are there now. Timothy, turn away from them."
Read on:

"For of this sort are they which creep into houses, and lead captive silly women laden with sins, led away with divers lusts, Ever learning, and never able to come to the knowledge of the truth."

"Timothy, stay away from that crowd. They are there now."

Read on:

"Now as Jannes and Jambres withstood Moses...."

That is in the Old Testament! Were people like that then? Yes, ever since the Garden of Eden!

We read on:

"...so do these...."

Present tense, right now, "Timothy, these people do it like they did." So you who talk about "the last days" ought to mean this whole New Testament Age.

III. NO ONE CAN KNOW WHEN JESUS WILL COME

But how are you going to know when Christ is coming? You won't know.

1. Neither Angels nor Christ Knew When He Would Return

The one thing the Lord said most often about the second coming was, "But of that day and hour knoweth no man, no, not the angels of heaven, but my Father only" (Matt. 24:36).

And in Mark 13:32: "But of that day and that hour knoweth no man, no, not the angels which are in heaven, neither the Son, but the Father."

When Jesus was here in the flesh, He did not know when He would come the second time. He knows now, but He didn't know then. And we are not supposed to know.

"But, Dr. Rice, don't you think there are signs by which we can tell?" No. In Acts, chapter 1, they asked, "Lord, wilt thou at this time restore again the kingdom to Israel?"

And He said unto them, "It is not for you to know the times or the seasons, which the Father hath put in his own power. But ye shall receive power, after that the Holy Ghost is come upon you: and ye shall be witnesses unto me." In other words, "Quit doting on prophecy, and go to doting on soul winning."

Now, why not get burdened about soul winning instead of being so wise on prophecy?

"Well, Brother Rice, do you think Jesus is coming soon?" He may come tonight. I have been looking for Him a long time. I will surely be glad to see Him! I hope He will smile and say, "John, well done."

But I don't know when He is coming, and neither do you. But we are supposed to be ready, "for ye know not the hour when the Son of man cometh."

2. Paul Looked for Christ to Come in His Lifetime

I rush on. By the way, Paul the apostle expected the Lord Jesus to come in his lifetime; for I Corinthians 15:51,52 says: "We shall not all sleep, but we shall all be changed, In a moment, in the twinkling of an eye, at the last trump: for the trumpet shall sound, and the dead shall be raised incorruptible, and we shall be changed."

"We shall be changed." "We"—Paul and all those Christians to whom he was preaching.

Paul said the same thing in I Thessalonians 4:16,17: "For the Lord himself shall descend from heaven with a shout. . . and the dead in Christ shall rise first: Then we which are alive and remain . . . ."

"We." Paul was doing exactly what Jesus said to do—expecting, watching. We, too, ought to watch for Jesus' coming. Quit getting on incidentals and riding hobbies and get back on New Testament Christianity. Preach the Gospel and work to keep people out of Hell.

IV. HOLY SPIRIT POWER NOW FOR EVERY CHRISTIAN

I come to a wonderful Scripture: "And it shall come to pass in the last days, saith God, I will pour out of my Spirit upon all flesh. . . and they will prophesy."

1. Not All Christians Had Holy Spirit Power in the Old Testament

In the Old Testament times, did people have the Holy Spirit power upon them? A few did, but only a few; now and then a prophet. The Holy Spirit of God "came mightily on Samson." The Spirit of the Lord came upon Gideon. The Spirit of the Lord came on David when he was anointed. The Spirit of God was on Elijah. Elisha wanted what Elijah had. You know the story. So when Elijah went to Heaven, his garment fell on Elisha; he put it on, and the Spirit of the Lord was on Elisha.

A few people were filled with the Holy Spirit in the Old Testament, but not many.

2. Seventy Men Received Holy Spirit Power in Moses' Day—a Great Surprise

Moses came to the Lord one day complaining, in Numbers 11. "Lord, do You want me to carry these 3 1/2 million people around in my arms like a baby? Lord, what am I going to do?"

The Lord told Moses, "Pick out seventy elders—good men of Israel. I will put part of the Spirit on them that is on you."

Moses pointed them out. God instructed, "Have them meet Me out here in the Tabernacle, outside the camp." When they went, the power of God fell on them, and they prophesied.

Wait a minute! There are only sixty-eight! Where are the other two? Eldad and Medad are back in camp. Perhaps their wives didn't get their shirts ironed in time. Nevertheless, the power of God fell on them, too.

They were praising the Lord and speaking in the power of God when Joshua came running to Moses, saying, "Moses, those men in the camp—make them shut up. Nobody but you is supposed to talk that way and have the power of God."

But Moses said, "Would God that all the Lord's people would have the Spirit!"

Moses, they can now have it, too. Now all can be filled with the Spirit. Old men, young men, sons, daughters, servants, handmaidens can witness for Jesus. All now may have the power of God. It is abnormal for a Christian not to have God's power.

3. Now Young Men, Old Men, Servants, Handmaidens, Sons and Daughters—All May Be Spirit-Filled

Young men see visions, and old men dream dreams.

When I was nine, I was converted. A year later we moved to a ranch in West Texas. I had a Stetson hat as big as my dad's. I drove a six-mule team plowing a field. The hired man helped me harness the mules and put them together. I drove them a mile to the field, hooked them to that triple-disk plow and got the work done. The big grain drill box had to be filled regularly; so there was this big stack of oatsacks. Every time I came around, I would stop and fill that seedbox with oats.

I would sit up on top and drive that mule team—at age ten, remember. I had the best time sowing oats! I got to seeing visions and dreaming dreams. I had been saved. I didn't know then that my mother and dad had given me to God to preach when I was born. But God was already doing something to me.

I enjoyed singing as I drove those mules. A favorite was "When the Roll Is Called Up Yonder." I would sit up there and sing, "When the rooooolllll. . . ." Every mule thought I said, "Whoa"—or hoped I did—so they stopped. As I drove, this ten-year-old saw great crowds and people come weeping to Christ.

Young men dream dreams; old men see visions.

I go back in my vision and see Kleinhan's Music Hall, Buffalo, New York, with 92 churches backing the campaign and a choir of 300 and Strat Shufelt leading the singing and thirty or forty or fifty preachers backing me up and that Hall jammed to the doors night after night, and 52 saved, 75 saved, 90 saved, night after night—997 people saved in that short revival—and in the late forties when great revivals were not being held.

I think about the Chicago Arena when Paul Rood preached six days, Dr. Bob Jones, Sr., seven days, and I had the last fifteen days, when 2,700 people came to Christ.

Oh, in a citywide campaign in Miami, with 40 Baptist churches in the Civic Auditorium or in Liberty Tobacco Warehouse, seating perhaps 3,000 at Winston-Salem—and hundreds coming to Christ in each campaign.

Old men dream dreams, too.

V. HOLY SPIRIT FULLNESS WAS FOR SOUL WINNING

Oh, if all we could think about was getting people saved! Oh, if all we could think about was the Gospel and getting people ready for Jesus to come and getting everybody we could, saved! We can! Young men, sons and daughters, children, women folks—everyone winning souls!

What is the fullness of the Spirit for? What happened at Pentecost? They were filled with the Spirit, and three thousand were saved. That is what God is talking about.

1. John the Baptist Filled With the Spirit to Win Many

Look at John the Baptist in Luke 1:14,15. Zacharias was praying, and the Lord said, "Zacharias, your prayer is answered. You have been begging God thirty-five years for a son. Now it is going to happen. And he will be great in the sight of the Lord. He will drink neither wine nor strong drink. He will be filled with the Holy Ghost even from his mother's womb."

Now note: **"Many of the children of Israel shall he turn to the Lord their God."**

What is the fullness of the Spirit for? For soul winning.

2. Barnabas Was Filled With the Holy Ghost

Here is Barnabas in Acts 11:24. We read of him: "For he was a good man, and full of the Holy Ghost and of faith: and much people was added unto the Lord." God's plan is for Christians to win souls.

"Tarry in Jerusalem"—for what? Until "ye be endued with power from on high" and "be witnesses unto me." God is talking about mighty power to win souls.

We get the incidentals and lose the fundamentals. We get some of the trappings and the show, the talk and the form of godliness, while the world is going to Hell, and we do nothing about it. Oh, everybody can have the power of God.

3. Many Terms for This Enduement of Power From on High

That leads to another thing. What is this for? You are to tarry till you win souls.

Endued with the power to win souls. The Lord used many terms for that, just as Jesus has many names. He is the Son of God, Son of David, Son of Abraham; He is Christ, the Messiah, the Lord; He is the Bright and Morning Star, Fairest of Ten Thousand; His name shall be called Wonderful, Counsellor, Mighty God, Everlasting Father. It takes lots of names to tell how wonderful He is.

Salvation, redemption, born again, children of God, new creatures—those terms are used for being saved.

So we need not be surprised when God used several terms, such as filled with the Spirit, baptized with the Spirit, the gift of the Spirit, anointed with the Spirit, endued with the power from on High. There is a definitive term, "endued with power" to witness.

VI. PENTECOST FOR EVERYBODY!

But now comes another point. Pentecost is for everybody.

You say, "No, sir! One baptism and many fillings," repeating what Dr. Scofield says.

1. Acts 2:4 and Acts 4:31 Exactly the Same

Turn to Acts 2:4 and Acts 4:31. That is Pentecost once, then Pentecost repeated.

"And when the day of Pentecost was fully come, they were all with one accord in one place. And suddenly there came a sound from heaven as of a rushing mighty wind, and it filled all the house where they were sitting. And there appeared unto them cloven tongues like as of fire, and it sat upon each of them." And what? *"AND THEY WERE ALL FILLED WITH THE HOLY GHOST."*—Acts 2:1-4.

Now let's see if that ever happened again.

"Lord, behold their threatenings: and grant unto thy servants, that with all boldness they may speak thy word, By stretching forth thine hand to heal: and that signs and wonders may be done by the name of thy holy child Jesus. And when they had prayed, the place was shaken where they were assembled. [Before, it was the sound like a cyclone; now it is an earthquake.] *And the place was shaken where they were assembled together;* [Watch it!] *AND THEY WERE ALL FILLED WITH THE HOLY GHOST."*—Acts 4:29-31.

Acts 4:31 and Acts 2:4 are word for word alike.

Now, if God says exactly the same thing twice, does it mean the same thing? Yes. Pentecost was repeated. They prayed, God gave power, and three thousand were saved.

They later prayed, "Lord, let us do it again. We want to win some more souls. Lord, do it again. Come and breathe on us again." And when they prayed, they were all filled with the Holy Ghost again, and "they spake the word of God with boldness . . . ."—word for word the same as at Pentecost: "They were all filled with the Holy Ghost." It was a repeat. So if you would win souls, then you need power every time you do it.

2. Same Promise Is for "All That Are Afar Off"

Pentecost is for everyone? Yes.

Look at Acts 2:38,39. These people had come and said, "What meaneth this? These men are full of new wine"—drunk.

Peter said, "These are not drunk."

"What is it?"

"You crucified Jesus. He, being raised up, is at the right hand of God. He hath shed forth this, which you now see and hear."

They said, "Men and brethren, what shall we do?" (Not, "What must I do to be saved?" They were talking about the power of God.)

Peter answered, "Repent [get saved], and be baptized every one of you in the name of Jesus Christ for the remission of sins. . . ." [*For* is the little Greek preposition of reference, *eis,* meaning "pointing to, referring to"; so, "be baptized, pointing to, referring to the remission of sins." And then what?] "and ye shall receive the gift of the Holy Ghost." [Get saved, get baptized; then you can be filled with the Holy Ghost, too.] "For the promise is unto you, and to your children."

The promise is to "*you,* and to your children." And who else? ". . . and to all that are afar off." A thousand miles away, yes, or a thousand years away—the promise is to "you, and to your children, and to all that are afar off." Pentecost is for everybody!

3. Was Pentecost for "a Day" or "Many Days"—Plural?

Turn back to Acts 2:17: "But this is that which was spoken by the prophet Joel. And it shall come to pass in the last days, saith God, I will pour out of my Spirit." A day, or days? Single or plural? Plural. It is just as good for the next day and the next week and the next month and the next year. Until when? "Until the great and notable day of the Lord." Pentecost is not just one day; the filling of the Spirit for soul winning is for every Christian every day.

4. All Christians Clearly Commanded to Be Spirit-Filled

Ephesians 5:18 commands: "Be not drunk with wine, wherein is excess; but be filled with the Spirit."

Every Christian can be filled with *the* Spirit. We not only can be, but we are *commanded to be* filled with the Spirit. Not being filled with the Spirit means disobeying God. Normal Christianity means to be filled with the Spirit, to have the power of God. If you live in sin, have dirty habits, read dirty literature, run with a bad crowd, work only for money and fame, seek pleasure in a hedonistic society, then you are not going to have a thirsty heart for the power of God. This is for all who mean business.

When I started out to preach, how God dealt with my heart! The fact is, I was preaching before I knew I was called to preach. I just couldn't keep out of it. At Pacific Garden Mission in Chicago I won a drunken bum to the Lord. Overnight he cleaned up, got a job and quit drinking. This so blessed my heart that I said, "Lord, this sure is a lot better than college teaching!" So I cancelled my contract with the college where I had accepted a position, left the University of Chicago Graduate School and came on back to Texas and started out preaching.

A preacher, hearing me tell the above story, said, "Is that the only call to preach you have?"

"I don't know," I answered.

"Then you are not called to preach," he told me.

I said, "I don't care whether I am or not, just so the Lord doesn't stop me."

The truth is, I am called. Oh, what a call in my heart!

But you listen to me! Everyone can and ought to have the mighty power of God for soul winning—old men, young men, servants and handmaidens—everybody. That promise is to you—the power of the Holy Ghost—and it is for soul winning.

VII. HOW HAVE HOLY SPIRIT POWER?

How are we going to have it? By waiting on God, like they did.

"Tarry in the city of Jerusalem, until ye be endued with power from on high."

"These all continued with one accord in prayer and supplication, with the women, and Mary the mother of Jesus, and with his brethren."

Steadfast, continuing in prayer, waiting ten days.

1. Give Yourself to Soul Winning

You wonder, *How can I be filled with the Spirit?* First, unless you are interested in soul winning, then you are not going to have this. This is for the Great Commission.

"And that repentance and remission of sins should be preached in his name among all nations. . . . And, behold, I send the promise of my Father upon you: but tarry ye in the city of Jerusalem, until ye be endued with power from on high."—Luke 24:47,49.

Ah, for soul winning! That is it!

2. Seek to Have a Holy Thirst for Souls

Oh, for a thirsty heart! I wish all here would get a fire burning you couldn't put out. I wish all here would get a hunger to get people saved. Isaiah 44:3 promises: "For I will pour water upon him that is thirsty, and floods upon the dry ground: I will pour my spirit upon thy seed, and my blessing upon thine offspring." God gives Holy Spirit power to the thirsty of heart that cannot be satisfied with other things. Oh, get thirsty tonight!

3. Plead With God for Power

We read in Luke 11:5:

"Which of you shall have a friend, and shall go unto him at midnight, and say unto him, Friend, lend me three loaves. . .?"

Here is a Christian man wanting three loaves, all the power of the Father, Son and the Holy Ghost, this bread from Heaven.

"For a sinner friend has come to me and I have nothing to set before him."

And he from within said, "Trouble me not. The children are with me in bed. I can't rise and give you."

Then verse 8:

"I say unto you, Though he will not rise and give him, because he is his friend, yet because of his importunity he will rise and give him as many as he needeth."

"I am a fundamentalist. I am a premillennial fundamentalist. I am a pre-tribulation rapture premillennial fundamentalist! Yes, sir! I wouldn't touch a sinner with a ten-foot pole. I am saved and sanctified and petrified." You don't get it by being all those things. He will not rise and give him because he is his friend; but *because of his importunity,* he will give him as many loaves as he needs. Importunity is the way we get.

Isaiah 40:29-31 tells us:

"He giveth power to the faint; and to them that have no might he increaseth strength. Even the youths shall faint and be weary, and the young men shall utterly fall: But they that wait upon the Lord shall renew their strength; they shall mount up with wings as eagles. . . . "

Some of you are crawling instead of mounting up on wings. Some of you got so weak, you quit. You want to go back to selling automobiles or teaching school or selling insurance, when your real need is to wait on God. They that wait upon the Lord renew their strength.

Then look at II Chronicles 7:14: "If my people, which are called by my name, shall humble themselves, and pray, and seek my face...." Crying, praying and sometimes fasting. If you feel that way about keeping people out of Hell, then you feel like Jesus felt. Anyone can have the power of God who means business. Oh, I know nothing we need more than that power.

When I started out preaching some said, "Get to talking about the Holy Spirit, and the first thing you know, you will be rolling on the floor and talking in tongues."

I said, "I don't think so, but I am going to do what the Bible says. I don't care if I am a nut, a fool and lose everything; I am going to have Holy Spirit power."

I told the Lord, "Lord, You gave power to Peter, James, John and Paul; You tell me to get drunkards saved, make harlots pure, infidels into saints, and shake towns. If You want me to do that, then You must give me the same kind of power You gave them."

It was so with D. L. Moody; it was so with all great soul winners of all times.

Dr. Bob Jones, Sr., once told me, "They argue about terminology. I don't care what they call it. I know there was a time when I went to an altar and I waited on God until something happened. Then I went out to win thousands of souls."

I am a very poor example, but I thank God that I know one can have the power of God, like He has given me. I won't live without it. I must, I must, I must have the power of God to win souls!

A Holy Commitment!

How many preachers will stand to your feet and by that you say you are committing yourself to seek the power of God, a mighty enduement of power upon your ministry? God grant it! I am not talking about tongues but about getting the power of God to win souls.

How many others have unsaved loved ones? You can't win them. The trouble is not with God, so it must be with you.

How many have neighbors and friends you try to get to church, but they won't come? Wouldn't you like to have power to get them there?

Jacob wrestled with God. At last the angel said, "We will change your name. For as a prince thou hast prevailed for power with God and with men."

Someone says, "I preach, and nothing happens." But nothing happened in that secret closet the night before.

Will you set out to persistently plead with God for the power of God, soul-winning power, Holy Spirit power?

God grant it!

JOE HENRY HANKINS
1889-1967

ABOUT THE MAN:

"He was a weeping prophet" is the way Dr. Hankins was characterized by those who knew him best—one of the 20th century's great soul-winning preachers.

BUT—Hankins preached sharply, strongly against sin. Would to God we had more men of his mettle in a ministry today that has largely been given over to namby-pamby, mealy-mouthed silence when it comes to strong preaching against sin.

Dr. John R. Rice wrote of him: *"His method and manifest spiritual power would remind one of D. L. Moody. He has the keen, scholarly, analytical mind of an R. A. Torrey, and the love and compassion of souls of a Wilbur Chapman."*

Hankins was born in Arkansas and saved as a youth. He graduated from high school in Pine Bluff, then from Quachita Baptist College. He held pastorates in Pine Bluff, Arkansas; in Whitewright, Greenville and Childress, Texas. His last and most productive pastorate was the First Baptist Church, Little Rock, Arkansas. There, in less than five years, 1,799 additions by letter, 1,144 by baptism—an average of 227 baptisms a year—made a total of 2,943 members added to the church. Sunday school spiralled to nearly 1,400; membership mushroomed to 3,200 despite a deletion of 882 to revise the rolls.

In 1942, Hankins gave up the pastorate for full-time evangelism.

In 1967, Dr. Hankins passed on to the Heaven he loved to preach about. Be sure that he was greeted by a thronging host of redeemed souls—saved under his Spirit-filled ministry.

IX.

Sinning Against the Holy Ghost

JOE HENRY HANKINS

(Sermon preached at Wheaton College Chapel, Wheaton, Illinois, 1943)

When one speaks of sinning against the Holy Ghost, most people think of the unpardonable sin. But there are a number of sins mentioned in the Scripture against the Holy Spirit which are not unpardonable sins but which deprive us Christians of our joy, our power, our assurance, our ability to pray, our fruit-bearing for the Lord, our spiritual growth and fellowship with the Lord.

We read from chapter 5 of Galatians, beginning with verse 16:

"This I say then, Walk in the Spirit, and ye shall not fulfill the lust of the flesh. For the flesh lusteth against the Spirit, and the Spirit against the flesh: and these are contrary the one to the other: so that ye cannot do the things that ye would."

I pause to explain that word *cannot*. The word translated "cannot" here is not the word we usually use. When we say "cannot," we mean it is impossible: here it means it is very difficult. So we read it this way: ". . . so that it is difficult for you to do the things that ye would."

"But if ye be led of the Spirit, ye are not under the law. Now the works of the flesh are manifest, which are these; Adultery, fornication, uncleanness, lasciviousness, Idolatry, witchcraft, hatred, variance, emulations, wrath, strife, seditions, heresies, Envyings, murders, drunkenness, revellings, and such like: of the which I tell you before, as I have also told you in time past, that they which do such things shall not inherit the kingdom of God. But the fruit of the Spirit is love, joy, peace, longsuffering, gentleness, goodness, faith, Meekness, temperance: against such there is no law. And they that are Christ's have crucified the flesh with the affections and lusts. If we live in the Spirit,

let us also walk in the Spirit. Let us not be desirous of vain glory, provoking one another, envying one another."—Gal. 5:18-26.

The Work of the Holy Spirit

Now before we speak specifically about sinning against the Holy Spirit, I give just this brief explanation of the work of the Holy Spirit.

First, He brings an unbelieving person to salvation.

God seeks out the unbeliever by the Holy Spirit. God always makes the first move in salvation. You who have been saved are very conscious of that. Maybe suddenly there once came a realization in your heart that you were lost; there came a hungering in your heart for the Lord; there was a tug at your heartstrings, a knock at your heart's door. That was the work of the Holy Spirit.

Jesus said in John 6:44, "No man can come to me, except the Father which hath sent me draw him." In other words, God must begin the work in our hearts when we are lost. It is God who calls us unto Himself. The Holy Spirit seeks us out. The Holy Spirit produces the conviction of sin in the unsaved heart and a sense of need of a Saviour.

Jesus said in chapter 16 of John, verse 8, "When he [the Holy Spirit] is come, he will reprove the world of sin, and of righteousness, and of judgment." Now that is the beginning, the groundwork of salvation— the moving of the Spirit upon the unsaved heart to arouse him to his lost condition and his sense of need and to woo and draw him unto Christ. Then the Holy Spirit takes the Word of God and plants it in that unsaved heart.

God tells us in I Corinthians 2:14, "The natural man receiveth not the things of the Spirit of God: for they are foolishness unto him: neither can he know them, because they are spiritually discerned." No person could ever understand the way of salvation if the Holy Spirit did not open his understanding and enable him to know, see and understand the way of salvation. Then the Holy Spirit regenerates that heart, and we are born of the Spirit.

Then the Holy Spirit seals that regenerated heart in Christ, says Ephesians 1:13,14: "In whom also after that ye believed, ye were sealed with that holy Spirit of promise, which is the earnest of our inheritance until the redemption. . . ." We are sealed by the Spirit.

Also, the Holy Spirit moves into the saved heart to take up His abode. We become temples of the Holy Spirit. He lives in us.

Now the purpose of His indwelling presence is to guide us, to teach us, to lead us out into service, to bear the fruit of the Spirit in our hearts, to make us happy in the Lord, to give us power and spiritual understanding and assurance of our salvation, to bear witness with our spirit that we are the children of God.

We are especially dependent upon the indwelling presence of the Holy Spirit for the assurance of our salvation. Many Christians have doubts come. They get to the place where they don't even know whether they are saved or lost. Having lost the assurance of their salvation, they are groping in darkness; they have lost the joy of their salvation; they have lost their first love; and they have lost the power to pray.

We are dependent upon the Holy Spirit for that warm glow of the first love that we experienced when we first found the Lord. The Scripture says, "The love of God is shed abroad in our hearts by the Holy Ghost which is given unto us."

We are dependent upon Him, as I said, for the assurance of our salvation, the joy of salvation and that first love. The fruit of the Spirit is love, joy, peace, longsuffering, gentleness, goodness, meekness, faith.

Oh, our faith is so weak! How we wish we might have stronger faith! Well, it is the fruit of the Spirit which enables us to have it. Then not only faith, but self-control, also a fruit of the Spirit, in the saved heart and life.

Now, what are some of the sins against the Holy Spirit?

I. GRIEVING THE SPIRIT

In Ephesians, chapter 4, verse 30, Paul exhorts, "Grieve not the holy Spirit of God, whereby ye are sealed unto the day of redemption." Grieving the Holy Spirit is one of the most common of the sins of the children of God against this indwelling divine Person. Yes, the Holy Spirit is the third Person of the Godhead. The Holy Spirit is not an *it*, not a mere influence. He is a Person; just as truly a Person as Jesus Christ is a Person, just as much as God the Father is a Person. God is a Trinity—three Persons—yet all merging into One, called the Godhead. God the Father, God the Son and God the Holy Spirit each has a distinct and separate work in salvation. The Holy Spirit's great work is in the fruitfulness, spiritual growth and development of the child of God.

"Grieve not the holy Spirit of God, whereby ye are sealed unto the day of redemption." How do we grieve the Holy Spirit? Remember this: the Holy Spirit has taken up His abode in the saved heart. There He lives. We hear Paul say in the verse just preceding the one I have just read, "Let no corrupt communication proceed out of your mouth," literally meaning, "Let no filthy conversation proceed out of your mouth."

Since the Holy Spirit lives in a child of God, then He must listen in on every conversation. The Holy Spirit is the most sensitive Person to sin in all the universe: infinitely more sensitive to sin than the holiest, sweetest saint; more sensitive to sin than the holiest, purest, sweetest, most godly and saintly mother. So filthy conversation grieves the Holy Spirit who dwells within.

Not only are we warned against filthy conversation, but in this same book of Ephesians, in chapter 5 and verse 4 we read, "Neither filthiness, nor foolish talking, nor jesting. . . . Let not one of these be named among you."

Oh, how we must watch our conversation! So many Christians are so careless here. I have heard Christians, even preachers of the Gospel, tell filthy, smutty stories. This grieves the Holy Spirit. Let no foolish talking, no filthiness of any kind, no jesting proceed out of your mouth. Be careful, child of God, about your conversation. You cannot be too careful nor too chaste in your speech.

More Christians are robbing themselves of the power of the Holy Spirit by grieving Him with their careless conversation and foolish jesting, to say nothing of the filthy conversation that proceeds out of many mouths, than any other one thing. Many professing Christians—I say it without a spirit of criticism—have veritably made a sewer out of their mouths. No wonder they have no power! No wonder they cannot pray! No prayer is answered unless it is prayed in the Spirit, and nobody who is grieving the Spirit of God can pray in the Spirit.

I am trying to give you something practical this morning.

Perhaps you have asked yourself, *Why do I find it impossible to pray? Why do my words seem to come back and mock me with their hollowness? I am so conscious that my prayers get nowhere with God.* Most likely the answer is, you have been grieving the Holy Spirit.

Listen again. Our attitude, especially our attitude of heart toward others, may grieve the Spirit. "Be ye kind one to another, tenderhearted, forgiving one another, even as God for Christ's sake hath forgiven you." If you have an unforgiving spirit or if you carry around malice or ill will or hard feelings against another, get it out; for it is grieving the Holy Spirit and it will rob you of your joy, peace, assurance, power to pray and fruitfulness.

Not only that, but "let all bitterness, and wrath, and anger, and clamour, and evil speaking"—it comes back again to the matter of speaking—"be put away from you, with all malice," for those things grieve the Spirit of God.

A young lady said to me the other night, "I want to know how to have the indwelling of the Holy Spirit." I told her what I tell you. One of the things you must know is that certain things grieve the Holy Spirit. You cannot have the infilling of the Spirit while at the same time you are grieving the Spirit by your attitude, by your conversation or by sin in your life.

Another thing that grieves the Spirit is the places we go. Many times a Christian will go into places and into groups where the atmosphere does not please the Holy Spirit or is not conducive to the Spirit's manifestation of Himself in his life.

One cannot be too careful about where he goes. There is a price to pay for a spiritual life. And there is a price to pay for a prayer life.

Let me stop here and say this: any price you have to pay, young people, will be worth it in the joy of the fulness of the Spirit of God. His constant presence, His witness in your heart, the fruit of love, joy, peace, longsuffering, gentleness, goodness, faith, meekness, self-control—when you are in possession of that, you will realize that the price you paid was well worthwhile. It is worth any price to be able to walk with God, to talk with God, to know that your prayers will be answered, to have the constant joy and assurance of salvation.

Now again I say, we must be careful where we go since the Holy Spirit must go with us. One reason I never go to picture shows is that I have never seen one where I felt the atmosphere would be conducive and pleasing to the Holy Spirit. Have you? Go into one of them. What do you see on the screen? A veritable orgy of lust, murder, crime, sex—everything that would be displeasing to the Holy Spirit and grieve Him. Yet a lot of Christians say, "I can see no harm in that." I will tell you why. They are not spiritual Christians, not Spirit-filled nor Spirit-led.

Do you want to be just a nominal Christian, which means one in name only? Have you an ambition to walk with the Lord? Have you an ambition in your heart, a hungering in your soul, to know more of the power of the Spirit? to have more power in prayer? When we pray in the Spirit, God tells us, "Ask anything, and it will be done for you." God throws the gate of Heaven wide open to those who can really pray. Do you want the kind Enoch had when he walked with the Lord?

The Devil tells us that we will be happier to follow him, to let down our standards. "Do not be narrow and fanatic; be broad," he urges. We have listened to the Devil, and he has cheated us out of the greatest blessing, the deepest joy, the sweetest peace, the most wonderful life possible for human beings on this earth.

If I believe there is a God—and I do—and I know Him as a child, then don't I know God's way, not my way, will be best? Don't I know if I follow Him, life will be sweeter, deeper, richer, happier, more glorious than it could be any other way? Surely you realize that. So quit grieving the Spirit because of the places you go.

Some Christians go to dances and see no harm in doing so. Can you imagine the Holy Spirit at home there with the sensuous jazz music, with young women and men in each other's arms whirling on the dance floor? No wonder so many have no peace. No wonder so many are groping in the dark. No wonder so many Christians have lost their assurance.

You say, "I just can't see a bit of harm in a social game of bridge." That thing you hold in your hand—a deck of playing cards—is the Devil's Bible, the Devil's favorite instrument and the favorite instrument of the gambler, drunkard and criminal. Go into the jails and penitentiaries and see how many inmates have a deck of cards handy. Go into the lowest dives, the underworld—every brothel, every haunt of the underworld has a deck of cards. I say, a deck of cards is the Devil's favorite instrument. Oh, but it grieves the Holy Spirit and robs us of our power, our joy as a Christian, our peace, our assurance, our fruitfulness for the Lord Jesus Christ.

II. QUENCHING THE SPIRIT

Another sin against the Holy Spirit I want to mention is found in I Thessalonians 5:19: "Quench not the Spirit." The Spirit, indwelling the heart of the believer, moves upon his heart and mind and impresses him especially in two respects: one is to urge him to service and impress him to do certain things; the other is to warn him against certain things he may be about to do or a course he is about to take which is displeasing to God.

What child of God hasn't felt very definite impressions from the Spirit to speak to certain persons about their souls or to undertake a certain service for the Lord? God's Word teaches that we may be and ought to be continually led by the Spirit. If we won't quench the Spirit but will yield to and follow His leadership, we will be led of Him to the glory of Christ.

The Holy Spirit is also on the job to warn us against sin and pitfalls of the Devil. Remember when you were first saved how something ripped you, how, all of a sudden, something got hold of your heart and tried to stop you when you were about to do wrong? A voice was hammering away at your conscience. There was, as it were, a red light swinging across your path like the light at the railroad crossing warning of an approaching train. What was that? The Holy Spirit trying to warn you against the dangers of your course.

But you ignored it, went on and overrode that warning, that urging, that prompting of the Spirit of God. If you continue such a course, soon you cannot hear His warnings. After awhile you won't see any harm in anything.

The saddest thing to see is when Christians lose their power to discriminate between right and wrong. That happens when you quench the Spirit, when you turn a deaf ear as He tries to warn you, prompt you, urge you against that thing and tries to lead you the other way around. After awhile nothing seems very bad. To lose your power to discriminate between right and wrong is one of the saddest things that can happen to a child of God.

The Prophet Isaiah said, "Woe unto them that call evil good, and good evil; that put darkness for light, and light for darkness; that put bitter for sweet, and sweet for bitter!" God means it is a sad day for a child of God when he has lost his power to discriminate between right and wrong. These are they who say, "I can't see any harm in this," "I don't see any harm in the dance," "I can't see any harm in card-playing, or in smoking," "I can't see any harm in taking a little drink." How tragic to get to that place in your life! But that is what will happen if you continually quench the Spirit of God.

III. THE SIN UNTO DEATH

Another sin I want to mention is described in I John 5:16. Talking to an unsaved person, he says, "There is a sin unto death: I do not say that he shall pray for it." Listen, you who may be here unsaved. Jesus said in John 6:44, "No man can come to me, except the Father which hath sent me draw him."

"Draw him!" Oh, that strange feeling that takes hold of our heart strings when the Gospel is preached, when you wake up in the wee small hours of the night with a strange feeling gripping your heart! Something seems to tell you that you ought to get right with God, that the way you are going is the way of destruction, that you ought to forsake this way and trust the Lord, that you ought to be a Christian. How many times has that knock come at your door! That is the most sacred, the most crucial hour that ever comes to an unsaved heart, when that knock comes at your door, when that call of the Holy Spirit comes. For you will never be saved without it. "No man can come to me, except the Father which hath sent me draw him."

God teaches in His Word that an unsaved person can resist the Spirit of God and drive Him away. Listen to Genesis 6:3: "And the Lord said, My spirit shall not always strive with man, for that he also is flesh." God says there will come a time when He will quit. Listen to Hosea 4:17, "Ephraim is joined to idols: let him alone." Can you imagine God speaking like that? "Let him alone." Here is a man who is married to sin, who loves it, who is determined he shall have it; loves his drink, loves lustful indulgence, loves to satisfy his lower nature and gives himself to it—"Let him alone!"

Three times in the first chapter of Romans, in verses 24, 26 and 28, God uses language like this: "God gave them up"!

The first time was because they didn't follow the light they had and deliberately turned away from God.

The second statement was because they loved the created things more than they did the Creator. Multiplied thousands, in order to get a little bit of this world's goods, a few things of this world, shut God out of their lives. God says when that happens, when men turn away from the God who created them, then He gives them up.

The third case was indulging of the lower nature. And because of this awful sin, they did not like to retain God in their knowledge, didn't like to think about God, and "God gave them up!" God says, "If you have lust as your god, all right, you can have it." Then God gives them up and turns them over to the Devil.

How many times, my unsaved friend, has there been that strange tug at your heart strings! How many times has there been that still Small Voice trying to turn you around for God! How many times has there been a whispering in your soul, telling you that you are in need of a Saviour and calling you tenderly, lovingly, knocking gently at the door of that heart!

God says, "There is a sin unto death: I do not say that he shall pray for it." There will come a time when God will say, "Let him alone!" You have resisted the Holy Spirit of God, you have insulted the Spirit of God; now God says, "Let him alone."

In Hebrews 10:26 we read, "If we sin wilfully after that we have received the knowledge of the truth, there remaineth no more sacrifice for sins. . . ." If we sin wilfully after we have come to the knowledge of the truth, after the Holy Spirit has opened the understanding, after He has knocked at the heart's door and called and drawn us to salvation and has aroused our mind and heart to a sense of a need of a Saviour, has opened our understanding to see the way of salvation in Christ, then we deliberately, willfully go away into sin, "there remaineth no more sacrifice for sins, but a certain fearful looking for of judgment and fiery indignation." Then what did He say? That person has "trampled under foot the Son of God, and hath counted the blood of the covenant, wherewith he was sanctified, an unholy thing, and hath done despite unto the Spirit of grace." Then Paul says, "It is a fearful thing to fall into the hands of the living God."

I repeat: the crisis of your life, the most crucial moment you will ever face this side of eternity, is when the Spirit calls at your heart's door and that gentle, loving, knocking and wooing draws you unto salvation. Don't turn Him away.

In Childress, Texas Clyde, a seventeen-year-old high school lad, sat in the service one night in the balcony. He sat near the rail and, leaning over, he listened intently. I saw him as the Holy Spirit gripped his heart and as he wiped perspiration from his brow. I saw him as we stood for the invitation. As we sang, Clyde gripped the balcony rail and trembled like a leaf in the wind. I saw him stand there and saw his face turn pale as he looked at me.

I kept motioning to him to come. I knew the Spirit of God was calling. I said, "Come! Come on!" Many times during that invitation I saw him start and then draw back and shake his head. After awhile I saw him step into the aisle. I called, "Come on!" I saw him step back. I kept calling. He stood there and trembled. I kept calling for him to come. I saw him shake his head and start down the steps of the balcony, but out the front door he went and ran out into the dark.

Three weeks later I went to the home of Clyde who then had leukemia. That awful blood disease enlarges the spleen and sometimes the abdomen distends to twice its normal size. The red blood corpuscles cease to be replenished and death gradually, slowly, inch by inch, comes.

I went that morning and sat by his bedside and tried to lead him to Christ. Finally he said something like this:

> Brother Hankins, I appreciate your coming, but I had my last call three weeks ago Sunday night. You kept urging me to come. You knew what was taking place in my heart. I started to come once. I just felt like I would have to come. I gripped the balcony rail, but when I started—you saw me step out in the aisle—the Devil whispered, "Clyde, you are the leader of the high school dancing crowd. You are the most popular young man in the high school. Are you going to give it up?" So I stepped back and shook my head and said, *I will go to Hell before I will do it!* And that is why I walked out.
>
> I want to tell you, something in here (pointing to his heart) died, and you need not talk to me about being a Christian. My heart is as cold, as dead as a stone.

Thinking perhaps he had not been told that his disease was fatal, I said, "Clyde, has the doctor told you what the trouble is?"

"Yes. He was here this morning. He told me I had just three or four more days to live."

I got on my knees beside that bed, and I read out of God's Word the plan of salvation. And if ever I prayed in my life for a young man, that God would give him another chance, I prayed then.

When I got up off my knees, he said, "Thank you, Brother Hankins, but I have had my chance. I can't! I can't! Something died in here." And that young man died without God.

You can't trifle with the Spirit of God. He is too sensitive to sin. Don't quench the Spirit. Don't grieve the Spirit. Don't resist the Spirit. When God's Spirit speaks, do what He commands. When the Spirit of God speaks, don't say no!

I wonder if God has shown some of you young people your need. This message has been for some of you. I wonder if God hasn't shown you where you have failed; why your prayers have not been answered; why you haven't had peace, joy, assurance and the power of the Spirit; why you haven't had a burden for lost souls.

When the Spirit is grieved, He can't work and you cannot bear fruit; you do not have any faith or power.

Oh, young people, how I covet for you a Spirit-filled and a Spirit-led life, a life glorious and happy and fruitful and sweet and deep and rich beyond words to describe. Has God shown you this morning what the trouble is? How I pray that He has!

ROBERT J. WELLS
1915-

ABOUT THE MAN:

Dr. Robert Wells was born in Winnepeg, Canada. When Robert was eight years old, his parents moved the family to the Chicago area. His father was a superintendent of missions in several parts of the United States. Robert went through the Chicago school system and then went briefly to Moody Bible Institute. He graduated from National Bible College in New York and took his first pastorate in 1936—the First Baptist Church of Fairbury, Illinois.

In 1937 Dr. Wells went to Burton Avenue Baptist Church, Waterloo, Iowa. He says, "We invited Dr. John R. Rice to hold a campaign for us, which really shook the city. From that point on, my life was impacted in a tremendous way by Dr. Rice."

In 1939 Dr. Wells succeeded Dr. John R. Rice at Galilean Baptist Church, Dallas, Texas, with a strong, successful ministry. This was during the World War II years, but still the Lord prospered. While in Dallas, he founded Dallas Bible Institute.

Dr. Rice knew of Dr. Wells' burden for evangelism, so in 1944 he invited Dr. Wells to join him in Wheaton, Illinois and become Associate Editor of THE SWORD OF THE LORD, to hold evangelistic meetings, and to direct some of the great conferences on revival, including the great conferences at Winona Lake. Tremendous crowds attended, and thousands were converted throughout America. Dr. Wells was with the Sword for twelve years.

In 1956 the Lord led him to pitch his Big Tent in Anaheim, California, blessing his work beyond measure. The Central Baptist Church was organized, growing to over 4,000 members. His largest Sunday school attendance was above 3,600. Heritage Christian Schools were founded and were widely recognized.

While still pastor at Central, Dr. Wells held many campaigns in foreign countries and started other churches throughout the U.S.A.

Following a serious stroke, he retired from the pastorate in 1986, after a blessed thirty years in the ministry. Recovery was good, and he is now holding conferences on revival again, making his headquarters in Palm Desert, California. Dr. Wells is a talented cornet player, as well as a great Bible teacher and preacher. This gifted writer is also spending much time writing.

X.

"Be Filled With the Spirit"

ROBERT J. WELLS

(Preached in 1945)

"And be not drunk with wine, wherein is excess; but be filled with the Spirit."—Eph. 5:18.

One of the most neglected, misunderstood and misused passages in the New Testament is the one which constitutes the text of this message. The negative part is not the source of the difficulty, for I have never heard of a Bible scholar nor any really born-again person for that matter, having the slightest difficulty in understanding Paul when he said: "Be not drunk with wine wherein is excess. . . ." All are quite agreed that Paul means just what he says.

But when we approach the positive injunction in the passage, we find ourselves on exceedingly controversial ground. It is not necessary, and this is not the place for us to go into discussion of the "pros" and "cons" which enter into the various theological considerations of the passage; but it is necessary to point out that the church of Christ has suffered tragically and the cause of evangelism and revival has received irreparable damage as the result of this controversy.

Without doubt the greatest hindrance to the progress of revival in our generation has been the refusal of conservative Bible teachers, evangelists, Bible institutes and seminaries to give due attention to the command of our text and to the doctrines that are associated with it.

I remember well an experience in my own life which illustrates the facts I will try to present.

A special ministers' conference was being held in a church in Evanston some years ago. I had been pastor of a small church on the far south side of Chicago for only a few months at a time. I was invited, together with about forty other ministers, to attend. We sat in the choir loft, and one of the brethren sat at a table on the platform leading the discussion on the subject: "Is the Filling of the Spirit for Us Today?" Being only a young man with rather limited experience and not having preached very long, I did not feel that I was entitled to enter into the discussion. But I listened very carefully and drank in everything that was said.

I recall that one man spoke something like this:

> The Bible says that the Spirit does not speak of Himself, and during this dispensation of the Spirit it is not God's desire that we emphasize the Holy Spirit but rather that we emphasize Christ. In my ministry I do not talk about the Holy Spirit, but I seek to emphasize the importance of the Christlike life.

He had not bothered to check the margin in his Bible for the correct translation of John 16:13. If he had, of course he would have discovered that the Bible actually says, "He shall not speak **from** Himself," and not "**of** Himself." It seemed that a little thing like a mistranslation of a word did not bother him, nor did it seem to bother any of the others.

Another brother stood and asked, "What about the testimony of men like D. L. Moody, Charles G. Finney, and R. A. Torrey concerning the work of the Holy Spirit in their lives?"

Here was admittedly a difficult problem to handle, and so the discussion lagged somewhat for a few moments. Then one of the brethren arose and said:

> I've been perturbed about this matter for quite a long time. I have searched my heart to see if there were anything hindering me from having the same kind of an experience that these other men had, for I greatly desired to be filled with the Spirit and to have the power that they had experienced. But I have come to this conclusion: I believe that God doesn't always work in the same way. He uses different means and methods and men. I believe God had a special work for these men to perform, and so He called them and gave them a special filling with the Holy Spirit to equip them for their special tasks.
>
> I do not feel that just because God did this for Moody, Wesley, Finney, Edwards, Torrey and others like them, He will do it for us today. I have come to the conclusion that the baptism of the Holy Spirit, or the filling of the Holy Spirit as these men experienced it, is only for those whom God calls and especially equips for particular and extraordinary tasks.

For some reason or another the other men who were in attendance upon this discussion seemed to like this explanation of the problem.

One after another they concurred with this suggestion, and so concluded that the ministry of the Spirit in filling men as in days gone by is limited to those whom God specially selects for the purpose of accomplishing particular objectives. They agreed that if God has a special job for a man to do, then it may be that He will fill that man with the Holy Spirit as He filled Moody, Wesley, Finney, Torrey and the many others whose names we do not have time to mention, but that we are not to be concerned about the matter and are most certainly not to presume to seek a similar blessing.

I well remember how I went from that place with a hungry heart. In my heart I was saying: *That's a lie! That isn't true! That's a lie. That isn't true!* I had felt that I did not have any right to speak in the conference, but I said, *I'm going to settle this thing for myself!*

I went to my home, and I sat down with my Bible. I said, "Lord, I don't believe that the conclusion of that conference was according to the teaching of Thy Word, and I am not willing to believe it. That kind of a conclusion makes You a respecter of persons, and my Bible says that You are not a respecter of persons. I believe that if You did something for D. L. Moody, You will do it for me if I am willing to meet the conditions that are laid down in Your Word. D. L. Moody had the same problems that we have, the same trials that we must face; his responsibilities were the same as ours, and his task no different from ours. He was commissioned to preach the Gospel to a dying world even as we have been. If he received special equipment for the task, then we are entitled to the same. And, anyway, Lord, Ephesians 5:18 still says, 'Be filled with the Spirit.'"

As a result of that experience, I searched my Bible for what I believed to be the truth concerning this passage, and I want to present that to you in this message.

I. SOME LOGICAL CONCLUSIONS CONCERNING THIS INJUNCTION

Consider first of all the Author of the words, "Be filled with the Spirit." If I were to ask you, "Who wrote these words?" your answer would no doubt be, "The Apostle Paul." But your answer would be incorrect. While Paul was the human instrument used, he was not the real author of the words. The Holy Spirit of God wrote them. These words are not of human but of divine origin.

So, it is important as we consider this command, "Be filled with the Spirit," that we realize it is the command of Almighty God! Since this is true, we had better give careful consideration, for no command from God is incidental! We do not have the authority to set it aside with a mere shrug and say, *It's a matter of controversy, so I won't bother giving it personal consideration.* Controversial or not, it is God's command and just as important as any other command in the Bible. And we will be held responsible for our attitude concerning it just as we will be held responsible for heeding the authoritative warning, "Ye must be born again!"

Now, let me ask you a question. Would God give a command if He did not expect obedience to that command? Would He give a command simply for the purpose of taking up space in His blessed Word, or perhaps, for the purpose of creating controversy? Surely it is not logical to assume that God, the all-wise and the all-understanding God, would give a command to His children without expecting them to obey it.

Then why should we treat this definite, clear, positive command of God in a different way than we treat His other commands? To ask the question is to reveal the foolishness that has so characterized our attitudes in this matter. It is quite obvious that, since this is a command of God, He expects obedience. That means that God's children are obligated to obey the solemn injunction: "Be filled with the Spirit."

Since this is a command of God, and since God expects obedience to this command, what naturally follows is that we can obey that command. God would never give a command to which He expected obedience, if it were not possible for us to obey. We must face the fact that we are not only obligated to obey this command, but we have the ability or the enablement to obey it. We are able to respond to the injunction with our obedience.

There is another step in this process of logic which we must not overlook. Since it is true that God has given us the command, "Be filled with the Spirit," and since it is obviously true that He expects obedience, and likewise, that we are able to obey, I think it naturally follows that we should obey! We are without excuse!

Those who have been emphasizing this great truth and spending much of their time urging Christians to face up to their responsibility and to be filled with the Spirit, have been the subjects of much ridicule and mocking. They have been laughed and scoffed at in contempt.

But beloved, what does this blessed Book have to say? After all, that is what counts. God's Word says, "Be filled with the Spirit." How many of us are facing these facts and obeying this part of our "marching orders"?

Let us now consider one other thing. If I as a child of God am obligated to be filled with the Spirit of God, there is another inescapable fact that I must face, a fact that follows just as surely as night follows day and day follows night: We can and should know whether or not we have obeyed the injunction and whether or not we have been filled with the Holy Spirit. We are faced with a definite command, and we must have a definite reaction to that command. It is either obedience or disobedience. There is no middle road in this.

Have you been filled with the Spirit? We have no right to hedge, no right to evade the issue. The command is so plain and so simple that there is not any room for excuse. We cannot truthfully say that we didn't understand.

Now we are ready to take one more step in the direction of logical conclusions concerning this injunction. Since this is a command of God, since God expects obedience to His command, since we have the ability to obey, since we know that it naturally follows that we should obey, since we can and should know whether or not we have obeyed, I think it is not at all presumptuous but rather definitely in order that we should proceed to the final step, which is: We can be so definite about it as to give thanks to God for having been filled with the Spirit!

We love to sing the chorus by Seth Sykes:

> **Thank You, Lord, for saving my soul;**
> **Thank You, Lord, for making me whole;**
> **Thank You, Lord, for giving to me**
> **Thy great salvation, so rich and free.**

I say, "We love to sing it," and we do. But, why? Because we know that we have been born again. We have accepted the truth of the Gospel, God's wonderful salvation has been appropriated by faith, and so we thrill at the opportunity to express our thanks in this great chorus.

My friends, I believe it should be even so in the matter of the filling of the Holy Spirit. I believe that we can know that we have been filled with the Holy Spirit even to the point of coming to God in the quiet of our prayer closets and saying, "Thank You, Lord, for filling me with the Holy Spirit of God!"

There is a need in America today which is pre-eminent, a need that transcends all other needs—the need of men and women who have been called of God into the service of God to know that they have been filled with the Holy Spirit of God. They need to know it with such confident assurance that they will get down on their knees in heartfelt praise and gratitude to God for the purpose of pouring out their thanksgiving for being filled with the Holy Spirit.

That is how definite I believe the filling of the Holy Spirit to be. I think anything short of this is a crime against the Word of God! Without danger of being contradicted, I remind you that in days gone by, the men who have been used mightily of God in the salvation of souls have been men who believed, experienced, preached and taught the very facts I am presenting to you just now!

Having considered these logical implications of the injunction, let us now give consideration to

II. THE ACTUAL MEANING OF THE PASSAGE

Our Authorized Version is inadequate in the translation of this particular passage. It reads: "Be filled with the Spirit." However, in the original it is not just that way. A literal and somewhat liberal translation of the passage clears away many of the problems which have entered into the controversies relative to it.

Actually, the words of Paul inspired by the Spirit of God are: *"Be ye continually being filled up to the brim with the Holy Spirit."* This clear translation should settle the matter once and for all for those who talk about a filling never again to be repeated, and for those who talk about a "second blessing" apart from any future or further blessings. The passage clearly teaches the very opposite of this.

In considering the actual meaning of the text, I would like for you to think with me concerning three very important matters: the crisis filling, the process filling and the problem involved.

A. The Crisis Filling

Some time ago I came upon the words of a British Bible teacher, Rev. W. W. Martin, whose message on the Holy Spirit was published in the 1938 English Keswick Report. He said, "The filling of the Holy Spirit is a crisis which becomes a process."

That is consistent with what this passage actually teaches and what the Greek demands. I am well aware that there are many who will immediately agree with me when I speak of the process and suggest that there are many infillings. But these same people are losing out on the blessings of this great doctrine so far as practical experience is concerned simply because they are not willing to consider the **crisis** as the supreme necessity!

I feel that we must lay a great deal more stress on the fact that we are commanded to be filled "up to the brim" with the Holy Spirit! We are not told that we must begin a process but that we are to be **filled**. Then we are told that this filling must be retained.

Every Christian who would be in the center of God's will must some time come to the place where he will face up to the command that he be filled with the Holy Spirit. This means that he must come to a **crisis** in his life. It also means that he must not be content until he has come to the place where he is able to say, "Thank Thee, Lord, for filling me with Thy Holy Spirit." It means that he will come into a definite experience, a crucial, crisis experience when he will have received the filling of the Holy Spirit.

I believe it is something that manifests itself in a very definite way. I am not suggesting that the one who is filled with the Spirit will necessarily be conscious of an overwhelming emotional reaction, nor am I contending that there will necessarily be any kind of physical manifestation. But I am satisfied that there will be an inner evidence bringing confirmation of the completed transaction. Then, without question, there will be the inevitable results that accompany the Spirit-filled life!

It is the lack of these evidences that casts such reflection upon the testimonies of so many of those who make profession of being filled. Looking back into the pages of history we read the testimonies of those who wrought mightily for God, and almost without exception they bear witness to the necessity of the **crisis** experience of which I am speaking. Wesley was filled with the Holy Spirit, and he knew it! Count Zinzendorf knew it! Finney knew it! Jonathan Edwards knew it! Brainerd knew it! Greenleaf knew it! Torrey knew it!

D. L. Moody was preaching to great crowds of people and was enjoying an unusual measure of success, a greater success than most preachers in our day are having. But there came that night when those two godly women called his attention to his need of the filling of the Holy Spirit. Then, one glorious day, as a result of the prayers of these women and the searching of his own heart, D. L. Moody was filled with God's Holy Spirit in such an unusual way that he could hardly live.

Moody testified that "from that day on my ministry was different." Instead of having a few people coming to Christ for salvation, they came by the hundreds and by the thousands, and the power of God was upon his ministry in a tremendous way. There was never any question on his part as to the reason why God so marvelously blessed him. Without hesitation he constantly declared that it was the result of, as he called it, the "baptism of the Spirit."

It is this kind of definite experience, definite in its transforming power, for which I am pleading and which I believe to be absolutely necessary if we are to know what is actually meant by the filling of the Holy Spirit. It is involved in the passage and cannot be overlooked!

B. The Process, the Continual Filling

I have emphasized the need for the **crisis**, or the initial filling; but I do not want to give the impression that I consider the one initial filling to be sufficient to meet the requirements of our text. As we have seen, our text demands, "Be continually being filled." That means, as this British Bible teacher put it, "The crisis becomes a process."

The one crucial, crisis, initial filling is of supreme importance, and there can be no process without it. But that one filling is to issue forth in a series of continued fillings. God is desirous of our being filled and being kept filled with the Holy Spirit as a process that will not end until we stand in His presence and likeness!

Now I do not want to be misunderstood here. There are some who will think I am suggesting that it is necessary to have a crisis experience of being filled with the Spirit, and that this is to be followed with an emptying out, a complete emptying out, and that this order is to be repeated throughout the Christian's lifetime.

No, that is not what God expects. He is saying, "I want you to be filled with the Spirit, and I want you to be filled constantly, continually, completely!" It is not the idea of filling a glass of water and emptying it out and filling it again. It is the idea of putting the glass of water under a faucet, filling it and keeping the glass under the running faucet so that the glass continues to be filled even to overflowing.

That is what God wants for you and for me and for every one of His children. He wants to fill us with His Holy Spirit, and He wants to keep us filled day by day, year in and year out, so that "rivers of living water" may flow from us to a dry and thirsty world.

C. The Problem Involved

Having considered briefly the fact that this experience of being filled with the Spirit is a crisis which becomes a process, we can now turn for just a moment to the consideration of the problem involved.

Wherever I have spoken on the subject of this message, I have inevitably been aware of the fact that many people were perplexed with one particular question: "Since the Holy Spirit is a Person, and since He already indwells us as believers, how can we have more of Him?"

It is because of the problem involved in this question that many teachers have given the suggestion, "It is not that we should have more of Him, but rather, that He should have more of us," as the final solution of the entire matter. As a consequence, they go up and down the land telling people that they are not to pray for the Spirit, nor for more of the Spirit, but they are to yield more of themselves, and having done that, they are just simply to accept the filling by faith. These folk insist that if we have met the requirement of yieldedness, all that remains is for us to believe, and having done so, God will not deny our faith, but is really obligated to fill us. So we are to take it for granted that, although there is no particular manifestation of the filling, the transaction has been completed nevertheless. It is because of this kind of teaching that many people make profession of this filling when there is an utter absence of evidence to support their contention because there is a total absence of the results that normally follow a Spirit-filled life.

The problem is: "considering the fact that the Holy Spirit is a Person and that, as such, He is already indwelling the believer, how can the believer have more of Him?"

Dr. W. E. Biederwolf said in his book, *A Help to the Study of the Holy Spirit*:

> To attempt such an answer as just indicated is for the finite to presume a knowledge sufficient to clarify the *most infinite mystery — the omnipresence of a Divine Personality*.
>
> We have thought long here, but have been left always as at the outset. The subject deals with Infinity, and while many have made statements conformable as they believe to Scripture, it is satisfying to note that not in a single volume is any attempt made to deal with this inscrutable mystery with a view to making it wholly intelligible to the

finite mind; we are in the presence of the Infinite, and it becomes us to say, "Speak, Lord, for thy servant heareth," and to be satisfied with what He ways.

This most precious bestowal we have been accustomed to explain by figurative expressions; indeed, we have been taught in this by the inspired writers themselves. Even baptism and filling are figurative as touching any relation the Holy Spirit can bear to an individual. We speak, as indeed does the Word, of His filling us, clothing us, being poured upon us, etc.; all of which are accommodations to the finite.

All the definitions in the world can never explain what God is, and no more can any amount of philosophizing explain how by His Spirit He enters into man, regenerates him or operates within him; this is a mystery more infinite than life itself, but we have not only the postulates of reason that it may be so, but the Word of God and our own experience that it is so, which is more powerful evidence than anything metaphysics could ever bring to us.

F. B. Meyer said, "Before undertaking any definite work for God, be sure you are equipped by a new reception of the Holy Ghost."

Andrew Murray said, "God has not given His Spirit in the sense of parting with Him."

Added to these witnesses is the testimony of the great scholar, Bishop Handley Moule, who said while commenting on Ephesians 1:17, "We are not to think of the 'giving' of the Spirit as an isolated deposit of what, once given, is now locally in possession."

The expressions of these men (and we could quote from many others) warn us that we are to remember that the Holy Spirit is in Heaven as well as in the believer, and that He is at the same time in every believer. We are dealing with the mystery of that wonderful attribute of the Holy Spirit (as of each member of the Trinity), the mystery of omnipresence.

There is no doubt at all that the answer to the question will still be lacking so far as complete satisfaction is concerned. Yet in the light of the things we have just considered and in the light of some references in the Word of God, we can be satisfied that in some mysterious, wonderful and perhaps amazing sense, we can have more of the Spirit.

Here we should notice that in John 3:34 we are informed that "God giveth not the Spirit by measure unto him"; in Acts 2:17,18, Luke speaks of the Spirit as having been "poured out"; then those who had been filled once are spoken of in Acts as having been filled again and again.

Since the Scripture uses such terminology, since the New Testament writers, inspired by the Holy Spirit, spoke in such manner, why should we hesitate for a moment to believe that it is possible in some wonderful way to receive an additional measure, an additional outpouring, or an additional "filling" with the Holy Spirit?

Once again, we have the same old quibbling about theological terminology which has hindered so many from enjoying the blessings and benefits which come from a wholehearted reception of the teaching of God's Word. I say, away with all doubts, away with all questionings concerning this matter: receive the testimony of the New Testament writers, the testimony of the eminent Bible teachers I have quoted, the testimony of God's great giants of days gone by who have moved entire continents for God, the testimony of contemporary Christian leaders who are winning multitudes to Christ! With complete unanimity they agree that, although we are dealing with the infinite in the consideration of this problem, and although our finite minds find it difficult to comprehend the infinite, we may come into the realization of what it is to be filled with the Spirit even in the sense, so to speak, of receiving more of a Person who already indwells us since we are born again children of God!

III. TO WHOM THE INJUNCTION IS GIVEN

Having seen that Ephesians 5:18 teaches a definite and continuous experience of being filled with the Spirit, it is necessary for us to consider to whom this injunction is given. As we consider what the Bible teaches in this regard we will be faced with inescapable evidence that will compel us to admit that this passage is addressed to all those who have experienced the new birth.

Please notice that Paul speaks to members of the Ephesian church in chapter 1, verse 13: "In whom ye also trusted, after that ye heard the word of truth, the gospel of your salvation: in whom also after that ye believed, ye were sealed with that holy Spirit of promise." Paul tells us here that the members had "heard the word of truth" and "trusted" in Christ. Then he adds, "After that ye believed, ye were sealed with that holy Spirit of promise." There can be no denial that here Paul is addressing born-again believers, indwelt by the Holy Spirit.

In chapter 4, verse 30, he writes to these same Christians: "And grieve not the holy Spirit of God, whereby ye are sealed unto the day of redemption." Once again he emphasizes the fact that he is writing to Spirit-sealed, Spirit-indwelt Christians.

Then in Ephesians 5:18 he commands these same born-again ones who have been indwelt by the Spirit to "be filled with the Spirit."

It is not an accident that the command comes to us in this setting. God wanted us to know that it is not enough to be born again, not enough to be indwelt or sealed by the Spirit; He forcefully impresses upon our minds the necessity of being filled with the Spirit.

To those of you attending this great conference at Winona Lake, I thank God that you have been born again. I rejoice with you in the fact of the new birth, and that you have been and are indwelt by the Holy Spirit. But I call upon you to believe God when He says you must be filled with the Holy Spirit, and I urge you to give solemn attention to this positive command to Christians! If you do not, at the judgment seat of Christ you will stand before the Lord Jesus Christ and give an account of your attitude concerning Ephesians 5:18.

When Jesus stands before you and asks, "What have you done about being filled with the Holy Spirit?" there will be no questions, no controversies aired. In that day no excuses will stand before Him. In that day you will face the facts as they are! Then you will say, "I believed it and I obeyed it," or, "I set it aside, I paid no attention to it, I disobeyed it."

My friends, every child of God who should be filled with the Holy Spirit, who is obligated to be filled with the Spirit, and who has disobeyed this divine injunction, no matter what the reason, will face the penalty of God in that day and the loss of reward, to say the least!

IV. THE RESULTS OF BEING FILLED WITH THE SPIRIT

Some of you will wonder, *How can I know whether or not I have been filled with the Holy Spirit?* The Bible has not left us ignorant concerning this all-important question. The verses immediately following our text will find at least part of the answer.

A. Spirit-Filled Christians Are Happy Christians

Notice a semicolon after "Spirit" in verse 18. Notice Paul says in verse 19: "Speaking to yourselves in psalms and hymns and spiritual songs, singing and making melody in your heart to the Lord." That is one way you can know whether you are filled with the Holy Spirit. You who go around with a long face, you who grumble, groan, murmur, complain most of the time will get over that. Those things will go out of your life when the Spirit of God comes in to take control.

When you are filled with the Spirit of God, you will have a song in your heart. You will start to sing as Elbert Tindley does if you get the Spirit of God in His fullness operating in your heart and life. It is not just singing with your voice; it is having a song in your heart. It is there in the morning when you awaken and stays all day long. It is there when you go to bed, and in the middle of the night. A song is in your heart because the Spirit of God is there. He takes away the sadness, the gloom, all bitterness. He takes away strife, envy, animosity. He takes out of your heart all those things which hinder you from living a victorious and happy life.

B. Spirit-Filled Christians Are Thankful Christians

Then in verse 20 God says: "Giving thanks always for all things unto God and the Father in the name of our Lord Jesus Christ." Now you would expect that of a person filled with the Holy Spirit, wouldn't you? We all know that Romans 8:28 is in the Book, and we all like to quote it: "And we know that all things work together for good. . . ."

But when some of us preachers wake up Sunday morning and see the clouds, we begin to murmur and grumble because of what we see in the sky, for we just know it is going to affect our service. When something happens to upset us a little bit, what do we do? We go around groaning and complaining in spite of Romans 8:28.

When we are filled with the Holy Spirit and are letting Him dominate and control our life, we will not be criticizing God's way of doing things. Rather, we will be giving thanks for all things, without exception, in the name of the Lord Jesus Christ. We will be thankful Christians in addition to being happy Christians.

C. Spirit-Filled Christians Are Humble Christians

There is another point here, for the thought is not completed until verse 21. Then the rest of the chapter continues and amplifies in detail what has been presented in verse 21: "Submitting yourselves one to another in the fear of God." That means that you will be a humble Christian. Instead of saying, "I want to be up there, I want this consideration, I want you to think about me"—instead of thinking of yourself more highly than you ought to think, you will be a humble Christian, down on your face before God. In the spirit of humility you will be thinking of others, esteeming yourself less than others. You will recognize your proper position, and you will respect those in authority.

If this congregation went from here as happy, thankful, humble Christians; if that spirit got contagious and spread out into all of the churches represented here, we would have revival all over America. The folks who are pointing their fingers at you and calling you hypocrites would not have the right nor the authority to do it anymore. They would have no evidence to substantiate their claims. You would live and act as a Christian.

That is what we need! You get the filling of the Holy Spirit, and you will be transformed by grace divine to such an extent that people will know it, will thank God for it and will want what you have.

A little Syrian girl was saved in Wichita, Kansas. She did not know very much. She was not very bright, but she was walking along the street singing:

> **To be like Jesus, to be like Jesus,**
> **All I ask — to be like Him.**
> **All through life's journey from earth to Glory,**
> **All I ask — to be like Him.**

She had no better sense than to sing it out loud in public. That is more than most of us would do. But as she was singing it there on the main street, a woman came up, tapped her on the shoulder and asked, "What are you singing? Sing it again!" So she sang for the woman the same song again. The tears came down the face of that woman as she said, "I'd like to be like Jesus; could you tell me how? More than anything else, I want to be like Jesus. Can you tell me how?"

The little girl thought for a minute, then said, "Well, all I know is John 3:16: 'For God so loved the world [and that means you], that he gave his only begotten Son, that whosoever [and that means you] believeth in him should not perish, but have everlasting life.' That's for you."

The woman said, "All right, can we pray?"

The little girl looked around (it was the main street, and she did not know what to do); then she said, "All right."

The two got down on their knees on the main street in Wichita, Kansas, and the little sixteen-year-old Syrian girl led that woman into the saving knowledge of Jesus Christ.

The world is looking for people like Jesus, and if you will only see it and live it, you will win them to Christ.

D. Spirit-Filled Christians Are Powerful Christians

If you are filled with the Holy Spirit, you will not only be a happy, thankful and humble Christian; you will be a powerful Christian. In John 7:37-39 we read:

"In the last day, that great day of the feast, Jesus stood and cried, saying, If any man thirst, let him come unto me, and drink. He that believeth on me, as the scripture hath said, out of his belly shall flow rivers of living water. (But this spake he of the Spirit, which they that believe on him should receive: for the Holy Ghost was not yet given; because that Jesus was not yet glorified.)"

This passage says that, when the Holy Spirit is given, the one who believes on Christ will have a wonderful experience, the experience of having rivers of living water flow from his innermost being.

Where are the rivers of living water? Do you see them anywhere? Wherever I go I find dry and barren, arid country, spiritually speaking. Oh, my heart ached this morning when I asked those who had not won a soul in at least a month to stand to their feet, and when the majority, the overwhelming majority, stood to their feet! That is a shame! It is a crime against our fellowmen who are lost and damned for eternity!

The reason this condition exists is that so many have not obeyed the injunction of God to be filled with the Spirit, and the living waters are not flowing from them. Oh, if the waters were pouring forth in streams and rivers from your life and mine, people could not help but drink of them and live. Our lives would be powerful in bringing the water of life to a thirsty world!

In Acts 1:8 we read: "But ye shall receive power. . . ." Notice the word "power." Power! POWER! Do you know where there is any power today? Someone says that the advent of the Holy Spirit took place at Pentecost and that when He came Christians were filled, and that is all that was necessary. If that be so, then show me the power to prove it! Someone says, "I am filled with the Holy Spirit." I say, "Show me the power to prove it."

"But ye shall receive power, after that the Holy Ghost is come upon you: and ye shall be witnesses unto me both in Jerusalem, and in all Judaea, and in Samaria, and unto the uttermost part of the earth."

The reason we are not successful witnesses is that we do not have the power. The reason we have no power is that we have not obeyed

Ephesians 5:18 to be filled with the Holy Spirit. That is our need more than anything else.

V. HOW TO BE FILLED WITH THE HOLY SPIRIT

That is our next point for consideration. Some of you ask, "Preacher, what can I do about it? How can I be filled with the Holy Spirit?" That is a message in itself, but let me give you some suggestions.

A. Get Thirsty

The first thing is to get thirsty, to **desire** to be filled with the Holy Spirit. Perhaps some of you do not want the filling of the Holy Spirit because you are afraid it will rid you of your dirty, filthy habits and sins; that it will send you forth to be honest men and women again; that it will make you live sacrificial lives; that it will make you put God, Christ, the Holy Spirit and lost, dying souls before yourself, your family, your home. You do not like that! It might make you a "fanatic."

Unless you desire, unless you are thirsty to such an extent that you are willing to pay whatever price necessary, you will never know what it means to be filled with the Spirit!

My friends, I say if being filled with the Holy Spirit of God makes fanatics of people, then God give us more fanatics!

B. Believe That God Can Do It

After you have desired to be filled, then believe that God can do it. Believe the Book. Believe that God meant what He said and that, because He is God, He is also able to fulfill His promise.

C. Obey!

Obey the Lord! In Acts 5:32 Peter declares, "And we are his witnesses of these things; and so is also the Holy Ghost, whom God hath given to them that **obey** him."

Someone says that's just for salvation. Absurd! Christ does not tell me to go out into the world and tell men, "Obey Me, and you will be saved." Rather, Christ tells me to preach, "Believe on the Lord Jesus Christ, and thou shalt be saved." But He says that those who would receive the power of God's Spirit, must **obey** Him! Obey Ephesians 5:18. Obey the other Scriptures, such as I John 1:9 and similar passages, which tell us that if we regard iniquity in our hearts He will not hear us; that in order to have forgiveness and cleansing, we must confess our sins.

D. Pray!

But this is not all. Maybe this will shock you, but listen carefully. You can thirst all you want, believe all you want, obey all you want; but unless that obedience includes praying to be filled with the Spirit, you will never be filled. Everything hinges on that.

Turn, please, to Luke 11:13. I would ask that you put all prejudices out of your hearts and minds. "If ye then, being evil, know how to give good gifts unto your children: how much more shall your heavenly Father give the Holy Spirit to them that ask him?"

We need to pray for the Holy Spirit today! In John 20:21 Jesus said to the disciples, "As my Father hath sent me, even so send I you." Then in verse 22 we read, "He breathed on them, and saith unto them, Receive ye the Holy Ghost."

Some people say nothing happened then. Some people say that was prophetic. Others say that was a foretaste. Still others say that was typical. But what right do they have to draw those conclusions? When Jesus spoke those words, He was the glorified Son of God, and something happened when He spoke them. After that event in Luke 24:49, He told the disciples: "Tarry ye in the city of Jerusalem, until ye be endued [or clothed upon] with power from on high." Not "until ye be indwelt by the Spirit of God," not "until the Spirit of God comes," but "until ye be clothed upon with power from on high."

Some people do not like that word *tarry*. Whatever you want to call it, God wants us to wait on Him concerning this matter.

Why do so many of you have trouble with sin in your lives? Because you do not tarry before the Lord. If you did, you would think of a multitude of things you had not thought of before. If down on your face before the Lord you would confess the sins you do know about, then if you would say, "Lord, if I have sinned that much, I must have sinned more. What have I said that was sinful? What have I thought that was sinful? What have I done that was sinful? O Spirit of God, reveal my sinfulness," then words, thoughts, deeds that have grieved the Spirit of God and need to be cleansed and forgiven will be brought to mind as you wait upon the Lord. You will not have victory until they are forgiven. Just as you need to wait upon God in getting rid of sin and getting victory over sin, just so it is for the blessing.

Those men who have prayed and worked mightily for God have not been those who have just prayed, "Now, Lord, I need $500.00. You love me. You have kept me. You are for me. Thank You. Goodnight." The men who have gone out and done mighty things for God have not been those who have just said, "Lord, You love sinners more than I do. You are more interested in them than I am. Your Word is powerful, and it will not return unto You void. So I'll give them the Word; then, Lord, You take care of the results." No, sir!

The men who have wrought wonderfully for God have been those who, though sick and brokenhearted and ready to die in some cases, got out in the midst of the woods and, in thick snow and below zero weather, poured out their hearts to God, pleading, "Lord, I have to have the victory, even if it kills me!"—like Brainerd did. They have been the kind who vowed, "Lord, I'll not be denied," and stayed on their knees until things happened!

People have been telling us that what I am preaching is not true. They have been saying, "Don't preach that doctrine anymore; just emphasize the grace of God." As a result, our institutions have gone over to the Devil and unnumbered multitudes have gone to Hell. A spiritual dearth has swept over the whole land, and our country has become like the dry desert.

Institutions that used to be flaming fires of evangelism for God have burned out. All they can do now is teach theology. Men who used to be on fire have cooled off; they cannot now get a baker's dozen out to hear them preach on Sunday night. Churches that used to be the centers of evangelism cannot even hold their own.

When I confronted the pastor of the First Baptist Church of a certain city with his lack of support of a union meeting I was then conducting, he said to me, "I'm not interested in mass evangelism." A few days later I learned from one of his deacons that on the previous Wednesday night, two people were out to prayer meeting. That following Sunday night fifteen hundred people were in our tent revival.

I said to the audience attending that tent revival, "I would like to know how many of you were saved in your homes?" Six people stood to their feet.

"How many of you were saved in Sunday school?" Twelve people stood.

"How many of you were saved in a midweek prayer meeting?" Three or four stood.

"How many of you were saved in a Spirit-filled evangelistic meeting?" Almost the whole audience stood to their feet.

Then I said, "Do you folks want to know why the pastor of the First Baptist Church will not cooperate in this meeting? He says that he does not believe in this type of evangelism. Any man who can face the facts that I have just placed before you—proving that the people who fill our churches have come through evangelistic fires—and say, 'I don't believe in that type of evangelism,' is just a plain fool!"

The thing that has killed, emptied and ruined our churches and our land has been a refusal to follow the Spirit of God.

Do you know what has happened in 1945? The tide has been turning. The thing is changing. Life is being rekindled. Evangelistic flames are burning brightly again. Now we have "Philadelphia for Christ," "Los Angeles for Christ," "Christ for Cleveland," "Christ for Buffalo" and "Christ for . . .," these other major cities up and down the land. Thousands are coming to God.

It is no accident either that "Youth for Christ" sweeps over the nation on Saturday nights; that hundreds of thousands are listening to the Gospel instead of playing with the Devil's crowd, and multitudes are being born again.

We have a Sword Conference on Evangelism like this, representing almost every state in the Union, with men and women coming with burdened, broken, bleeding hearts and finding joy, peace and satisfaction, coming to shake our hand and saying, "I'm going back with new life, new fire, new determination. May God help me to kindle the flames in the home church."

Why is all this happening? Because once again men are recognizing the need for being filled with the Spirit and are working in the might of His power!

Here is a tremendous fact. If you will study the history of revivals, you will learn that without one single, solitary exception, those who have been mightily used of God have believed the truth I am preaching this morning.

If you will go back just a few years to the close of the ministries of Torrey, Chapman, Billy Sunday and Paul Rader, then if you will search this land over up to the present day, you will discover that great dearth has come as a result of a lack of preaching on this particular subject.

But now with a renewed emphasis of this doctrine, the situation is rapidly changing. Cast your eyes about and listen to the voices of those who know. Ask Jesse Hendley, Hyman Appelman, Bob Jones, Sr., Joe Henry Hankins, John Rice and these other men. They will tell you that what I am saying is true. Thank God, we are waking up and once again witnessing revival blessings all over the land!

I close now with this illustration.

I heard Jesse Hendley tell this in my church a number of years ago. He said:

> There are three kinds of Christians. They can be illustrated by three kinds of boats. The **rowboat Christian**—pulling with might and main at his oars as he tries to row up the stream. It is pretty hard going against the current. Although he makes some progress, he gets worn out. He rests at his oars a little bit. But when he has recuperated and has sufficient strength to go on and starts to work again, lo and behold, he discovers that he is farther down stream than when he first began. There are a lot of Christians like that—struggling, struggling, in the energies of the flesh to get the job done.

Then he said:

> There is the **sailboat Christian**. When the wind of revival is blowing, the sails are put up to the wind. My, how they lift! The boat just sails along. For a time everything is wonderful, just sailing along on a surge of emotionalism. But when the wind stops blowing, when the revival is over, the boat stops and just drifts along. They get down in the dumps and amount to nothing much for God until the wind of revival starts blowing again.

Then he said:

> There is the **steamboat Christian**. The steamboat does not care about the current, nor about the wind, because the fire and water make the motors go, turn the propellers. It moves right on, the same one day as another, weather or no weather, wind or no wind!

The water of the Word of God, heated by the flame of the Holy Spirit, makes a Christian a "steamboat Christian," one who can plow on when the winds are blowing favorably or adversely, when the current is against him or with him. It makes not a bit of difference; he goes on and on and on for God.

That is what we need. We have the Word of God; don't ever let it go. But now, take the Spirit of God, let Him become a flame in your soul as He fills you. Then you will go forth under steam to do business for God.

May God grant it for every child of His in these dark days.

(From *How to Have a Revival*, now out of print, Sword of the Lord Publishers)

XI.

Grieving the Holy Spirit of God

WILLIAM E. BIEDERWOLF

"And grieve not the holy Spirit of God, whereby ye are sealed unto the day of redemption."—Eph. 4:30.

What a wonderful epistle this one of Paul's to the Ephesians really is! My own heart always takes a bound as I pass from the one just before it, so impassioned and so full of controversy, to this one, so unimpassioned and so exalted. It is like coming from the battlefield into the very hush and stillness of the Temple.

As I have read it over and over I have found myself saying, *If there is a sweeter or more helpful letter anywhere among the inspired epistles, I do not know which one it is.*

This letter of Paul to the Ephesians tells me of my redemption when it was but a silent thought in the mind of God; tells me of its glorious consummation in the faraway hereafter; and if I would accomplish the will of God on my way through this life, He sets before me here the marvelous possibility of "being strengthened with might by his Spirit in the inner man" to do it.

This is the epistle that speaks so often of the "heavenly places," but before it closes the apostle turns to deal with the more practical affairs of human life and relationships. "It begins in Heaven," as someone has said, "and ends in the kitchen."

Its last chapters are packed with practical suggestions concerning purity of life, false witnessing and proper relationships in the home. Right in the midst of these we find this most serious and affectionate exhortation of the text, "And grieve not the holy Spirit of God, whereby ye are sealed unto the day of redemption." As if we could grieve Him with the improper use of our lips and by wrong relationships in our home; and this, of course, is true.

There are three things that lie almost on the very surface of this text of Scripture.

It shows us that the Holy Spirit is a Person. If that were not so, He could not be grieved. Some people think the Holy Spirit is just an influence from God, some sort of an impersonal force or energy of the Almighty. But you cannot grieve an influence; you cannot grieve an impersonal force. It takes someone with a heart to be grieved.

Listen! We need to appreciate this fact more than we do, and it is only when we do appreciate it that we will come to appreciate Him in the way we should. And when He is so appreciated, you will find it exceedingly painful to hear others speaking of this blessed Personality as "it." How inconsiderate, to say the least, and how painful it must be to the Holy Spirit Himself! You would not appreciate being called an "it."

In the next place, the Holy Spirit is a Person who loves the child of God.

How long has it been since you heard a sermon on "The Love of the Holy Spirit"? We hear all too little about it. God loved us enough to give His Son, and the Son loved us enough to give Himself, but the Holy Spirit loved us enough to apply and to work out in us salvation which the love of the Father and the Son made possible. His love must be great, indeed, to deal as patiently and with such forbearance as He has been compelled to deal with most of us; in fact, with the best of us.

How do we know He loves us? How could it be otherwise, if what we have just said is true? We know it because the Word says it. And if we had no other verse than the one before us, how very plain it is made here; because, if He did not love you, you could not grieve Him.

You could not grieve an enemy. You could not grieve someone who is indifferent to you. He doesn't care. But you might grieve your mother because she loves you. The measure of her grief, when you wound her, can always be taken as the measure of her love. The deeper the love, the profounder the grief.

And something of the Holy Spirit's love for you and me may be measured by this, that the word used for *grief* here is the very same word used to express the awful grief, sorrow and agony of the Saviour in the Garden of Gethsemane.

Oh, how He loves! Think of it! Such infinite sorrow in the heart of the Holy Spirit because of the thoughtlessness, the worldliness and sin of those who have been sealed by Him unto the day of redemption! No wonder some have sought to find in the Holy Spirit the mother-part of Divine Love.

In the next place, He is a Person to whose agency we are indebted for the most unspeakable gift it is possible for us to know. It is *"with Him,"* we are told, or rather *"in him,"* as one version puts it, that we have been sealed unto the day of redemption.

Paul is working upon the Ephesians through love and not through fear. It is not because the day of wrath and revelation of the righteous judgment of God is coming that we are urged not to grieve the Holy Spirit; it is because, through His great love, we are so much indebted to Him.

No one but a child of God can grieve the Holy Spirit; and this is the sad thing about it. Others may *resist* Him, but only the Christian can grieve Him.

Every Christian is sealed with the Holy Spirit, and the seal is security—made secure unto the day of redemption. If you are a child of God, it is not proper for you to pray for the sealing of the Holy Spirit. That sealing took place at your conversion. This is the Person concerning whom Paul says, "And grieve not the holy Spirit of God."

How do we grieve Him? Whenever we set Him aside; whenever we pull away from Him; whenever we smother His voice; whenever we sin in any way, His sensitive heart is made sorrowful.

But I want just now to call your attention more especially to three ways in which this grief is brought about. They all begin with the same letter and the same sound. This may help you to remember them.

We grieve the Holy Spirit by:

1. Disregarding His presence within us;
2. Distrusting His Word about us;
3. Disobeying His counsel to us.

Disregarding His Presence Within Us

By that I mean giving Him an unclean place in which to dwell. At the moment of our regeneration, He becomes our guest, indwelling and abiding with us forever. "Know ye not that ye are the temple of God, and that the Spirit of God dwelleth in you?" That verse every Christian should memorize and ponder.

Now, suppose an aged mother were dwelling with her son and he should so disregard her presence as to make no provision for her comfort and let her live without one token of gratitude for what she has meant to him. Yes, more; suppose he made that home the scene of deep offense to her and brought into it unholy companions in whose presence he allowed her to be ridiculed and insulted! There are no words in language severe enough to characterize a disposition like that.

But do you know what I think? I think you might better so treat the one who gave you your first birth than to be born a second time of the Holy Spirit of God and be so utterly unmindful of His presence and feeling as to poison the atmosphere of His temple with unholy thoughts and fill the place of His abiding with that which is repulsive and unclean, which His eyes must behold and His heart endure, though it throb with unspeakable grief all the while.

"The Spirit of God dwelleth in you." Have you ever seriously considered what that means? It means, of course, that you can go nowhere without taking Him with you.

I heard of a young man who was asked to go to a questionable place. He replied that he could not go because he had a Friend who loved him and whom he loved very much in return, and He would not want to go with him. And said the young man, "I cannot go without Him."

His companions said, "Come, let us meet Him, and we will ask Him to go."

"But, it's no use," said the young man. "He will not want to go."

"Who is He?" they inquired.

With all the dignity of his heroic manliness, he answered, "My Friend is Jesus Christ."

Christ would not want to be found in many a place where those who bear His name sometimes go. But Paul says, "Christ liveth in me." That indwelling is through the Holy Spirit, and, in a very certain sense, where we go He must go. I wonder how many of us, under the same circumstances, would have declined to enter where we felt He would not wish to accompany us.

But His indwelling means more. It means that He hears all we say, sees all we do, and is conscious of our every thought. God pity us if we do not care.

They tell us King Menzentius was driven out by his own people because of his detestable cruelty. He was a stranger to mercy, and no torture which his cruel heart could invent was too horrible to gratify hi' vengeance. One of his methods of punishment was to fasten the living to the dead, hand in hand, face to face, lip to lip, and thus leave the wretched victim to die in this terrible and disgusting embrace.

Paul cried, "O wretched man that I am! who shall deliver me from the body of this death?" What a striking illustration of the thing Paul had in mind! He was crying for deliverance from sin, from the impure and unholy passions and appetites which use this body, with its weakness and its lust, as the instrument of their activity, and so bring us under the power of death.

What a picture it is of the real nature of sin—foul, offensive and polluting. It may not appear so at first to the sinner who loves his sin, but to the one who has found the way and experienced the delights of a holy life in Christ, the cry of Paul comes with telling significance.

If sin can thus appear to a mortal like Paul and like you and me, how must it appear in the eyes of Him in whose sight our very best is unclean?

It would not be pleasant, and it ought not to be necessary, for me to dilate on the unholy things which God's own people often tolerate to their own hurt and the Spirit's grief. If they cared to know and would listen, they might hear His voice telling them where to go and what to avoid; but it is hardly worth His while to speak if there isn't any disposition to obey when His voice is heard.

You may have a Christian heart and yet not have a clean heart, though it would be a very poor Christian heart, to be sure. It may not be possible for me to be great, but it is possible for me to be holy if I really want to be.

Listen again: "Know ye not that ye are the temple of God, and that the Spirit of God dwelleth in you?" If I want to be holy, it will please Him not only to indwell with His presence but to infill with His power until my life shall no longer be a disappointment to Him and a source of constant grief, but one in which, thank God, even He, the Holy Spirit, will delight.

I said we grieve Him also by

Distrusting His Word About Us

What about the assurance of your salvation? Why are you always in doubt about it?

When Chapman told Moody his trouble along this line, Moody said to him with characteristic bluntness, "Whom are you doubting?"

Dr. Chapman saw that he was doubting God, and from that day the good doctor said he stopped this unintentional sin.

Dear friend, it is yours to know that you are a child of God. "These things have I written," says John, "that ye may know that ye have eternal life."

And what are some of the things that are written? Well, here are some of them: "And this is the record that God hath given to us eternal life, and this life is in his Son." John wrote that. Then, here are the words of Jesus Himself: "He that...believeth on him that sent me, hath everlasting life, and...is passed"—not going to pass merely when you die, but *is* passed—"from death unto life."

There never was a time when a Christian had any right to sing,

> 'Tis a point I long to know,
>   Oft it causes anxious thought;
> Do I love the Lord or no?
> Am I His, or am I not?

I know it is all right with me at this point, not because I am any better than you, but because "I know whom I have believed, and am persuaded that he is able to keep that which I have committed unto him against that day."

My dear child, it is not a question as to how you feel about it. An ounce of faith is worth a ton of that sort of stuff.

> Believe, and the feeling may come or may go;
> Believe in the Word that was written to show
> That all who believe their salvation may know;
> Believe, and keep right on believing.

Said an old Scotch woman to her persecutors who threatened her with the loss of everything if she did not renounce her faith, "Ah, you may take my property; you may take my husband; you may take my child; you may take my life; but you canna take my Christ."

Isn't that great! Isn't that wondrously fine! But, oh, how it must grieve Him to have us always doubting His Word and mistrusting His love when we ought to be giving ourselves to doing His will. "And grieve not the holy Spirit of God."

We are told in Romans 8:16 that the Holy Spirit bears witness with our spirit that we are the children of God; and if that witness with your spirit is not as deep as it might be, I am sure you will find the reason in the shallowness of your whole Christian life and experience.

The Bible is the Holy Spirit's Word, and this Word is the great instrument in all His operations. Willful sinning will dampen anyone's assurance. I wouldn't give a fig for it if it didn't.

Then here is something very much akin to what we have been saying: it is our distrust of His Word about our final inheritance.

A pastor once said to me, "I wish you would come with me to the bedside of an old saint; her case is a very peculiar one."

We entered her room and I said, "Well, Mother, you have some sweet experiences waiting for you very soon."

She whispered, "Do you really think it is all true?"

I replied, "Certainly, Mother. We have His Word for all that."

"Oh," she said, "if I were only sure, it would be so easy to go."

I helped her as best I could, going from promise to promise throughout His Word. After prayer, as we left the pastor said to me, "I have done that each time I have called, but each time I return I find her doubting and trembling lest after all death will be the end."

Not willing to trust His Word! Oh, how it grieves Him!

The Bible is crammed full of promises for the life to come. There are many men—millions of them—who can lay a little piece of paper on a bank counter with nothing back of it but a human promise to pay and it will instantly turn to money; and yet here we are, some of us, fearful that the promises given to us through the Holy Spirit of the Mighty God will not produce face value in the life to come.

I read of a man who began to crawl over a frozen river on his hands and knees, fearful lest the ice would not bear his weight. While a great way from shore, a man drove past him with a big sled filled with pig iron.

Some of us are like that with the promises of God. We seem to be afraid lest they will break down under the strain of any faith we might place upon them. "And grieve not the holy Spirit of God, whereby ye are sealed unto the day of redemption." The seal is the sign of security, and God knows His own.

Then there is a third way by which we grieve the Holy Spirit, and that is by

Disobeying His Counsel or His Command to Us

Friends, isn't it about time some of us stop singing, "I'll go where You want me to go; I'll be what You want me to be," and begin walking in that way and be something of what His grace and power have made it possible to become?

Oh, how often He has given to us some new vision of Christ that has called for increased devotion and deeper consecration! And just because the way of consecration and devotion has always been the way of the altar and the cross we have shrunk back, and His tender, sensitive heart has been grieved.

The story is told of a young lady from a fashionable home who had given her heart to Christ and was a most earnest Christian. She was always speaking to others about Christ and refrained from anything that might bring the sincerity of her profession into question. She was bitterly opposed in her own home. Her earnest life brought her no little embarrassment. Once when she was repulsed and wounded, Satan whispered to her that possibly she was a bit too conscientious and that it would be just as well if she were a bit more like the average Christian.

Just then came an invitation to spend the holidays with the guests of a friend among whom she was not very well known. She made up her mind not to speak openly to any of them about Christ and not to put herself in the way of being known as especially religious.

She carried out her purpose, but not without considerable pain to herself.

The visit closed. On the day of her leaving, a very fashionable society lady was walking with her alone when suddenly the lady asked, "Where is your sister? Why did she not come? I mean your religious sister, the one who is sometimes called 'the religious Miss J.' It was because I heard that she was to be here that I accepted the invitation. I am so tired of the vain and empty and unsatisfying life I am leading that I just longed to have a talk with a real Christian. Why did your sister not come?"

It was then that the poor, unhappy girl burst into tears. With shame she was obliged to confess that she had no sister, that she was the one who had sometimes been called "the religious Miss J.," but she had been ashamed of Christ and of the badge she should so proudly have worn for Him.

"And grieve not the holy Spirit of God."

Do you know, my friend, there is a life that always honors God and always glorifies Christ, a life that will never bring us to a place of shame. It is the Spirit-filled life.

Paul said, "Be not drunk with wine. . . but be filled with the Spirit." It is just as much of a command to "be filled with the Spirit" as to "be not drunk with wine." And if you should ask me what the "filling of the Spirit" means, I would say that in a word it is the yielding of myself so completely to the already indwelling Spirit of God that He may have His way altogether with me.

It is this, and this only, that can cause us to walk and not stumble and in all things be well-pleasing to Him. "And grieve not the holy Spirit of God, whereby ye are sealed unto the day of redemption."

And if I do grieve Him, what then?

Well, if in a moment of temptation my feet have slipped and I have gone down, Christ will lift me up and His forgiveness will be mine.

But if I trifle with sin and persist in self-indulgence, it means shame, defeat and failure all along the way—no peace of mind, the lashing whip of a guilty conscience and, in the end, being saved as if by fire.

A man waited for me at the close of a meeting. He stood midway in the room, and as I came near I saw the blood rush from his fingers as he almost drove them into the seat before him.

I asked, "Well, my friend, what is it?"

Looking into my face he said, "Lost!" And before I could reply he said, "I used to know God, but I've lost Him altogether out of my life."

I said, "Well, Sir, you know the reason why."

Looking still more intently into my face, he leaned forward and said, "Sin! Sin!"

I could hear the hiss of the serpent in the word.

His story is pitiful in the extreme. He had been a minister of the Gospel but had so incessantly, so continuously grieved the Holy Spirit by persisting in sin—in something that was grossly questionable, to say the least—that God was no longer using him. God stripped him of his power, took the influence of His Holy Spirit from him, removed him from the place where he had set his feet, and reserved his crown for service for someone more worthy to wear it.

May Heaven spare you, and may Heaven spare me, from ever coming to a place like that!

Paul says in I Corinthians 9:27, "I keep under my body. . .lest that by any means, when I have preached to others, I myself should be a castaway." I know what some people say that means. I also know what I very much fear it means: The word is *adokimos*—"castaway." It means not losing one's salvation but becoming a useless Christian.

May Heaven spare you and me an experience like that—of being in a place where God will have no further use for us because we have become ambitious for ourselves and not for Christ; because we have so long refused to obey the promptings of the Holy Spirit, and have so long indulged ourselves at a point where God has said, "Thou shalt not"; until God must strip us of our power and leave us to drag our impoverished lives out to their disappointing end, and then go up, saved as if by fire, when we might have had an abundant entrance because of what the Holy Spirit of God would have done for us had we only been yielded to Him.

"And grieve not the holy Spirit of God, whereby ye are sealed unto the day of redemption." May the indwelling Holy Spirit help us now.

> **Lord, for tomorrow and its needs I do not pray;**
> **Keep me, my God, from stain of sin, just for today.**

And may we have the grace to say, be it by water or by fire,

> **So wash me, Thou, without, within,**
> **Or purge with fire, if that must be;**
> **No matter how, if only sin**
> **Die out in me, die out in me.**

CHARLES HADDON SPURGEON
1835 - 1892

ABOUT THE MAN:

Many times it has been said that this was the greatest preacher this side of the Apostle Paul. He began preaching at the age of 16. At 25 he built London's famous Metropolitan Tabernacle, seating around 5,000. It was never large enough. Even when traveling he preached to 10,000 eager listeners a week. Crowds thronged to hear him as they came to hear John the Baptist by the River Jordan. The fire of God was on him as on the Prophet Elijah facing assembled Israel at Mount Carmel.

Royalty sat in his Tabernacle, as did washerwomen. Mr. Gladstone had him to dinner; and cabbies refused his fare, considering it an honor to drive for this "Prince of Preachers." To a housewife kneading bread, he would say, "Have you ever tried the Bread of life?" Many a carpenter was asked, "Have you ever tried to build a house on sand?"

He preached in all the principal cities of England, Scotland and Ireland. And although invited to the United States on several occasions, he was never able to visit this country.

HOW GREAT WAS HIS HEART: for preachers, so the Pastors' College was founded; for orphans, so the orphans' houses came to be; for people around the world, so his literature poured forth in an almost immeasurable volume. He was a national voice; so every national issue affecting morals, religion or the poor had his interpretation, his counsel.

Oh, but his passion for souls! You can see it in every sermon.

Spurgeon published thousands of poems, tracts, sermons and songs.

HIS MESSAGE TO LOST SINNERS WILL LIVE AS LONG AS THE GOSPEL IS PREACHED.

XII.

The Personality of the Holy Ghost

CHARLES H. SPURGEON

"And I will pray the Father, and he shall give you another Comforter, that he may abide with you for ever; Even the Spirit of truth; whom the world cannot receive, because it seeth him not, neither knoweth him: but ye know him; for he dwelleth with you, and shall be in you."— John 14:16,17.

You will be surprised to hear me announce that I do not intend this morning to say anything about the Holy Spirit as the Comforter. I propose to reserve that for another discourse. In this discourse I shall endeavor to explain and enforce certain other doctrines which I believe are plainly taught in this text and which I hope God the Holy Ghost may make profitable to our souls.

John Newton once said that there were some books which he could not read—they were good and sound enough, but "They are books of halfpence; you have to take so much in quantity before you have any value. There are other books of silver and others of gold; but I have one book that is a book of banknotes; and every leaf is a banknote of immense value."

So I found with this text, that I had a banknote of so large a sum that I could not tell it out all this morning. I should have to keep you several hours before I could unfold to you the whole value of this precious promise, one of the last which Christ gave to His people.

I invite your attention to this passage because we shall find in it some instruction on four points: first, concerning the true and proper personality of the Holy Ghost; second, concerning the united agency of the glorious Three Persons in the work of our salvation; third, we shall find something to establish the doctrine of the indwelling of the Holy Ghost in the souls of all believers; and, fourth, we shall find out the reason why the carnal mind rejects the Holy Ghost.

I. THE PERSONALITY OF THE HOLY SPIRIT

First, we shall have some little instruction concerning the proper *personality of the Holy Spirit.* We are so much accustomed to talk about the influence of the Holy Ghost and His sacred operations and graces, that we are apt to forget that the Holy Spirit is truly and actually a Person—that He is a subsistence—an existence; or, as we Trinitarians usually say, one Person in the essence of the Godhead.

I am afraid that, though we do not know it, we have acquired the habit of regarding the Holy Ghost as an emanation flowing from the Father and the Son, but not as being actually a Person Himself. I know it is not easy to carry about in our mind the idea of the Holy Spirit as a Person.

I can think of the Father as a Person, because His acts are such as I can understand. I see Him hang the world in ether; I behold Him swaddling a newborn sea in bands of darkness. I know it is He who formed the drops of hail, who leadeth forth the stars by their hosts and calleth them by their names. I can conceive of Him as a Person because I behold His operations. I can realize Jesus, the Son of Man, as a real Person because He is bone of my bone and flesh of my flesh.

It takes no great stretch of my imagination to picture the Babe in Bethlehem, or behold the "man of sorrows and acquainted with grief," as He was persecuted in Pilate's hall or nailed to the accursed tree for our sins. Nor do I find it difficult at times to realize the Person of my Jesus sitting on His throne in Heaven; or girt with clouds and wearing the diadem of all creation, calling the earth to judgment and summoning us to hear our final sentence.

But, when I come to deal with the Holy Ghost, His operations are so mysterious, His doings so secret, His acts so removed from everything that is of sense and of the body, I cannot so easily get the idea of His being a Person. But a Person He is.

God the Holy Ghost is not an influence, an emanation, a stream of something flowing from the Father: He is as much an actual Person as either God the Son or God the Father.

I shall attempt this morning to establish the doctrine and to show you the truth of it—that God the Holy Spirit is actually a Person.

The first proof we shall gather from the pool of holy baptism. Let me take you down, as I have taken others, into the pool where believers put on the name of the Lord Jesus; and you shall hear me pronounce the solemn words, "I baptize thee in the name"—mark, "in the name," not names—"of the Father, and of the Son, and of the Holy Ghost."

Everyone who is baptized according to the true form laid down in Scripture must be a Trinitarian; otherwise his baptism is a farce and a lie, and he himself is found a deceiver and a hypocrite before God. As the Father is mentioned, and as the Son is mentioned, so is the Holy Ghost; and the whole is summed up as being a Trinity in unity, by its being said, not the names, but the "name," the glorious name, the Jehovah name, "of the Father, and of the Son, and of the Holy Ghost."

Let me remind you that the same thing occurs each time you are dismissed from this house of prayer. In pronouncing the solemn closing benediction, we invoke on your behalf the love of Jesus Christ, the grace of the Father, and the fellowship of the Holy Spirit. Thus, according to the apostolic manner, we make a manifest distinction among the Persons, showing that we believe the Father to be a Person, the Son to be a Person, and the Holy Ghost to be a Person. Were there no other proofs in Scripture, these would be sufficient for every sensible man. He would see that, if the Holy Spirit were a mere influence, He would not be mentioned in conjunction with two, whom we all confess to be actual and proper Persons.

A second argument arises from the fact that the Holy Ghost has actually made different appearances on earth. The Great Spirit has manifested Himself to man; He has put on a form, so that, whilst He has not been beheld by mortal men, He has been so veiled in an appearance that He was seen, so far as that appearance was concerned, by the eyes of all beholders.

See you Jesus Christ our Saviour? There is the river Jordan, with its shelving banks and its willows weeping at its side. Jesus Christ, the Son of God, descends into the stream, and the holy Baptist John plunges Him into the waves. The doors of Heaven are opened; a miraculous appearance presents itself; a bright light shineth from the sky, brighter than the sun in all its grandeur, and down in a flood of glory descends something which you recognize to be a dove. It rests on Jesus—it sits upon His sacred head, and as the old painters put a halo round the brow of Jesus, so did the Holy Ghost shed a resplendence around the face of Him who came to fulfill all righteousness, and therefore com-menced with the ordinance of baptism.

The Holy Ghost was seen as a dove, to mark His purity and His gentleness; and He came down like a dove *from Heaven* to show that it is from Heaven alone that He descendeth.

Nor is this the only time when the Holy Ghost has been manifest in a visible shape. You see that company of disciples gathered together in an upper room waiting for some promised blessing. By and by it shall come.

Hark! there is a sound as of a rushing, mighty wind; it fills all the house where they are sitting and, astonished, they look around them, wonder-ing what will come next. Soon a bright light appears, shining upon the heads of each; cloven tongues of fire sat upon them. What were these marvelous appearances of wind and flame but a display of the Holy Ghost in His proper Person?

I say, the fact of an appearance manifests that He must be a Person. An influence could not appear—an attribute could not appear. We can-not see attributes—we cannot behold influences. The Holy Ghost must, then, have been a Person, since He was beheld by mortal eyes and came under the cognizance of mortal sense.

Another proof is from the fact that the personal qualities are in Scrip-ture ascribed to the Holy Ghost. First, let me read to you a text in which the Holy Ghost is spoken of as having understanding.

In the first epistle to the Corinthians, chapter 2, you will read,

"But as it is written, Eye hath not seen, nor ear heard, neither have entered into the heart of man, the things which God hath prepared for them that love him. But God hath revealed them unto us by his Spirit: for the Spirit searcheth all things, yea, the deep things of God. For what man knoweth the things of a man, save the spirit of man which is in him? even so the things of God knoweth no man, but the Spirit of God."

Here you see an understanding—a power of knowledge is ascribed to the Holy Ghost. Now, if there be any persons here whose minds are of so preposterous a complexion that they would ascribe one at-tribute to another and would speak of a mere influence having under-standing, then I give up all the argument. But I believe every rational man will admit that when anything is spoken of as having an under-standing, it must be an existence—it must, in fact, be a person.

In chapter 12, verse 11 of the same epistle, you will find a *will* ascribed to the Holy Spirit: "But all these worketh that one and the selfsame Spirit, dividing to every man severally as he will." So it is plain that the Spirit has a will. He does not come from God simply at God's will; but He has a will of His own, which is always in keeping with the will of the infinite Jehovah, but is, nevertheless, distinct and separate. Therefore, I say He is a Person.

In another text, *power* is ascribed to the Holy Ghost, and power is a thing which can only be ascribed to an existence. In Romans 15:13 it is written, "Now the God of hope fill you with all joy and peace in believing, that ye may abound in hope, through the power of the Holy Ghost."

I need not insist upon it, because it is self-evident that wherever you find understanding, will, and power, you must also find an existence. It cannot be a mere attribute; it cannot be a metaphor; it cannot be a personified influence, but it must be a person.

But I have a proof, which, perhaps, will be more telling upon you than any other. Acts and deeds are ascribed to the Holy Ghost; therefore, He must be a Person.

You read in the first chapter of the book of Genesis that the Spirit brooded over the surface of the earth when it was as yet all disorder and confusion. This world was once a mass of chaotic matter. There was no order. It was like the valley of darkness and the shadow of death. God the Holy Ghost spread His wings over it; He sowed the seeds of life in it. He impregnated the earth so that it became capable of life.

Now, it must have been a Person who brought order out of confusion; it must have been an existence who hovered over this world and made it what it now is.

But do we not read in Scripture something more of the Holy Ghost? Yes. We are told that "Holy men of old spake as they were moved by the Holy Ghost."

When Moses penned the Pentateuch, the Holy Ghost moved his hand.

When David wrote the Psalms, and discoursed sweet music on his harp, it was the Holy Spirit that gave his fingers their seraphic motion.

When Solomon dropped from his lips the words of the proverbs of wisdom or when he hymned the Canticles of love, it was the Holy Ghost who gave him words of knowledge and hymns of rapture.

Ah! and what fire was that which touched the lips of the eloquent Isaiah?

What hand was that which came upon Daniel?

What might was that which made Jeremiah so plaintive in his grief?

Or what was that which winged Ezekiel and made him, like an eagle, soar into mysteries aloft and see the mighty Unknown beyond our reach?

Who was it that made Amos, the herdsman, a prophet?

Who taught the rugged Haggai to pronounce his thundering sentences?

Who showed Habakkuk the horses of Jehovah marching through the waters?

Or who kindled the burning eloquence of Nahum?

Who caused Malachi to close up the book with the muttering of the word *curse*?

Who was it in each of these save the Holy Ghost? And must it not have been a Person who spake in and through the ancient witnesses? We must believe it. We cannot avoid believing it when we read that "Holy men of old spake as they were moved by the Holy Ghost."

And when has the Holy Ghost ceased to have an influence upon men? We find that still He deals with His ministers and with all His saints.

Turn to the Acts and you will find the Holy Ghost said, "Separate me Paul and Barnabas for the work." I never heard of an attribute saying such a thing.

The Holy Spirit said to Peter, 'Go to the centurion, and what I have cleansed, that call not thou common.'

The Holy Ghost caught away Philip after he had baptized the eunuch and carried him away to another place.

And the Holy Ghost said to Paul, "Thou shalt not go into that city, but shalt turn into another."

And we know that the Holy Ghost was lied unto by Ananias and Sapphira when it was said, "Thou hast not lied unto man, but unto God."

Again, that power which we feel every day, who are called to preach—that wondrous spell which makes our lips so potent—that power which gives us thoughts which are like birds from a far-off region, not the natives of our soul—that influence which I sometimes strangely feel, which, if it does not give me poetry and eloquence, gives me a might I never felt before and lifts me above my fellowman—that majesty with which He clothes His ministers, till in the midst of the battle they cry, of Job, and move themselves like leviathans in the water—that power which gives us might over men and causes them to sit and listen as if their ears were chained, as if they were entranced by the power of some magician's wand—that power must come from a Person; it must come from the Holy Ghost.

But is it not said in Scripture, and do we not feel it, dear brethren, that it is the Holy Ghost who regenerates the soul? It is the Holy Ghost who quickens us. "You hath he quickened who were dead in trespasses and sins." It is the Holy Spirit who imparts the first germ of life, convincing us of sin, of righteousness, and of judgment to come. And is it not the Holy Spirit who, after that flame is kindled, still fans it with the breath of His mouth and keeps it alive? Its author is its preserver.

Oh, can it be said that it is the Holy Ghost who strives in men's souls, that it is the Holy Ghost who brings them to the foot of Sinai, then guides them into the sweet place that is called Calvary—can it be said that He does all these things, yet is not a person? It may be said, but it must be said by fools; for He never can be a wise man who can consider that these things can be done by any other than a glorious Person—a divine existence.

Allow me to give you one more proof, and I shall have done. Certain feelings are ascribed to the Holy Ghost which can only be understood upon the supposition that He is actually a Person.

In the 4th chapter of Ephesians, verse 30, it is said that the Holy Ghost can be grieved: "Grieve not the holy Spirit of God, whereby ye are sealed unto the day of redemption."

In Isaiah, chapter 63, verse 10, it is said that the Holy Ghost can be vexed: "But they rebelled, and vexed his holy Spirit: therefore he was turned to be their enemy, and he fought against them."

In Acts, chapter 7, verse 51, you read that the Holy Ghost can be resisted: "Ye stiffnecked and uncircumcised in heart and ears, ye do always resist the Holy Ghost; as your fathers did, so do ye."

And in the 5th chapter, verse 9, of the same book, you will find that the Holy Ghost may be tempted. We are there informed that Peter said to Ananias and Sapphira, "How is it that ye have agreed together to tempt the Spirit of the Lord?"

Now, these things could not be emotions which might be ascribed to a quality or an emanation; they must be understood to relate to a person. An influence could not be grieved; it must be a person who can be grieved, vexed, or resisted.

And now, dear brethren, I think I have fully established the point of the personality of the Holy Ghost; allow me now, most earnestly, to impress upon you the absolute necessity of being sound upon the doctrine of the Trinity.

I knew a man, a good minister of Jesus Christ he is now, and I believe he was before he turned his eyes to heresy—he began to doubt the glorious divinity of our blessed Lord, and for years did he preach the heterodox doctrine, until one day he happened to hear a very eccentric old minister preaching from the text,

"But there the glorious Lord will be unto us a place of broad rivers and streams; wherein shall go no galley with oars, neither shall gallant ship pass thereby. . . . Thy tacklings are loosed; they could not well strengthen their mast, they could not spread the sail."

"Now," said the old minister, "you give up the Trinity, and your tacklings are loosed, and you cannot strengthen your masts. Once give up the doctrine of three Persons, and your tacklings are all gone; your mast, which ought to be a support to your vessel, is a rickety one and shakes."

A Gospel without the Trinity! It is a pyramid built upon its apex. A Gospel without the Trinity! It is a rope of sand that cannot hold together. A Gospel without the Trinity! Then, indeed, Satan can overturn it. But give me a Gospel with the Trinity, and the might of Hell cannot prevail against it. No man can any more overthrow it than a bubble could split a rock or a feather break in halves a mountain. Get the thought of the three Persons, and you have the marrow of all divinity.

Only know the Father and know the Son and know the Holy Ghost to be one. Then all things will appear clear. This is the golden key to the secrets of nature; this is the silken clue of the labyrinths of mystery. And he who understands this will soon understand as much as mortals e'er can know.

II. THE UNITED AGENCY OF THE GLORIOUS THREE PERSONS IN THE WORK OF OUR SALVATION

Now for our second point—the *united agency* of the three Persons in the work of our salvation. Look at the text, and you will find all the three Persons mentioned. "I"—that is the Son—"will pray the Father, and he shall give you another Comforter." There are the three Persons mentioned, all of them doing something for our salvation. "I will pray," says the Son; "I will send," says the Father; "I will comfort," says the Holy Ghost.

Now let us for a few moments discourse upon this wondrous theme—the unity of the three Persons with regard to the great purpose of salvation.

When God first made man, He said, "Let *us* make man"—not let *me* but, "Let us make man in our own image." The covenant Elohim said to each other, "Let us unitedly become the creator of man." So, when in ages far gone by, in eternity, they said, "Let us save man," it was not the Father who said, "Let *Me* save man," but the three Persons conjointly said, with one consent, "Let *us* save man."

It is to me a source of sweet comfort to think that it is not one Person of the Trinity engaged for my salvation; it is not simply one Person of the Godhead vowing that He will redeem me; but it is a glorious trio of Godlike ones, and the three declaring unitedly, "*We* will save man."

Now, observe here that each Person is spoken of as performing a separate office. "I will pray," says the Son—that is intercession. "I will send," says the Father—that is donation. "I will comfort," says the Holy Spirit—that is supernatural influence.

Oh, if it were possible for us to see the three Persons of the Godhead, we should behold one of them standing before the throne with outstretched hands, crying day and night, "O Lord, how long?" We should see one girt with Urim and Thummim, precious stones, on which are written the twelve names of the tribes of Israel. We should behold Him crying unto His Father, "Forget not Thy promises, forget not Thy covenant." We should hear Him make mention of our sorrows and tell forth our griefs on our behalf, for He is our intercessor. And could we behold the Father, we should not see Him a listless and idle spectator of the intercession of the Son, but we should see Him with attentive ear listening to every word of Jesus and granting every petition.

Where is the Holy Spirit all the while? Is He lying idle? Oh, no. He is floating over the earth; and when He sees a weary soul, He says, "Come to Jesus; He will give you rest." When He beholds an eye filled with tears, He wipes them away and bids the mourner look for comfort to the cross. When He sees the tempest-tossed believer, He takes the helm of his soul and speaks the word of consolation. He helpeth the broken in heart and bindeth up their wounds; and, ever on His mission of mercy, He flies around the world, being everywhere present.

Behold, how the three Persons work together! Do not then say, "I am grateful to the Son"—so you ought to be, but God the Son no more saves you than God the Father. Do not imagine that God the Father is a great tyrant and that God the Son had to die to make Him merciful. It was not to make the Father's love flow towards His people. Oh, no. One loves as much as the Other. The Three are cojoined in the great purpose of rescuing the unsaved from damnation.

But you must notice another thing in my text, which will show the blessed unity of the Three—the one Person promises to the Other. The Son says, "I will pray the Father. . . ." "Very well," the disciples may have said, "we can trust You for that." "And he will send you. . . ." You see, here is the Son signing a bond on behalf of the Father—"He will send you another Comforter." There is a bond on behalf of the Holy Spirit, too—"And he will abide with you for ever."

One Person speaks for the Other. But how could They, if there were any disagreement between them? If One wished to save and the Other not, They could not promise on Another's behalf. But whatever the Son says, the Father listens to; whatever the Father promises, the Holy Ghost works; and whatever the Holy Ghost injects into the soul, that God the Father fulfills. So, the Three together mutually promise on one Another's behalf. There is a bond with three names appended— Father, Son and Holy Ghost. By three immutable things, as well as by two, the Christian is secured beyond the reach of death and Hell. A Trinity of securities, because there is a Trinity of God.

III. THE INDWELLING OF THE HOLY GHOST
IN BELIEVERS

Our third point is, the *indwelling* of the Holy Ghost in believers. Now, beloved, these first two things have been matters of pure doctrine; this is the subject of experience. The indwelling of the Holy Ghost is a subject so profound and so having to do with the inner man that no soul will be able truly and really to comprehend what I say, unless it has been taught of God.

I have heard of an old minister who told a fellow of one of the Cambridge colleges that he understood a language that *he* never learned in all his life. "I have not," he said, "even a smattering of Greek, and I know no Latin, but thank God, I can talk the language of Canaan, and that is more than you can."

So, beloved, I shall now have to talk a little of the language of Canaan. If you cannot comprehend me, I am much afraid it is because you are not of Israelitish extraction; you are not a child of God nor an inheritor of the kingdom of Heaven.

We are told in the text that Jesus would send the Comforter who would abide in the saints forever; who would dwell with them and be in them.

Old Ignatius the martyr used to call himself Theophorus, or the God-bearer "because," said he, "I bear about with me the Holy Ghost." Truly every Christian is a God-bearer. 'Know ye not that ye are the temples of the Holy Ghost? for he dwelleth in you.'

That man is no Christian who is not the subject of the indwelling of the Holy Spirit. He may talk well; he may understand theology. He will be the child of nature finely dressed but not the living child. He may be a man of so profound an intellect, so gigantic a soul, so comprehensive a mind, and so lofty an imagination that he may dive into all the secrets of nature. He may know the path which the eagle's eye hath not seen and go into depths where the ken of mortals reacheth not. But he shall not be a Christian with all his knowledge; he shall not be a son of God with all his researches, unless he understands what it is to have the Holy Ghost dwelling and abiding in him; yea, and that forever.

Some people call this fanaticism and say, "You are a Quaker; why not follow George Fox?" Well, we would not mind that much; we would follow anyone who followed the Holy Ghost. Even he, with all his eccentricities, I doubt not, was, in many cases, actually inspired by the Holy Spirit. And whenever I find a man in whom there rests the Spirit of God, the Spirit within me leaps to hear the Spirit within him, and we feel that we are one. The Spirit of God in one Christian soul recognizes the Spirit in another.

I recollect talking with a good man, as I believe he was, who was insisting that it was impossible for us to know whether we had the Holy Spirit within us or not. I should like him to be here this morning because I would read this verse to him: "But ye know him, for he dwelleth with you, and shall be in you."

Ah! you think you cannot tell whether you have the Holy Spirit or not? Can I tell whether I am alive or not? If I were touched by electricity, could I tell whether I was or not? The shock would be strong enough to make me know where I stood. So, if I have God within me—if I have Deity tabernacling in my breast—if I have God the Holy Ghost resting in my heart and making a temple of my body, do you think I shall know it? Call it fanaticism if you will, but I trust that there are some of us who know what it is to be always, or generally, under the influence of the Holy Spirit—always in one sense, generally in another.

When we have difficulties, we ask the direction of the Holy Ghost. When we do not understand a portion of Holy Scripture, we ask God the Holy Ghost to shine upon us. When we are depressed, the Holy Ghost comforts us. You cannot tell what the wondrous power of the indwelling of the Holy Ghost is; how it pulls back the hand of the saint when he would touch the forbidden thing; how it prompts him to make a covenant with his eyes; how it binds his feet, lest they should fall in a slippery way; how it restrains his heart and keeps him from temptation. O ye, who know nothing of the indwelling of the Holy Ghost, despise it not.

But before closing this point, there is one little word that pleases me very much—*forever*. You know I should not miss that. You were certain I could not let it go without observation. "Abide with you *for ever*."

I wish I could get an Arminian here to finish my sermon. I fancy I see him taking that word *forever*. He would say, "for—forever"; he would have to stammer and stutter, for he could never get it out all at once. He might stand and pull it about, and at last he would have to say, "The translation is wrong." Then I suppose the poor man would have to prove that the original was wrong, too.

Ah! but blessed be God we can read it—'He shall abide with you forever.' Once give me the Holy Ghost, and I shall never lose Him till "for ever" has run out, till eternity has spun its everlasting rounds.

IV. THE REASON THE CARNAL MIND REJECTS THE HOLY GHOST

The unregenerate world of sinners despises the Holy Ghost, "because it seeth him not." Yes, I believe this is the great secret why many laugh at the idea of the existence of the Holy Ghost—because they see Him not. Tell the worldling, "I have the Holy Ghost within me," and he will say, "I cannot see it." He wants it to be something tangible—a thing he can recognize with his senses.

Have you ever heard the argument used by a good old Christian against an infidel doctor? The doctor said there was no soul and asked, "Did you ever see a soul?"

"No," said the Christian.

"Did you *ever* hear a soul?"

"No."

"Did you *ever* smell a soul?"

"No."

"Did you *ever* taste a soul?"

"No."

"Did you *ever* feel a soul?"

"Yes," said the man—"I feel I have one within me."

"Well," said the doctor, "there are four senses against one; you have only one on your side."

"Very well," said the Christian. "Did you *ever* see a pain?"

"No."

"Did you *ever* hear a pain?"

"No."

"Did you *ever* smell a pain?"

"No."

"Did you *ever* taste a pain?"

"No."

"Did you *ever* feel a pain?"

"Yes."

"And that is quite enough, I suppose, to prove there is a pain?"

"Yes."

So the worldling says there is no Holy Ghost because he cannot see Him. Well, but we feel Him. You say that is fanaticism and that you never felt Him.

Suppose you tell me that honey is bitter and I reply, "No, I am sure you cannot have tasted it; taste it and try."

So with the Holy Ghost. If you felt His influence, you would no longer say there is no Holy Spirit because you cannot see Him.

Are there not many things even in nature which we cannot see?

Did you *ever* see the wind? No; but ye know there is wind when ye behold the hurricane tossing the waves about and rending down the habitations of men; or when, in the soft evening zephyr, it kisses the flowers and maketh dewdrops hang in pearly coronets around the rose.

Did ye *ever* see electricity? No; but ye know there is such a thing, for it travels along the wires for thousands of miles and carries our messages. Though you cannot see the thing itself, you know there is such a thing.

So you must believe there is a Holy Ghost working in us, both to will and to do, even though it is beyond our senses.

But the last reason why worldly men laugh at the doctrine of the Holy Spirit is because they do not know it. If they knew it by heartfelt experience, if they recognized its agency in the soul, if they had ever been touched by it, if they had been made to tremble under a sense of sin, if they had had their hearts melted, they would never have doubted the existence of the Holy Ghost.

And now, beloved, it says, "He dwelleth with you, and shall be in you." We will close up with that sweet recollection—the Holy Ghost dwells in all believers and shall be with them.

One word of comment and advice to the saints of God and to sinners, and I have done. Saints of the Lord, ye have this morning heard that God the Holy Ghost is a Person; ye have had it proved to your souls. What follows from this? Why, it followeth how earnest ye should be in prayer *to* the Holy Spirit, as well as *for* the Holy Spirit. Let me say that this is an inference that you should lift up your prayers to the Holy Ghost, that you should cry earnestly unto Him, for He is able to do exceeding abundantly above all you can speak or think.

See this mass of people. What is to convert it? See this crowd. Who is to make my influence permeate through the mass? You know this place now has a mighty influence; and, God blessing us, it will have an influence not only upon this city but upon England at large; for we now employ the press as well as the pulpit. And certainly before the close of the year, more than two hundred thousand of my productions will be scattered through the land—words uttered by my lips or written by my pen.

But how can this influence be rendered for good? How shall God's glory be promoted by it? Only by incessant prayer for the Holy Spirit, by constantly calling down the influence of the Holy Ghost upon us. We want Him to rest upon every page printed and upon every word uttered. Let us then be doubly earnest in pleading with the Holy Ghost that He would come and own our labors, that the whole church at large may be revived thereby—not ourselves only, but the whole world share in the benefit.

Then, to the ungodly, I have this one closing word to say. Ever be careful how you speak of the Holy Ghost. If thou hast despised the Holy Spirit, if thou hast laughed at His revelations and scorned what

Christians call His influence, I beseech thee, stop! This morning seriously deliberate. Let fear stop you. Sit down. Do not drive on so rashly as you have done, Jehu! O slacken your reins! Thou who art such a profligate in sin—thou who hast uttered such hard words against the Trinity, stop! Ah! it makes us all stop. Let us think of this; and let us not at any time trifle either with the words or the acts of God the Holy Spirit.

(From *Spurgeon's Sermons*, Vol. I)

CURTIS HUTSON
1934-

ABOUT THE MAN:

In 1961 a mail carrier and pastor of a very small church attended a Sword of the Lord Conference, got on fire, gave up his route and set out to build a great soul-winning work for God. Forrest Hills Baptist Church of Decatur, Georgia, grew from 40 people into a membership of 7,900. The last four years of his pastorate there, the Sunday school was recognized as the largest one in Georgia.

After pastoring for 21 years, Dr. Hutson—the great soul winner that he is—became so burdened for the whole nation that he entered full-time evangelism, holding great citywide-areawide-cooperative revivals in some of America's greatest churches. As many as 625 precious souls have trusted Christ in a single service. In one eight-day meeting, 1,502 salvation decisions were recorded.

As an evangelist, he is in great demand.

At the request of Dr. John R. Rice, Dr. Hutson became Associate Editor of THE SWORD OF THE LORD in 1978, serving in that capacity until the death of Dr. Rice before becoming Editor, President of Sword of the Lord Foundation, and Director of Sword of the Lord Conferences.

All these ministries are literally changing the lives of thousands of preachers and laymen alike, as well as winning many more thousands to Christ.

Dr. Hutson is the author of many fine books and booklets.

XIII.

The Fullness of the Spirit

CURTIS HUTSON

(Preached at Nationwide Sword Conference in Atlanta Civic Center, Atlanta, Georgia)

I call attention to two verses:

"And be not drunk with wine, wherein is excess; but be filled with the Spirit."—Eph. 5:18.

"Not by might, nor by power, but by my spirit, saith the Lord."— Zech. 4:6.

When God called me to preach, I was only twenty years old. I had never heard a sermon on the fullness of the Holy Spirit. I had great ambitions and great dreams. Since some thought that to be ambitious or to dream too big was sinful, I didn't share them with too many.

But I did dream. The night I told a friend that God had called me to preach, I cried and we talked until 2:30 in the morning.

The group I was then with didn't believe in paying a preacher. They thought he should preach on the weekends and do something else during the week for his livelihood. But I told my friend then, "Someday I will preach full-time." I dreamed big!

I saw that day come. In God's providence a number of wonderful things have happened in my life. One was finding THE SWORD OF THE LORD in my mail truck and attending that Sword Conference in 1961 at Antioch Baptist Church in Atlanta. In that conference I noticed something was different about those speakers.

Dr. John R. Rice, Dr. Jack Hyles and Dr. Tom Malone were on the program. I was younger then, and curious. I listened. What I heard did something to my heart. I heard preaching that made sense.

Dr. Rice preached on "How to Get Your Prayers Answered." I

watched him. I knew there was something different about him. He was not the average run-of-the-mill preacher.

I remember walking by the book table and looking. I looked at all the books. Dr. Rice had then written nearly fifty hardback books. As I glanced them over, I thought, *I have never read that many books.* When I heard him preach, I was moved by him. One thing came through to me as he preached—soul winning is the most important thing in the world! And you can't do it without being filled with the Holy Spirit.

I heard Dr. Jack Hyles preach. I wanted to see him. I wanted to meet him. He came in late and was in the men's room in the basement shaving when I first saw him. I didn't know who he was then. When he got up to preach a few minutes later, I said to myself, *That is the man I saw in the men's room shaving!*

His sermon was, "What is man, that thou art mindful of him?" He told of an old man who wanted to talk with him in his church. He almost turned him away, but one of the secretaries insisted that he see him.

My heart burned and hungered. I thought, *I don't love people. I preach on Sundays—kind of a part-time activity. I enjoy the occasional pat on the back if I happen to say something worthy of a pat. But I don't love people.*

I had never led a soul to Christ, though I had been pastoring for six years.

I looked at Dr. Hyles. I later memorized his sermon and went back and preached it to my small congregation. I thought, *If I preach that sermon, "What is man, that thou art mindful of him?" to my congregation, it will have the same effect on them that it had on me.*

I preached it. Nobody moved. Nobody was affected. I wondered why they didn't respond. I had responded. I wondered why they were not hurting inside like I was hurting when I heard it. It was the same sermon; the same verses.

I heard Dr. Tom Malone speak on Deacons from Acts 6. When he finished giving the requirements for deacons, I left the church shaking my head and asking myself, *Have I ever seen a deacon? Would I know a deacon if I met one?*

Driving home from the meeting I thought, *I don't even meet the qualifications for being a deacon, let alone a preacher.*

For some time I considered resigning my small church and joining a good soul-winning church. I heard about the Highland Park Baptist

Church in Chattanooga, Tennessee, baptizing over 1,000 a year for a number of years. I seriously considered commuting to Chattanooga every weekend to be in a good church and learn what it was all about. But God wouldn't let me.

I thought, *What is different about those men? There are thousands of preachers in America! What is different about them?*

Last night Dr. Lee Roberson gave us seven mountain peaks in his life. He mentioned conversion, soul winning, the second coming, etc. I kept waiting, thinking, *He is going to say it.* He got down to the sixth thing and said, "I don't know when I first got hold of it, but the Spirit-filled life. . . ." The Spirit-filled life!

One thing all great preachers have in common—they are Spirit-filled. They may not all agree on everything; they might not all preach alike; their delivery may be different; but they are all filled with the Spirit.

One day I went to a bookstore. I roamed through, checking the books on the shelves. I came across a dark blue book with gold letters on the front entitled, *Deeper Experiences of Famous Christians*, by J. Gilchrist Lawson. I thumbed through the Table of Contents to see what it was about. Many of the names I did not know. I recognized the name of D. L. Moody. I recognized the name Billy Sunday. I didn't know A. J. Gordon, Savonarola, and many of the others.

Something seemed to say to me, *You ought to read the book.* So I purchased it, rushed out of the building, hurried home and read it. It was what the title implied—deeper experiences of famous Christians.

As I read the experiences of Billy Bray, the shouting Cornish miner, I wished that Billy Bray were alive and I could sit on the front porch and talk with him.

Billy shouted everywhere he went. Billy said, "I can't help praising God. As I go along the street I lift up one foot, and it seems to say, 'Glory!' I lift up the other, and it seems to say, 'Amen!' So they keep on like that all the while I am walking."

When the doctor told him that he was going to die, Billy said, "Glory! glory be to God! I shall soon be in Heaven!" He then added, in his own peculiar way, "When I get up there, shall I give them your compliments, Doctor, and tell them you will be coming, too?" This made a deep impression on the doctor.

Some little time before dying, he said: "What! me fear death! me lost! Why, my Saviour conquered death. If I were to go down to Hell I would shout Glory! Glory! to my blessed Jesus until I made the bottomless pit ring again, and the miserable old Satan would say, 'Billy, Billy, this is no place for thee: get thee back!' Then up to Heaven I should go, shouting Glory! Glory! Praise the Lord!"

Billy's dying word was "GLORY!"

My heart hungered for something I didn't have. I said, "Lord, where are the Billy Brays in Atlanta, Georgia? Where are the Billy Brays of my day? I don't even know them."

Then I read about Christmas Evans, the one-eyed Christian who made a thirteen-point covenant with God. In one point he said, "Oh, prosper me as Thou didst prosper Bunyan, Vassar, Powell, Howel Harris, Rowlands and Whitefield. The impediments in the way of my prosperity remove."

I said to myself, *I would like to talk with this gentleman. Here is a man with ambition, a man who is unafraid to say, 'Prosper my ministry and make something out of me.' Most men I talk with about that don't understand me. I would like to talk with Christmas Evans.*

I kept reading more and more. I read where Savonarola sat on his platform in a trance for five hours. You could hear a pin drop for five solid hours.

I thought, *I have never preached in my life. I am ashamed to even call myself a preacher.*

I read where D. L. Moody told of two ladies coming to his meetings and saying, "Mr. Moody, we are praying for you, because you need the power of the Spirit," and of Mr. Moody saying, "I need the power? Why, I thought I had power. I had the largest congregation in Chicago, and many conversions."

But one day walking down Wall Street in New York, Moody said, "The power of God came on me in such a fashion that I ran to borrow the room of a friend. I closed the door and in the room I prayed that God would stay His power, lest I die."

The difference between preachers is not dress, mannerisms, voice, delivery, length of sermon or current jokes. The difference between great preachers and mediocre preachers is one thing—being Spirit-filled.

Ephesians 3:20 doesn't say, "Unto him that is able to do exceeding abundantly above all that we ask or think, according to personality or ability or education or according to who promotes you or what fellowship you are out of," but ". . . according to the power that worketh in us."

A tongue-tied man like Uncle Buddy Robinson can have it. An eloquent man like Charles Spurgeon can have it. A demonstrative man like Billy Bray can have it. A simple man like D. L. Moody can have it. A deep man like John R. Rice can have it. When it comes to being filled with the Holy Spirit, everybody can have it.

For years I never heard a sermon on the subject. I was afraid to talk about it. I was so afraid I would get out on a limb that I never bothered to climb the tree. But by and by I got to the place where I had to have it.

The Comparison

Three times in the Bible a drunk man is compared to a Spirit-filled man. That is not by accident; that is by design.

Ephesians 5:18, my text, reads, "Be not drunk with wine . . . but be filled with the Spirit." A drunk man; a Spirit-filled man.

In Luke 1:15 it is said of John the Baptist, "For he shall be great in the sight of the Lord, and shall drink neither wine nor strong drink: and he shall be filled with the Holy Ghost."

In Acts 2, on the day of Pentecost, Peter said in verses 15 to 17: "For these are not drunken, as ye suppose, seeing it is but the third hour of the day. But this is that which was spoken by the prophet Joel; And it shall come to pass in the last days, saith God, I will pour out of my Spirit upon all flesh."

Why does the Bible compare the drunk man to a Spirit-filled man? A drunk man is controlled by another power. When a man is drunk, he is a different person. Spirit-filled men are also different.

You take a fellow who is shy, timid and backward and let that fellow get drunk; suddenly he is talking out loud, and the drunker he gets, the louder he talks. He gets so talkative you would think he had been vaccinated with a Victrola needle.

You take a shy, timid, backward Christian who is too timid to suck his thumb, get him filled with the Holy Spirit, and he will start talking out loud in front of crowds and not be embarrassed.

The fellow who would not sing in public gets drunk; suddenly he sings three or four hours and thinks everybody is enjoying it. I have never seen an unhappy drunk in my life. He may lose everything he has, but he is still happy. You can't discourage a drunk man. You may as well wait until he is sober. He is a different man when he is drunk.

The poor, inhibited creature who was afraid of his own shadow, when he gets drunk, becomes as bold as a lion.

An uncle of mine used to drink. He asked me to take a ride with him in his brown Pontiac. We went down Georgia 12 Highway, before there was an I-20. That speedometer went as far as it would go—I think it registered 85 or 90. It scared me to death! He was as drunk as Cooter Brown—whoever he is.

In Covington, Georgia, the State Patrol sounded the siren and pulled us over. It didn't bother my uncle a bit—he was drunk. He wasn't a bit nervous. He cussed a little.

The State Patrol said, "Let me see your license."

He gave the officer his license.

The officer said, "You were speeding."

"Yeah, I know it."

"You can pay me now or come to court."

"How much is it?"

"Ten dollars."

My uncle handed him a $20 bill. When the patrolman started to hand him $10 back, my uncle said, "Just keep it."

He said, "What do you mean, keep it?"

"I'm coming back through here in a few minutes, and I don't want you slowing me down."

Now he wouldn't have talked like that had he not been drunk. Had he been sober, he would have been scared to death.

The poor, inhibited creature who is afraid of his own shadow, when he is filled with drink becomes as bold as a lion and does things he would not otherwise do.

I used to work at a fire station in DeKalb County. One day a little drunk came in with a tablet and pencil and said, "What's your name?" I told him, and he wrote it down. He asked another fellow, "What's your name?" He told him, and he wrote it down. He asked another guy. He told him, and he wrote it down. He made a whole list of names.

Then he came to this big engine driver, about 6'5". He said, "Boy, what's your name?" That engine driver said, "My name's Glen So-and-So." He wrote it down. Then the engine driver said, "What do you want my name for?" The drunk never looked up but just kept writing and said, "I'm writin' down everybody's name on this paper that I'm going to whip. When I get my list up, I'm going to whip every one of 'em."

That big engine driver reached down, picked him up, shook him and said, "I tell you right now, you are not about to whip me!" He said, "Put me down. I'll just scratch your name off the list."

Had he been sober, he wouldn't have acted in this manner. When a man is drunk, he will attempt anything.

I read of one drunk who was up in a hotel room with a friend. Actually believing he could fly, he leaped out the window to fly around the block. Several days later he came to, arms all bandaged up, legs stretched out and in casts with weights on them, his face skinned and stitches everywhere.

His friend went to visit him. He said to his friend, "Why did you let me do that?" He said, "I thought you could fly." Both of them were drunk.

You get preachers drunk on the Holy Spirit, and one will say, "I'm going to build the biggest church in the world." Another one will say, "I think you can do it." He may wind up in the hospital with a broken leg, but he is more apt to fly than the fellow who doesn't try.

A drunk man is talkative.

Too many Christians are like arctic rivers. They are frozen at the mouth; afraid to say, "Boo!" to the Devil.

The way a drunk man talks you would think his father was an auctioneer and his mother was a woman!

I was in the St. Louis airport, and a drunk came in. (They are funny to me.) He had a paper bag under one arm and a red cap on his head that said "Caterpillar" across the top. He looked wild-eyed at me and said, "Did you come in here on a flying saucer?" To this nut I answered, "Yeah, I always fly on flying saucers. They are faster and more convenient." I figured that would shut him up. But he said, "Yeah, they fly good, but they sure do make you dizzy, don't they?"

I carried on the conversation with him. In a few minutes he looked into the mirror and when he saw that cap that said "Caterpillar," he said, "I'm a caterpillar! Yesterday I was a butterfly!"

That drunk guy had no inhibitions. If I could have told him later what he did, he would have been embarrassed, but at the moment he didn't care.

The Command

"And be not drunk with wine, wherein is excess; but be filled with the Spirit."

"Be filled with the Spirit." The same Bible, same book, same chapter, same verse, gives two commands. Let us take the first one. "Be not drunk with wine."

If I asked you all tonight, "How many think it is wrong to get drunk?" everybody here would answer, "It is wrong to get drunk." The command is, "Don't get drunk."

There is not a pastor here who would allow a single choir member to sing in the choir who came into the church drunk next Sunday morning.

There is not a preacher here tonight who would lay hands on a man's head to ordain him if you knew he was a drunkard.

There is not a pastor who would have a deacon if you knew that deacon got drunk. And you are right to feel that way.

But the same Bible that says, "Don't get drunk," says "... but be filled with the Spirit."

If I understand the Bible, then, it is just as wrong not to be filled with the Holy Spirit as it is to get drunk. Yet we seldom talk about the other command in that verse, but one is as important as the other. The verb is in the imperative mood: it is a command, "be filled."

There is no command in the Bible to be sealed with the Holy Spirit. There is no command in the Bible to be indwelt by the Holy Spirit. Those things are positional. The moment I was saved I was sealed: "And grieve not the holy Spirit of God, whereby ye are sealed unto the day of redemption" (Eph. 4:30). The moment I was saved, the Holy Spirit came into me as a person to take up His permanent abode. That happens automatically without any action on my part (I Cor. 6:19,20). Every believer has the Holy Spirit; every believer is sealed with the Holy Spirit. That is why there is no command to be sealed or indwelt.

But being filled with the Holy Spirit is not positional; it is a command—"... be filled with the Spirit." The responsibility of the fullness of the Holy Spirit lies with each individual Christian.

You come to my house, and my wife fixes a big meal. I say, "Sit down and be filled." If you leave without being filled, it is not my fault.

"... be filled with the Spirit" is a command. Notice to whom the command is given. Ephesians is a letter to the church at Ephesus. Notice in verse 1 to whom it is written: "... to the saints which are at Ephesus, and to the faithful in Christ Jesus." The command is to every individual Christian, not to just preachers.

Most people who experience the fullness of the Holy Spirit have been saved for a number of years before they are filled with the Holy Spirit. But there need not be a time lapse. The time lapse is brought about because of our ignorance concerning our responsibility to be filled with the Holy Spirit.

In my case I knew nothing about it. You don't have to wait five, ten or fifteen years to be filled with the Spirit.

The command is not only for the pastor and the deacon and evangelist, but it is addressed to every single Christian for all time and for every generation.

Let me tell you something. Most of what you think is trouble in your local congregation is only a symptom. Your members don't tithe. That is not the problem; that is a symptom. They don't win souls. That is not the problem; it is a symptom. Most of the trouble can be traced back to one thing: Christians are not Spirit-filled.

In I Corinthians 3:1 Paul said, "And I, brethren, could not speak unto you as unto spiritual, but as unto carnal, even as unto babes in Christ." He goes on to say there is envying and strife and division among them. Why? They were not spiritual. You don't have problems with Spirit-filled Christians.

The command is to every individual Christian.

The Conditions

I said you are not filled automatically. There are certain conditions. Since I don't have time to list them all, I will give you a few that stand out clear to me from the Scriptures.

The first condition for the fullness of the Holy Spirit is **thirsting.**

Ray Hart sang a moment ago a song based on a verse from Isaiah that says, "I will pour water on him who is thirsty."

John 7:37 says: "In the last day, that great day of the feast, Jesus stood and cried, saying, If any man thirst, let him come unto me, and drink. He that believeth on me, as the scripture hath said, out of his belly shall flow rivers of living water. (But this spake he of the Spirit, which they that believe on him should receive . . .)."

Thirsting. Thirsting. Thirsting. I doubt seriously if anyone in this building has ever been thirsty. You say, "I got thirsty today." No, you wanted water today. You see, the moment you want water, it is there in the faucet. You don't have to wait even five minutes to get it. But

you go without water for a day, two days, three days; go without water
until your lips swell three times their normal size and your tongue swells
and begins to crack and parch; go without water until you would give
your automobile and your house and everything you have in the bank
for one drop of water—then you are thirsty!

The prime reason many Christians do not have the fullness of the
Holy Spirit is that they just absolutely are not thirsty enough. If you can
take it or leave it, you will leave it. You have to get to the place where
you say, "I have to have it or die! I don't care what happens, I won't
give up!"

Pardon the personal reference, but I got to the place where I said,
"Lord, if it means speaking in tongues, I'll join the Pentecostals and
get out of the Baptist church. But I don't want to live without it. I've
got to have it!"

Uncle Buddy Robinson is one of my favorite characters. He was saved
in a Methodist meeting, got what he called the second blessing in a
Presbyterian meeting. Later he was thrown out of the Methodist Church
and died a Nazarene.

Uncle Buddy said:

> I went to hear this Methodist preacher preach, and he preached
> on Heaven till I wanted to go there. Then he preached on Hell till
> I thought I was going there. When he gave the invitation that night
> I couldn't read my name in boxcar letters, but when I got up from
> the altar I could read my title clear to mansions in the sky!

Then Uncle Buddy said:

> Awhile later this sanctified, second-blessing Presbyterian preacher
> came through town preaching on the second blessing. I went to hear
> him. When he preached, I wanted it so bad. I prayed, "O God, give
> it to me!" But the Lord didn't give it to me. Then I said, "O Lord,
> give it to me!"
>
> I threw away my deck of cards and my old pistol. I put my two
> mules and a bale of hay on the altar, and I still didn't have it. I put
> my Presbyterian mother and my drunken brother on the altar, and
> I still didn't have it. Then I prayed, "O God, give it to me!" And the
> Lord said, "Buddy, there is too much between you and Me and the
> altar." I said, "O God, if You will give it to me, I'll give every neighbor
> I've got a jug of molasses." And I can make the best molasses a man
> ever wallowed his biscuit in!

He wanted it. He never gave up till he got it. He called it the second blessing. I don't even believe in the second blessing, but I have an old recording of Uncle Buddy preaching on the second blessing and all through the sermon I have to keep working not to believe it!

Uncle Buddy said:

> This man in the Bible was blind, and the Lord touched him. And He said to him, "What do you see?" And the man said, "I see men walking like trees." He needed the second blessing. The Lord touched him the second time and said, "Now, what do you see?" And the man said, "I see all men clearly."

Uncle Buddy said:

> When I just had the first blessing, I saw the denominational bosses like great big old trees. But when I got the second blessing, I saw all men clearly.

I said, "Buddy, you are about to sell me on the second blessing! I can't call it what you call it, Bud, but I've got to get it!"

We argue over the right expression and die for a lack of the experience. Uncle Bud got it. He believed in complete sanctification with annihilation of the old sinful nature, which never happens, but I must say that he was closer to being sanctified than I am.

He went to New York City, and they showed him all the sites. When he got back to his room that night, as he prayed he said, "Dear Lord, I thank You for all the sites of New York City, but I thank You most of all that I didn't see anything I wanted."

When I went to New York, I saw something I wanted.

One day Buddy went to his doctor because he couldn't hear out of one ear. The doctor checked him out and said, "Bud, it isn't a thing in the world but old age." Buddy said, "I don't understand it. I can't hear a word out of this ear and I hear perfectly clear out of this other ear, and you say it is old age. Both ears were born at the same time."

I said, "Buddy, come back down here and let me talk to you. Sit down, Buddy, and tell me about this second blessing. I want it, Buddy! I want it! I don't like these basement buildings and these outside toilets with nobody ever getting saved. I want something else!"

The first condition is thirsting. Are you thirsty for it? My soul, I hope before this meeting is over somebody gets thirsty for it!

The second condition is **believing.** Look at those verses again in John 7:37-39. Jesus stood that last day of the feast and said, "If any man thirst, let him come unto me, and drink." And the next verse says,

"He that believeth on me, as the scripture hath said, out of his belly shall flow rivers of living water."

Underline two words: *thirsting* and *believing*. Believing. I didn't believe.

I heard Dr. Hyles tell about kneeling on his father's grave and praying until he was filled with the Holy Spirit. I thought: *He's just talking. He didn't have an experience like that. Well, maybe he did, but if he did, it is not for me, a poor country preacher with nobody to promote me, out of nobody's fellowship, out of nobody's school, left the crowd I was with. . . it's not for me. Oh, it's for Dr. Lee Roberson. It's for Dr. Jack Hyles. It's for Dr. Rice and Moody and Torrey and Spurgeon and others I have read about, but not for me!* But down inside, my heart kept saying, *Yes, it is for you, too. You can have it, too!*

If you are sitting here tonight saying, "I don't believe it," then you will never have it. But if you can leave here tonight saying, "If it is for Lee Roberson, if it is for John R. Rice, if it is for John Rawlings, if it was for J. Frank Norris, if it was for Gipsy Smith, Ira Sankey and R. A. Torrey, then it is for me, too," then you can have it.

Don't you get tired of just swinging the ax handle with no head on it? Don't you get tired of going through the motions, knowing nothing is going to happen but thinking that the show must go on? If you did some Sunday mornings what you felt like doing, you would stand and say, "Let's be dismissed. This place is as dead as a doornail, as dead and empty and dry as last year's bird nest."

Spurgeon said, "When you meet together, pray that the power of the Holy Spirit will be there. If you pray and He is not there, dismiss the congregation and pray He will be there next Sunday."

The first condition is thirsting. The second condition is believing, believing that it is for you and you can be filled with the Holy Spirit.

The third condition is **asking.** Luke 11:13: "If ye then, being evil, know how to give good gifts unto your children: how much more shall your heavenly Father give the Holy Spirit to them that ask him?"

Just keep on praying. Just keep on praying till light breaks through.

James 4:2 says, "Ye have not, because ye ask not." Some of you will die and go to Heaven a mediocre preacher. You know I am telling the truth. You don't have any ambition. You are satisfied. In Heaven you will know you could have done more if you had had the fullness of the Holy Spirit. God says, "Ye have not, because ye ask not." If you would have asked, He would have given you power to do His work.

Acts 4:31 says, "And when they had prayed, the place was shaken where they were assembled together; and they were all filled with the Holy Ghost."

I have time for one other condition, and it is very important. We must want the fullness of the Holy Spirit **for the right reason**. Some want to have an ecstatic experience. They want to feel something. They want their hair to stand on end. They want to get lightheaded. Some want to talk in what they think is a heavenly language.

But in Acts 2 there is no ecstatic, heavenly language. There were languages of people present on the day of Pentecost. They didn't speak in an ecstatic tongue on the day of Pentecost. They spoke with "other tongues"—plural languages. And every man heard them in his own language. And they marveled and said, "Behold, are not all these which speak Galileans? And how hear we every man in his own tongue [language], wherein we were born?"

You want to get it so you can feel good and lightheaded and run around and shout. I'm not against shouting, but that is not the reason God wants you to have the fullness of the Spirit.

What is the reason God wants you to have it? Acts 1:8: "But ye shall receive power, after that the Holy Ghost is come upon you: and ye shall be witnesses unto me both in Jerusalem, and in all Judaea, and in Samaria, and unto the uttermost part of the earth."

You won't shut up until you reach the whole world with the Gospel! You will be fanatical about soul winning when you are filled with the Holy Spirit.

We want the blessing to end in ourselves. We want to hem it all up. We want to get in our little prayer experiences. The Bible doesn't say you will have that. It says you will have power to be a witness.

The word *witness* is found 33 times in the book of Acts. Compare that with the number of times they talked in tongues—three times: in Acts 2, Acts 10 and Acts 19.

You must want it for the right reason. If you are not willing to sell out and make soul winning the main business of your life, then you will never be filled with the Holy Spirit. Never. You must want it for the right reason.

The Consequences

Today I listed eighteen things from the Bible that the Holy Spirit does for us. I am not saying there are only eighteen, but I listed eighteen. I will mention a few.

1. The Holy Spirit strengthens the believer in the inner man (Eph. 3:16).

2. The Holy Spirit leads the believer (Rom. 8:14). You don't have to go around guessing what you ought and ought not do. When you are Spirit-filled, you can make your decisions much quicker and better. You can have clear directions from God.

3. The Holy Spirit produces Christian graces in the believer's life—love, joy, peace, longsuffering, gentleness, goodness, faith, meekness, temperance.

4. The Holy Spirit helps the believer understand the Bible (I John 2:27). You need illumination. The Holy Spirit gives you that.

5. The Holy Spirit improves your memory. "The Comforter, which is the Holy Ghost, whom the Father will send in my name, he shall teach you all things, and bring all things to your remembrance, whatsoever I have said unto you" (John 14:26). He improves the memory.

6. He helps you to preach the Word effectively.

7. He improves your preaching and makes it effective. First Thessalonians 1:5 says, "For our gospel came not unto you in word only, but also in power, and in the Holy Ghost."

8. He guides the believer in prayer (Rom. 8:26). We don't know what to pray for as we ought, "but the Spirit itself maketh intercession for us with groanings which cannot be uttered."

These are but eight of the things I listed that the Holy Spirit does in the believer's life.

Now I want to talk about the main one—the consequences of the fullness of the Spirit—"and ye shall be witnesses unto me."

I don't mean this critically or to be mean, but I must tell our Pentecostal friends that it is not speaking in tongues. Not one time does the Bible say when you are filled with the Holy Spirit that you will speak in tongues. The Bible does say in Acts 1:8 that we will be witnesses.

Open your Bible to Luke 1:15. Speaking of John the Baptist, the Bible says, "For he shall be great in the sight of the Lord, and shall drink neither wine nor strong drink; and he shall be filled with the Holy Ghost, even from his mother's womb."

Notice the next verse: "And many of the children of Israel shall he turn to the Lord their God." He would get a lot of people saved.

A man stood in the balcony in one of Moody's meetings and said, "Mr. Moody, let me tell you about my mountaintop experience."

Moody asked, "How many souls have you led to Christ since you have been on the mountain?"

"Why," he said, "none."

Moody said, "Sit down! We don't care to hear about that kind of mountaintop experience!"

I don't see how anybody reads Acts 2 and gets ecstatic utterances out of it. These are the words of Acts 2: "other tongues," "in his own language," "our own tongue." How can anyone read Acts 2 and miss the latter part of the chapter where it says three thousand souls were saved?

Here is what happened on Pentecost. At least three thousand unconverted had gathered at that place. How do we know? Because when three thousand got saved, there had to be that many. There were probably many more.

Here some men knew the Gospel and could present it and win people to Christ, but they had a problem: They did not know the languages of the people who needed to hear the Gospel.

God had a problem. He said, "There are three thousand people who need to get saved, and those men who know how to tell them can't speak their language." So in Acts 2 God leaped a language barrier and allowed men to speak in languages they had never spoken before, not to magnify the language but to magnify the importance of getting the Gospel to the lost and getting them saved.

It is foolish to magnify the language that the message which resulted in three thousand conversions was carried in, yet never talk about the message and never talk about the conversions!

That is like my bringing you a million dollars in a brown paper bag and you dumping the million out and running through the house shouting over the brown paper bag. You are more interested in the vehicle that brought it to you than what came to you in the vehicle.

The most important thing at Pentecost was the message and the three thousand saved. Tongues were secondary and incidental.

"And be not drunk with wine, wherein is excess; but **be filled with the Spirit."** —Eph. 5:18.

The comparison, the command, the conditions, the consequences— "...and ye shall be witnesses unto me...."

How many want to be filled with the Holy Spirit? Maybe you are not as thirsty as you ought to be, but there is some longing in your heart. You are not satisfied with mediocrity.

Let us have several preachers form a line across the front. When the choir starts singing, will you start moving? Go to the nearest preacher and tell him, "I want the fullness of the Holy Spirit, and I don't intend to stop until I get it"; then go back to your seat.

(As the choir sang, hundreds came forward and said, "I want to be filled with the Holy Spirit.")

R. G. LEE
1886-1978

ABOUT THE MAN:

R. G. Lee was born November 11, 1886, and died July 20, 1978.

The midwife attending his birth held baby Lee in her black arms while dancing a jig around the room, saying, "Praise Gawd! Glory be! The good Lawd done sont a preacher to dis here house. Yas, sah! Yes, ma'am! Dat's what He's done gone and done."

"God-sent preacher" well describes Dr. Lee. Few in number are the Baptists who have never heard his most famous sermon, "Payday Someday!" If you haven't heard it, or read it, surely you have heard some preacher make a favorable reference to it.

From his humble birth to sharecropper parents, Dr. Lee rose to pastor one of the largest churches in his denomination and head the mammoth Southern Baptist Convention as its president, serving three terms in that office. Dr. John R. Rice said:

"If you have not had the privilege of hearing Dr. Lee in person, I am sorry for you. The scholarly thoroughness, the wizardry of words, the lilt of poetic thought, the exalted idealism, the tender pathos, the practical application, the stern devotion to divine truth, the holy urgency in the preaching of a man called and anointed of God to preach and who must therefore preach, are never to be forgotten. The stately progression of his sermon to its logical end satisfies. The facile language, the alliterative statement, the powerful conviction mark Dr. Lee's sermons. The scholarly gleaning of incident and illustration from the treasures of scholarly memory and library make a rich feast for the hearer. The banquet table is spread with bread from many a grain field, honey distilled from the nectar of far-off exotic blossoms, sweetmeats from many a bake shop, strong meat from divers markets, and the whole board is garnished by posies from a thousand gardens.

"Often have I been blessed in hearing Dr. Lee preach, have delighted in his southern voice, and have been carried along with joy by his anointed eloquence."

XIV.

The Power That Transforms

R. G. LEE

(A Message Given at a Conference for Young People)

"Be ye transformed."—Rom. 12:2.

What is transformation? What does transformation mean?

In alchemy it means to change into a different substance, or the change of one metal into another.

In mathematics it means to change one mathematical expression or operation into another equivalent to it, or having similar properties, by substituting new variables or elements for the original ones.

In the electrical realm it means to change the potential of, or the type of, as a current, from higher to lower voltage, or from alternating to continuous.

In mechanics it means to change the energy of, as mechanical into electrical.

In physiology it means the change that takes place in the blood during its passage through the capillaries of the vascular system.

In physics it means the change from a solid to a liquid, or from a liquid to a gaseous form, or the reverse—all in all it means the change of one form of energy into another.

In pathology it means a morbid change of tissue into a form not proper for the organ.

In life and matters of the soul it means to change the character or nature of—as Paul going to Damascus as a red-handed murderer and returning as a preaching saint and apostle.

And it is the transformation in life that we are concerned about in this message and—in your young lives.

And the greatest thing in the world is life. And the greatest thing in life is love. And the greatest thing in love is joy. And the greatest joy is the joy of the Lord as it comes in the transformed life consecrated to His service!

That you may have the abundant life in life, that you may have the sweetest love in life, that you may have the greatest joy in the greatest love in life, and that you may live the life that is ever fascinating and never wearisome and have the joy that is ever rich and abiding and an influence for God that is not calculated by mathematics and not deducible by logic and that is not made up of propositions and definitions, I speak to you of "The Power That Transforms."

I. NOTE THE TRANSFORMATIONS WROUGHT IN NATURE'S REALM—BY CHEMISTS AND SCIENTISTS

A gay pair of hydrogen atoms seize an oxygen atom and begin to fox-trot about among the molecules, the three of them together—and the transformation is water, a different looking thing entirely from the gas each of them was before the chemical fox-trot.

Mercury drowns itself—commits mercurial suicide—in naphthalene; and the transformation is phthalic acid. Quite a transformation.

The chemist marries oxygen and carbon; and the result of this chemical matrimony is flame, fire! Quite a transformation.

The chemist takes turpentine, potatoes, sawdust, pitch, petroleum, coal and lime. He mixes them. The transformation wrought is rubber— identical in every respect with natural rubber.

Coal tar, taken from our coke ovens, is transformed into dyes with all the colors of the rainbow. And 900 dyes in 5,000 shades have been made from black carbon tar. Fruit flavors that we eat in cake and ice cream come from tar.

Take tolvene, a coal tar distillate. It smells like gasoline. Combine it with chlorine, one of the poisonous gases used in the war; and, by treating it with another deadly poison, cyanide, we get a non-poisonous, health-aiding substance which is a harmless medicine for children.

Take hydrogen—a colorless, tasteless, odorless gas, fourteen and one-half times lighter than an equal volume of air and 11,160 times lighter than water. Man combines this with tasteless black carbon and with colorless, tasteless oxygen and gets—what do you suppose—white sugar.

Wonderful the transformation wrought by the chemist and scientist in the realm of nature. But time will not permit us to go more into detail just here. So we pass on, asking you to

II. NOTE THE TRANSFORMATIONS IN MODES OF TRANSPORTATION AND COMMUNICATION WROUGHT BY THE INVENTOR

Once it was the horse, the scythe, the sailing ship. Now it is the locomotive, the reaper, the ocean greyhound. Once it was the beacon signal fire, the tallow candle, the bellows. Now it is wireless telegraphy, the incandescent light, the blast furnace. Once it was the kite. Now it is the airplane. Once the milk jar; now the cream separator. Once the flint musket; now the Winchester and the machine gun. Once the goose-quill pen; now the fountain pen, the typewriter, the linotype. Once it was the hourglass and the lantern. Now the stop watch and the flashlight. Once the handbrake; now the airbrake. Once the stairway, the tread-mill, the spade. Now the escalator, the elevator, the steam shovel. Once the crowbar and sledge hammer; now the derrick and the pile driver. Once the washpot and clothesline; now the steam laundry. Once the bateau and oar; now the steel leviathan.

When it comes to transportation and communication and modes of living, the inventor has wrought marvelous transformations. He has added the telescope to our eyes, enabling us to see landscapes millions of miles away. He has added the microscope to our eyes, enabling us to see a world in a drop of water. He has added the spectrograph to our eyes, enabling us to learn the constituent elements of the remotest astral bodies.

He has added the X-ray to our eyes, enabling us to see the marrow in men's bones. He has added the telephone to our tongues, enabling us to talk across continents. He has added the telegraph to our fingers, enabling us to write around the world. He has added the radio to our ears, enabling us to hear whispers from all corners of all the continents. He has added the phonographs to our mouths, enabling us to preserve the accents and tones of the human voice for centuries.

He has added the cotton gin to man's hands, enabling him to gather his cotton crop. In 1792 Eli Whitney, a Connecticut schoolteacher working in Georgia, invented the cotton gin. Then the little patches of white that had clung around the cabin doors began to spread until they covered the Southland like snow. And at the call of the cotton gin, the idle streams were harnessed and made to turn myriads of spindles, the red hills were reared into factory walls, and the sleeping ore of the mountains was transformed into roaring machinery.

In this country, in 1800, there were no macadam roads. News of

Madison's election was three weeks in reaching Kentucky. Jefferson voyaged to represent our nation at the court of Paris with hardly more advantage of travel than Columbus enjoyed. Colonial trade was carried over sea by sail and over land by caravan as when Venice was queen of commerce. Mails and messages were speeded on their way as when David watched from the city walls for news of his wayward boy. Washington's death was announced in Charleston sixteen days after he died. But today ships cross oceans, trains traverse continents in four days! Garfield was the first President to use a telephone. Now twenty million telephone stations exchange daily approximately one hundred and seventy-five million messages for the welfare of the American people.

The boast of Puck that we would "put a girdle about the earth in forty minutes" is a fact in this century when three hundred thousand miles of ocean cables are aquiver with the news of the world. Jules Verne's fancy conceived a journey 'round the globe in eighty days. The Siberian railway made it possible in thirty-three. The world is at our very doors. We view its acts of yesterday at the breakfast table. Today mills are linked to mills, cities to cities, nations to nations in a vast mutualism of intercommunication—all the resultant of the inventor's accomplishments. Thus we see that the union of effort upon which modern civilization is based is made efficient by the inventor—who has wrought such marvels of transformation in matters of transportation and communication.

III. NOTE THE TRANSFORMATIONS THAT HAVE BEEN WROUGHT IN HUMAN LIVES

These are the greatest transformations of all—the transformations seen in the personalities that become a torch for God to kindle His fires. Transformations of human lives that were saved out of a life of which self was the center into a life of which love is the center.

Names once besmirched with dishonor, now resplendent with honor.

Names once black with the soot of sin, now white with the snow of righteousness.

Names once scarlet with shame, now fragrant with the perfume of love.

Names once a hiss and a byword in the mouths of multitudes, now mentioned with praise and gratitude by multitudes.

Men once ditchdiggers for Satan; now roadbuilders for God. Men once beer bums; now soldiers of the cross enduring hardness for Christ.

Men once the Devil's debauchees; now God's dynamos. What transformations! What a change in nature and character!

John Bunyan, once a swearing drunken tinker, mending old pots and pans and kettles. Transformed into a preacher he was—a preacher who got in jail for preaching and who, in jail, wrote a book that crawled out from the bars of the jail and traveled more highways and walked more bypaths and knocked at more doors and spoke to more people in their mother tongue than any book the world has ever known, save the Bible.

Jerry McAuley, a river thief, a jail-bird, degraded by inheritance, degraded by practice. But Jerry's life was transformed, his character was changed. He found thousands of priceless jewels for Jesus' crown.

John B. Gough, considered a hopeless drunkard; bankrupt in character and in purse he was. But he was changed—and, in turn, he led tens of thousands to Christ and to the Christian life.

And there was Matthew—despised, vulgar, greedy. But his life was transformed; and he wrote the first Gospel.

And there was Peter—blundering, cursing fisherman. He lied; he sulked; he swore; he denied. But the blasphemer became the preacher, the coward became the hero, the quicksand became the rock.

And there was the woman at the well—poor, bruised, soiled, brutalized, dirty toy of dirtier men. A woman with five husbands, living illicitly with another. But her life was transformed—and "many believed on Jesus because of the word of the woman."

And there was Saul of Tarsus. Bitter as a persecutor, thirsting for the blood of those who believed in Jesus, consenting to the death of Stephen, persecuting Christians into strange cities and rejoicing in their tortures. But his life was transformed. He became as gentle as a woman, yet as brave as a lion. He compassed the earth with the truths of redemption, storming the capitals of proud empires, smashing the temples of Greece, taking the hinges off the doors of nations, glorying in bearing in his body the marks and scars of the Lord Jesus.

And there was Moody—a shoe clerk, rude, crude, unlettered. But he was transformed. Through the regenerative transformation that took place in his heart and life, he took one continent in one hand and another continent in the other and rocked them both toward God.

And there was Jane Addams of Chicago. In the transformation of her life, she turned her back on society and frivolity and went down to Hull House. But today Jane Addams enjoys the reputation of being one of the foremost women—and her opinions on social questions are sought after in Europe and America.

And there was Dr. Grenfell. He turned from a life that could have been, and would have been, selfish had he followed the lure of the world. He lost his life among the fisherfolk of Labrador. But he found it again in the tongue of every man and woman in the English-speaking world.

IV. NOTE THE POWER THAT WORKS THESE TRANSFORMATIONS SEEN IN HUMAN LIVES

That power is oft mentioned in the Bible, where names are not merely incidental, where names of persons and places have definite and significant meanings. That power is a Person. And, in the Bible, He is called names which are not accidental or unnecessary. He is called "The Spirit of Glory," "The Spirit of Life," "The Spirit of Grace," "The Spirit of Truth," "The Spirit of Christ," "The Spirit of God," "The Holy Spirit."

This power that transforms is this Person of power—the Holy Ghost. And this Holy Spirit who transforms is not a mere attribute of Deity. Not a divine influence proceeding from God, corresponding to the influence which proceeds from a human being. Not the will or energy of God under certain forms of activity. Not an emanation proceeding from God, as heat comes from fire, as perfume comes from flowers. No. But a Person of power—working and bringing to pass transformations in human hearts and lives and purposes and achievements beyond all words to describe.

And to say that young people are not interested in the work of the Holy Spirit is to do them injustice. For the entire Bible doctrine of the personality and work of the Holy Spirit is quite in harmony with the instinct and knowledge of modern youth—as others have written.

There is even something exceedingly youthful, as one has said, in the manner in which Jesus speaks of the coming of the Holy Spirit; for the commentators tell us that when He is quoted as saying, "I will send you another Comforter," the phrase would be well translated, "I will send you another Comrade," or, reverently, "another Pal."

The great possibilities of these days in the science of radio and psychic phenomena make it not incredible that there could exist a noncorporeal Being whose influence could be exerted upon us and our affairs. Many think there was a day for materialism, when materialism held the upper hand and the crushing heel on us. But now scientists themselves are compelled to talk about some spiritual power and influence beyond the electrons. Living in such an atmosphere, why should these young people be expected to sneer at the doctrine of the Holy Spirit?

Moreover, the entire bearing of the work of the Holy Spirit is in favor of that which delights youth at its best. Whether when directing the prophets of the Old Testament or guiding the apostles of the New Testament or developing in the Christians the fruit that is the glory of the Christian life, the Holy Spirit is always and everywhere the enemy of formalism, the champion of sincerity and the revealer of new vistas of Christian glory.

It was the Holy Spirit who inspired Isaiah to speak for national righteousness and international peace.

It was the Holy Spirit who directed John the Baptist to denounce hypocrisy and sin in high places, calling for repentance as he did so.

It was the Holy Spirit who uncovered the deceit of Ananias and Sapphira. And on—and on.

Because the Holy Spirit comes as a guest into every converted soul, that soul has the power to grow in the Christian graces. The Christian is the temple, the tabernacle, the sanctuary for the Spirit. And to the degree that the Spirit is given opportunity, He develops that fruit— love, joy, peace, long-suffering, kindness, goodness, faithfulness, meekness and self-control. And it is not without significance that Paul writes the Galatians of liberty in the same paragraph in which he urges them to walk by the Spirit.

What liberty we enjoy we have by coming to the truth. "Ye shall know the truth, and the truth shall make you free." Every live young person knows that verse. Does he know also the companion verse: "He [the Holy Spirit] will guide you into all truth"? To the extent that we receive the truth given by the Holy Spirit we develop into true freedom—freedom that is the finest use of God's property.

> Somebody says that young people want what is evident—what can be shown to the eye, what can be touched with the hands. This must be a slander. Youth is practical. But young people know that the most real and practical things are unseen and intangible. Young people believe in love. Young people believe in personality. Young people believe in goodness and sincerity. Young people believe in courage. Young people believe in power. Young people believe in faith. The fact that the work of the Spirit presents mystery is no hindrance to belief in His reality and His effectiveness. Young people are not frightened away by mystery. Young people are challenged by mystery.

Whoever wrote the paragraph I have quoted in substance, wrote words of truth and glory.

What we need to do is to give the Holy Spirit an opportunity. We need to allow Him to develop in us the fruit. We need to show that those who claim belief in Him are different from those who do not. Life, liberty, spontaneity, sincerity, aggressive evangelism, heroic self-sacrifice, growth into the likeness of God Himself—these are the words used to express the objectives of the Holy Spirit—and they are words that belong peculiarly to young people.

V. NOTE THE WORK THE HOLY SPIRIT DOES

The Holy Spirit reproves, rebukes, convicts. When we see what this means in connection with the unbelief of the world, with our own personal righteousness and with the Devil, we understand how we need this power to work in our lives.

"And when he is come, he will reprove the world of sin, and of righteousness, and of judgment. Of sin, because they believe not on me; of righteousness, because I go to my Father, and ye see me no more. Of judgment, because the prince of this world is judged!"—John 16:8-11.

The Holy Spirit gives the new birth.

"Except a man be born of water and of the Spirit he cannot enter into the kingdom of God."—John 3:5.

"That which is born of the flesh is flesh; and that which is born of the Spirit is spirit."—John 3:6.

Those who are born of the Spirit have the new heart—are new creatures in Christ Jesus. And there is no transformation without this new birth. Thievery is in the heart before the hand steals. Lust is in the heart before the body is yielded to lustful indulgence. Lying is in the heart before it is on the lips. Deception is in the heart before it finds expression in the life, for "out of the heart are the issues of life."

The Holy Spirit gives assurance.

"The Spirit himself beareth witness with our spirit, that we are children of God."—Rom. 8:16.

"And because ye are sons, God hath sent forth the Spirit of his Son into your hearts, crying, Abba, Father."—Gal. 4:6.

Hardly anything is more potent in Christian service than assurance. Mr. Moody said he had never seen a successful soul winner who had not reached the point of assurance in Christian experience.

The Holy Spirit produces Christlike graces.

"But the fruit of the Spirit is love, joy, peace, long-suffering, gentleness, goodness, faith, Meekness, temperance."—Gal. 5:22,23.

Growth in grace must be growth in experience with the Holy Spirit. Victory over the flesh life is delegated to Him. This victory may be as instantaneous as the surrender is complete.

And time would fail me to tell of His work in the believer: how He assures the believer of sonship—of how He seals, as a manifestation of God's keeping power and the pledge of future glory (II Cor. 1:22; 5:5; Eph. 1:13,14; and 4:30); how He fills for a victorious life (Acts 2:4 and Eph. 5:18)—how He sanctifies, or separates, to God for His use (II Thess. 2:13 and I Pet. 1:2)—how He abides forever (John 14:16). And of how He teaches with the Word as His textbook and us as learners (John 14:26 and I Cor. 2:13). And of how He brings to remembrance the things we have learned (John 14:26).

And of how He testifies of and opens the Word to us concerning Jesus (John 15:26). And of how He guides into all truth (John 16:13). And of how He glorifies Jesus in and through us (John 16:14). And of how He takes the things of Jesus and shows them to us (John 16:14). And of how He gives power to obey God (Ezek. 36:27). And of how He gives power to obey the truth (I Pet. 1:22). And of how He gives freedom from the law of sin and death (Rom. 8:2). And of how He causes us to fulfill the righteousness of the very law which we, as sinners, could not fulfill (Rom. 8:3,4). And of how He gives power to please God by giving victory over the flesh (Rom. 8:5-9).

And of how He gives victory over disease (Rom. 8:11). And of how He gives power to mortify the deeds of the body (Rom. 8:13). And of how He directs in the prayer life (Rom. 8:26,27; Eph. 6:18; Jude 20). And of how He gives victory over the desires of the flesh (Gal. 5:16,17). And of how He delivers from the bondage of the law or places one up on a higher plane than that of mere law (Gal. 5:18). And of how He gives blessed substitutes for the works of the flesh, the fruit of the Spirit (Gal. 5:19-23). And of how He gives a holy walk (Gal. 5:25). And of how He puts away the things that displease the Father (Eph. 4:30-32). And of how He puts Satan to flight by lifting up a standard against him (Isa. 59:19, margin; James 4:7).

And of how He gives soul rest (Isa. 63:14). And of how He makes Jesus Lord (I Cor. 12:3). And of how He gives liberty (II Cor. 3:17). And of how He gives divine love (Rom. 5:5; Col. 1:4,8). And of how He gives fullness of joy (Acts 13:52; I Thess. 1:6). And of how He strengthens the inward man with power (Eph. 3:16). And of how He gives righteousness, peace and joy (Rom. 14:17; 15:13). And of how He reveals, interprets and applies the deep things of God (I Cor. 2:9-14). And of how He empowers us to impart truth to others (Acts 1:8; I Cor. 2:1-4; I Thess. 1:5).

And of how He inspires worship, or adoration of God Himself (John 4:23,24; Phil. 3:3). And of how He edifies (Acts 9:31). And of how He calls men and directs in their service (Acts 8:27,29; 13:2-4). And of how He leads, even in the details of life and service (Matt. 4:1; Rom. 8:14; Acts 10:19,20; 11:12; 16:6,7). And of how He makes known our redemption rights, the things that are freely given to us of God (I Cor. 2:12). And of how the Christian must recognize the Holy Spirit as a person and definitely appropriate Him for each one of these items and trust Him to make it real.

This is the person who is working such wonders in the believer and working with such immeasurable power, whom we need to direct our lives—to prompt us in all perplexities, to help us in all hazards, to direct us in all doubts, to enable us to be channels through which God Himself is articulate.

In Joseph's day that Spirit of God gave Joseph strength to resist a lustful woman's dirty proposal and to become fruitful in the land of his affliction and a ruler in the land of his imprisonment. So will He work within us today, helping us to wear the white flower of a blameless life.

In Samson's day that Spirit of God came mightily upon Samson, so that the ropes upon his arms became as flax that was burnt with fire, and made his hand with only the jawbone of an ass in it mightier and more terrible than an army with banners. So will He strengthen us today, seeing to it that no weapon formed against us shall prosper, giving us victories over evil majorities.

In King Saul's time, the Spirit of God came upon Saul and he opened his mouth with amazing prophecies. So will that Spirit be with our mouths today, filling them with the praises of God and giving us messages the world needs to hear.

In Ezekiel's day the Spirit of God set Ezekiel down "in the midst of the valley which was full of dry bones"—bones that were very dry. That valley was a graveyard turned upside down, the ghastly, disjointed bones scattered over all parts. Scavengers had done their work. Sinews gone. Flesh gone. Skin gone. But as Ezekiel, by the command of God, prophesied, "there was a noise, and behold a shaking, and the bones came together, bone to his bone." And then, as Ezekiel looked upon that scene, "the sinews and the flesh came upon them, and the skin covered them above."

But "there was no breath in them." The organized bones were as impotent as a gun in dead men's hands—as impotent as when they lay scattered over the desolate fields. "Noise." "Shaking." "Coming together," "getting together." Yes. But no enlivening power from the heart of God. Noise, shaking, coming together. But no inspiration, no aspiration, no pervading breath, no sacrifice, no shedding of blood. Just an organized corpse!

"Then said he unto me, Prophesy unto the wind, prophesy, son of man, and say to the wind, Thus saith the Lord God; Come from the four winds, O breath, and breathe upon these slain, that they may live."—Ezek. 37:9.

Then "the breath came upon them, and they lived, and stood upon their feet, an exceeding great army!"

When the breath comes! Jowett said the breath of God converts an organization into an organism. It transforms a combination into a fellowship, a congregation into a church, a body of believers into an army of soldiers of Jesus.

Watkinson said:

> Give that despairing musician an atom of Mozart's melodious brain or Beethoven's spirit—and music will swell from his instrument like thunder from the waves of the sea or whispers from summer zephyrs. Give the halting poet a spark of Shakespeare's fire—and verses will drop from his pen like golden pollen from the stems of shaken lilies. Give that struggling painter a nerve of Turner's color sense—and his brush will catch the waves and the winds and the mountains in it, and that brush will spread crude paint into wondrous landscapes. Give that stammering speaker a lick of Demosthenes' tongue—and people will listen like children frightened at the roar of a storm or like slaves to an emancipation proclamation. Give that baffled scientist a bit of Faraday's investigative skill—and the mysteries of Nature will stand revealed!

And when that same breath of God comes into our hearts and upon our lives, we shall be giants wherever we have been pygmies, be clear speakers with tongues on fire where we have been only a fraction of what we might have been, be spiritual athletes where we have been chilly and unresponsive corpses.

I know, I know. For that breath came upon a little disciple band—a band that was envious, a band that was jealous, a band that was weakened by timidity and fear; and that breath changed that band into a spiritual army that carried the Gospel to the uttermost frontiers of heathendom, quenched the altar fires of Diana, crushed the temples of Greece, lit a lamp in Caesar's palace—a spiritual army before which "the world, the flesh and the devil" became impotent—a spiritual army of the living God.

"And Jesus returned in the power of the Spirit into Galilee" (Luke 4:14). Jesus emerged from the wilderness scene of combat and wrestling and temptation with the Devil—will you listen?—in the power of the Spirit.

That is the thing above all other things that I pray shall be the portion of each of you when you return from this conference—that you, young men and young women upon whom our hopes center in this bewildered world—yes, that it may be recorded of you in Heaven and known of you on earth and experienced in your own lives, that you returned in the power of the Spirit into Texas, into Oklahoma, into Alabama, into Virginia, into all the states from which you come, in the power of the Spirit.

So we pray, "O Breath of God, come from behind matter and energy and ether and sin and death and Hell, and slain hopes, our slain wills, our slain minds, our slain ideals, and cause them to stand upon their feet and live, an exceeding great army, that we may go forth conquering and to conquer in the name of the Christ who loved us and gave Himself for us."

"Not by might, nor by power, but by my spirit, saith the Lord."—Zech. 4:6.

"But ye shall receive power after that the Holy Ghost is come upon you."—Acts 1:8.

LEE ROBERSON
1909-

ABOUT THE MAN:

When one considers the far-reaching ministries of the Highland Park Baptist Church and pauses to reflect upon its total outreach, he has cause to believe that it is close to the New Testament pattern.

In the more than forty-one years—from 1942 when Roberson first came to Highland Park until his retirement in April 1983—the ministry expanded to include Camp Joy, reaching some 3,000 children annually; World Wide Faith Missions, contributing to the support of over 350 missionaries; 50 branch churches in the greater Chattanooga area; Union Gospel Mission, which feeds and sleeps an average of 50 transient men daily; a Sunday school bus ministry, which covers 45 bus routes; a deaf ministry; "Gospel Dynamite," a live broadcast held daily over 2 radio stations, now in its 44th year; a church paper, THE EVANGELIST, being mailed free twice monthly to over 73,000 readers; and Tennessee Temple University, Temple Baptist Theological Seminary, and Tennessee Temple Academy.

He is an author of many books.

Preaching to thousands, training preachers, supporting the mission cause, Dr. John R. Rice called him the Spurgeon of our generation.

XV.

It's Dynamite!

LEE ROBERSON

"God hath spoken once, twice have I heard this; that power belongeth unto God."—Ps. 62:11.

"For I am not ashamed of the gospel of Christ: for it is the power of God unto salvation to every one that believeth; to the Jew first, and also to the Greek."—Rom. 1:16.

Both David and Paul knew the power of God. David often sang of God's mighty power. In Psalm 21:13 we hear him lift up his voice with: "Be thou exalted, Lord, in thine own strength: so will we sing and praise thy power."

In II Samuel 22 David sings a song of deliverance. The entire song concerns itself with the power of God. David sang,

"The Lord is my rock, and my fortress, and my deliverer; The God of my rock; in him will I trust: he is my shield, and the horn of my salvation, my high tower, and my refuge, my saviour; thou savest me from violence."

He sang, "God is my strength and power: and he maketh my way perfect."

Not only did David sing of the power of God, but he also prayed and gave thanks for that power. When the people brought in generous offerings for the building of the Temple, David lifted up his voice and prayed:

"Blessed be thou, Lord God of Israel our father, for ever and ever. Thine, O Lord, is the greatness, and the power, and the glory, and the victory, and the majesty: for all that is in the heaven and in the earth is thine; thine is the kingdom, O Lord, and thou art exalted as head above all. Both riches and honour come of thee, and thou reignest over

all; and in thine hand is power and might; and in thine hand it is to make great, and to give strength unto all."—I Chron. 29:10-12.

David knew well the power of God in his own life.

It was the power of God working through an humble shepherd lad which enabled him to kill the giant Goliath.

It was the power of God which preserved him from the anger of King Saul.

It was the power of God which gave him great victories over the enemies of Israel.

The Apostle Paul knew the power of God by experience also. His life was altogether different from that of David, but no less miraculous.

It was the power of God which arrested Paul on the road to Damascus. A blaspheming, egotistical persecutor of Christians was changed into a quiet, humble missionary.

It was the power of God which healed the lame man at Lystra, at the word of the apostle.

It was the power of God manifested in the city of Philippi when Paul and Silas prayed and sang praises unto God. It was God's power which shook the prison and also the power of God which brought the jailor and his household unto salvation.

Paul knew the power of God and never ceased to talk about it. He was never ashamed of the Gospel of Christ, for he knew it was the power of God unto salvation to all who believed. He knew the power of God was sufficient to smash evil and to save souls and transform lives.

It was the power of God upon which Paul rested in all of his ministry. He wrote to the church in Corinth:

"And I was with you in weakness, and in fear, and in much trembling. And my speech and my preaching was not with enticing words of man's wisdom, but in demonstration of the Spirit and of power: That your faith should not stand in the wisdom of men, but in the power of God."—I Cor. 2:3-5.

We come now to consider the power of God and its relation to our lives and our times.

I. THE NEED FOR POWER

Everyone will agree that we need the power of God in this day. Everyone will agree that demonstrations of divine power are sorely lacking. This we know is not the fault of God, but the fault of man.

We see the powerlessness of Christians in daily living. The average Christian seems powerless to live victoriously. Professing Christians do as much fretting and worrying as those who make no profession at all. Homes and hospitals are filled with whining, complaining, defeated Christians.

In the realm of witnessing, powerlessness is just as evident. God is unable to use the average Christian because he refuses to pay the price for power. Hence his witnessing is without effect. Yes, it is even ridiculed in many instances. The lost world is keenly sensitive to the powerlessness of Christians.

Consequently homes are divided and the years roll on without any changes taking place. Souls are lost and perishing for want of a witness that tells.

Think of the powerlessness of churches to touch cities and communities; the powerlessness of churches to move and shake the forces of unrighteousness; the powerlessness of churches to claim respect from a lost world.

When Paul moved about, one of two things happened. Wherever he stopped, there was either a revival or a riot. The apostle was not ignored. He was charged and surcharged with the power of God so that things happened wherever he stopped.

Our churches are so powerless that they quite often are ignored by the city. Civic affairs are arranged without any consultation with the churches. Prayer meetings are ignored. Even Sunday services are forgotten.

I do not say that people must like all of our churches, but they should have respect for them. I am not asking that the entire city of Chattanooga like Highland Park Baptist Church; but because of the power of this place, they should have respect for the work being done there. They should have respect for its standards and for the zeal which is manifested.

Think, too, of the powerlessness of church organizations and plans. How often we are guilty of worshiping the machinery made by men's hands and set up by men's mind, instead of looking for the power of God.

I was interested in a simple little story told of an arid region in South Africa. The missionaries received from the homeland a gasoline engine with which to pump water for irrigation. Among the many gods worshiped by the natives, there was one favorite deity who was supposed to preside over the sending of moisture.

After the new equipment had been tried out and was working successfully, the missionaries were greatly surprised one day to find about a hundred natives bowed down upon their faces, worshiping the gasoline engine.

The comment which went along with this little story was: "And they were not the first, and probably will not be the last to make the machinery an object of reverence."

What mighty power could be sent forth for God and for good through our churches! It is impossible to estimate the latent power in our churches. The power of steam engines, electricity and nuclear bombs is nothing as compared to the power hidden and sleeping in the churches.

Let us confess in our individual lives our need for power. Let us face with frankness and honesty our failures, both in living and witnessing.

II. THE REASON FOR POWERLESSNESS

First, powerlessness comes from the failure to seek the face of God. In our lives we plan and proceed without waiting for Him. The same is true in most churches. Programs are launched without sufficient prayer. The Holy Spirit and His leadership are not sought. We profess to know God and to believe in Him, but we fail to seek Him daily.

Second, powerlessness comes because of broken contact with God. Sin breaks fellowship, and broken fellowship means no power. Inconsistent worldly living accounts for the powerlessness of many. Power will not return until correction is made.

Suppose I went out to my car, stepped on the starter, but received no response. By simple investigation I discovered that the battery cable was broken. It would do me no good to polish the headlights, clean the spark plugs, or to change the oil. If my car is going to run, the battery cable must be replaced. There must be contact with the power.

Years ago in *The Prairie Overcomer* the following appeared. A newspaper reporter in Germany asked General Von Rundstedt why Germany lost the war. The great general listed four causes. We Christians lose our war through these same four failures:

1. *Broken communications.* What about replacements, men to fill the gaps, money to send them?

2. *Lack of air power.* Must God's men advance without the barrage of prayer power?

3. *Lack of oil.* The great Commander-in-Chief said, "Ye shall receive power, after that the Holy Ghost is come upon you: and ye shall be witnesses unto me." Of the first missionaries, we read, "They being sent forth by the Holy Ghost."

4. *Failure at the source of supply.* Failure indeed, but not with God, for the cattle upon a thousand hills are His. But man has his hands upon them—has choked the supply. "Will a man rob God?"

A third reason why we are powerless is that of dependency upon the flesh. This is implied in all else that we have said, but let us understand that we can never succeed in living a Christian life, nor can we be victorious in any way as long as we depend upon ourselves, "The arm of flesh will fail you, ye dare not trust your own." Samson failed when he turned away from God and rested upon his own power. Simon Peter failed when he depended upon the flesh.

It is clearly dependence upon the flesh when we fail to read our Bibles, pray or attend worship services and look toward God in everything.

God has prescribed a way whereby we are to live victoriously. Failure to take His way will bring defeat and powerlessness.

III. GOD GIVES POWER TO MEN

May we keep before our minds that God has all power. Read through this divine Book, the Bible, and note the mighty working power of our Almighty Heavenly Father. Surely "power belongeth unto God."

Trace Israel's journey out of Egypt, and you will see that God has all power. The Red Sea stands open to provide a highway for the chosen people. Manna rains down from Heaven to feed the thousands who journey toward the Promised Land. Desert rocks burst open and yield fountains of water. When finally Israel crosses into the promised land, she does so through the Jordan River. The mighty city of Jericho falls without a battle.

Study God's power as evidenced in the ministries of Elijah, Elisha and Daniel.

See the power of God as revealed in God's Son, the Lord Jesus Christ. Blind eyes were opened, lame limbs were healed, incurable diseases were banished by a word, the dead were raised. Thousands were fed with a few loaves and fishes. The storms were quieted by a word from the Son of God. These are just a few of the miracles which tell us again and again that God has all power.

Pompey boasted that with one stamp of his foot he could rouse all Italy to arms. But God, by one word of His mouth, can summon the inhabitants of Heaven, earth and the undiscovered world to His aid or bring new creatures into being to do His will.

Now, let us think upon this glorious truth: God gives power to men.

He gives power to men to glorify His name. His power will never be given if it is to be used in defiling His holy name.

He gives power to men! He gives power to live victoriously. What is the victorious life? It is to go forward with Christ in spite of all opposition of the world, the flesh and the Devil. It is to grow in grace and knowledge of our Lord and Saviour Jesus Christ.

Truly victorious Christians are hard to find. Some of you have already felt that it is impossible to be victorious. If so, listen to these words of Jesus: "The things which are impossible with men are possible with God."

We must learn the lesson, that by ourselves we can accomplish nothing; but with God all things are possible. On the human side, there is only feebleness; from the divine side, there is omnipotence.

Your daily life is to be a series of impossibilities made possible by God's almighty power.

Also, God gives power to men to serve and witness. He has decreed that the message should go out. It must go out through His power and not ours. The Apostle Peter made it very clear after the healing of the lame man that it was not by his power that the man was made to walk. We need to make it very clear to this world that the winning of souls, the transforming of lives is not the work of man, but the work of God.

The early disciples had power to witness. They laid their all upon the altar. They were filled with the Holy Spirit. "And with great power gave the apostles witness of the resurrection of the Lord Jesus, and great grace was upon them all."

The Christian needs to be mighty careful in this matter of desiring the power of God. Simon the sorcerer saw the mighty work of Peter and said, "Give me also this power, that on whomsoever I lay hands, he may receive the Holy Ghost." God's power is for God's work, not for your personal satisfaction or pleasure.

Let it also be remembered that the power of God given to you by the Holy Spirit does not mean popularity or freedom from suffering. You have only to turn to Acts 6 and 7 and find the story of Stephen to realize that this is true. "And Stephen, full of faith and power, did great wonders and miracles among the people." In spite of his power, he became the first martyr.

The Apostle Paul was a man of mighty power, yet he suffered greatly and finally gave his life for the Gospel.

Conclusion:

How to Live Victoriously and Witness Successfully

In closing, let us consider what is necessary for spiritual power to live victoriously and to witness successfully.

First, there must be recognition of God's power. We must say, "Not by might, nor by power, but by my Spirit, saith the Lord." All ideas of attainment by personality, persistence or personal power must be laid aside. God's power must be recognized and desired.

Second, there must be full surrender to the will of God. Every room of your heart must be opened to Him. Every key to your life must be surrendered. You must be sold out to the Lord.

Third, there must be contact with God. This contact can be made and maintained in five ways: (1) by the reading of the Bible; (2) by prayer; (3) by worship; (4) by meditation; (5) by faithful service.

Fourth, if there is to be spiritual power, there must be *daily* contact with God, unbroken by sin. Yesterday's power will not suffice for today. A man of spiritual power at thirty or forty may be the person of great weakness at sixty or sixty-five.

I am thinking now of a man who lived a life of great usefulness, who was known as one filled with the Holy Spirit. He accomplished a work which gave evidence of spiritual power. But in his later years he became weak, defeated and powerless. Contact was broken.

It's Dynamite

The power about which I am speaking is the power of the Holy Spirit. Paul said, "Be filled with the Spirit." This filling is available for every child of God who is willing to pay the price. I have plainly stated the conditions to spiritual power.

As many of you survey your lives, you feel that all is in ruins. If this be true, then let me remind you that out of the ruins God can bring great victory. If tonight you have come to the end of yourself and if you will look Heavenward and depend wholly on God, a life of power can be brought forth from apparent ruins.

It is said that a painting was presented to a small New England church. At first this typical New England landscape scene seemed very unsuited for display in the beautiful building. Cows grazed leisurely on a rolling country-side, and in the foreground was an abandoned cellar and bare granite foundation stones. Charred timbers jutted crazily from beneath a summer's growth of grass and trailing vine. Stone steps ascended majestically into space where once was a friendly door. Disaster had overtaken what once had been a home.

But the center of interest in the painting was not in the ruins. One's eyes did not remain focused on the charred wreckage but shifted to a sturdy oak, full leaved and beautiful in its symmetry and color. It grew in the black, fertile soil beneath the old cellar floor. Out of the abandoned cellar, God had brought forth glorious life.

Out of tragedies and loss, God can make victorious souls. God can turn your defeat into victory. "Power belongeth unto God."

For Reference
Do Not Take From the Library